Word-Spirit Communal Revelationalism

Word-Spirit Communal Revelationalism

The Brethren-Evangelical Theological Epistemology of Dr. J. Allen Miller (1866–1935)

JASON S. BARNHART

WIPF & STOCK · Eugene, Oregon

WORD-SPIRIT COMMUNAL REVELATIONALISM
The Brethren-Evangelical Theological Epistemology of Dr. J. Allen Miller (1866–1935)

Copyright © 2022 Jason S. Barnhart. All rights reserved. Except for brief quotations in critical publications or reviews, no part of this book may be reproduced in any manner without prior written permission from the publisher. Write: Permissions, Wipf and Stock Publishers, 199 W. 8th Ave., Suite 3, Eugene, OR 97401.

Wipf & Stock
An Imprint of Wipf and Stock Publishers
199 W. 8th Ave., Suite 3
Eugene, OR 97401

www.wipfandstock.com

PAPERBACK ISBN: 978-1-6667-3342-6
HARDCOVER ISBN: 978-1-6667-2902-3
EBOOK ISBN: 978-1-6667-2903-0

10/27/22

Contents

Acknowledgments		vii
Introduction		xi
1	The Confluence That Became the Schwarzenau Brethren	1
2	Brethren in America: Schwarzenau, Germany, to Ashland, Ohio	29
3	The Liberal Controversy	56
4	The Theological Pilgrimage and Witness of J. Allen Miller	92
5	The Theological Epistemology, Biblical Hermeneutic, and Pedagogy of J. Allen Miller	134
6	Word-Spirit Communal Revelationalism and Brethren Engagement with American Evangelicalism	175
Concluding Remarks		213
Bibliography		217

Acknowledgments

It would not be a Brethren book without a community of people that made it possible. Many people have spoken into this project. I first thank the Mt. Olive Brethren Church, my home congregation, in McGaheysville, Virginia. They took a teenager, helped him find Jesus, and then assisted him in discerning his call to ministry. The centrality of the Word and Spirit marked that community and their posture of love toward my life. I am especially grateful to their senior pastor, my first pastor, Fred Miller. Fred's mentoring was formative in my call to ministry. I thank Doug and Pat Gravatt, longtime members of that congregation, for their continued support of me in my calling. Their generosity made the printing of this work possible.

Next, I would like to acknowledge the huge debt that I owe to the Park Street Brethren Church in Ashland, Ohio. I've served on staff there and find some of my most meaningful friendships within this fellowship. Many people, far too many to mention here, have helped shape this project from this congregation. I am especially indebted to two lead pastors of the church, Arden Gilmer and Nate Bebout. Numerous conversations with them have served as helpful catalysts for this endeavor.

The late Brian Moore (1943–2015) deserves recognition as he sparked a love for the Brethren in me that has sustained me throughout this project. I spent many an evening with him and his wonderful wife, Amanda, enjoying a piece of blackberry pie, a warm cup of coffee, and numerous conversations on Brethren historical theology, Christian mysticism, Civil War history, and pastoral ministry. It was Brian who inspired both me and a fellow colleague, Bill Ludwig, to reclaim the Brethren witness once more. It was Brian who encouraged me to do further graduate work in Brethren thought.

Jayne Wilcox, a La Salle University alumna, is another person that deserves special mention. Her encouragement to apply to La Salle's Doctor of Theology program was one of the most important decisions of my life. I have spent several summers chatting with both Jayne and her husband, Keith. I am eternally grateful for their hospitality toward me.

My doctoral cohort, ThD Cohort D, has been essential in completing this program. From day one, we connected. The many laughs, prayers, encouraging texts, and conversations have made each time we return to La Salle like a homecoming. As one of the token Protestants, along with my friend Alan Rudnick, I have always felt welcomed and affirmed by this Catholic community.

Over the course of two years, I have learned from many faculty tutors who journeyed with me for seven weeks each. They listened to my rambling, provided profound insights that shaped the dissertation that became this book, and became good friends in the process. I am grateful to Br. John Crawford, Anthony Paul Smith, Jeff Bach, Christian Collins-Winn, Chris Gehrz, George Marsden, and Carl Bowman. They each challenged me in their own way. I hear their contributions through the pages of this work.

Some of my tutors, not mentioned above, served on my dissertation committee. I am thankful, deeply honored, and humbled by this group of four individuals. Their feedback on my original dissertation was challenging. They pushed me to write with greater clarity, no small feat, and pulled out of me the deeper insights that I wanted to share. All in all, they set the bar high for this project. My heartfelt appreciation goes to Joel Garver, my advisor, who was a constant source of encouragement. He guided me through the program with great clarity and care. Fr. Frank Berna was a conversation partner who constantly reminded me of, and modeled for me, the unique call I have to be a "pastor-theologian" who has feet in both the church and the academy. Brenda Colijn was extremely helpful in making sure my writing was coherent and that a natural flow to the arguments being made was evident. She is a brilliant scholar and I am sure my writing frustrated her. She was always patient, always offered helpful advice, and believed in what I was trying to say. Lastly, and most significantly, my mentor and friend, Dale Stoffer, has proven more helpful than words on a page will ever convey. From being one of his graduate students, to serving as his graduate assistant, to being one of his doctoral students, I can say that Dale is one of the most generous scholars I have ever worked alongside. Dale believed in the project, he believes in the Brethren, but in those moments when the work frustrated me, Dale reminded me that he believed in me. I merely ride his coattails with what I write.

Jerry Flora has been my spiritual director for almost thirteen years. Over those many years we have met every other Friday to discuss life and faith. This project would not be complete without the many conversations I have shared with this gentle giant of the faith. Jerry has always been the one to ask how my heart is doing when I seem to get lost in my mind.

Laura Kollar has been indispensable in reading over the drafts and looking for typos and other grammatical errors. She has been gracious in her critique of each chapter and inquisitive about the subject manner. I have benefited from my many conversations with her.

John Swope has been a wonderful friend on this journey. Over coffee at a local shop, John succinctly stated the core truth of this dissertation, "Affirming that Jesus is God does not necessarily make you a Christian, it just makes you correct." John's reflections and solidarity on this journey have made the work less burdensome and reminded me of the larger purpose for this writing.

Cherith Fee-Nordling deserves special thanks. I first heard her speak at a conference in Chicago on the role of the Spirit in spiritual formation. "People," she declared, "do not want to merely be formed in spiritual formation. They want the Spirit." Her challenge to allow the Spirit to be our guest in formation helped move this project forward significantly. The Word and Spirit are constitutive of a Brethren epistemology. I thank Cherith for unclogging the dam that was my writer's block with her call for the Spirit.

To Steven Cole, the executive director of the Brethren Church, and the rest of the Brethren Church National Office staff, I am highly indebted. They have afforded me the opportunity to be both employed and complete this undertaking simultaneously. Steven has also allowed parts of this project to shape pertinent resources for the Brethren. Thanks to friends and coworkers like Patrick Sprague, this project has already started accomplishing one of its stated purposes, namely, to educate the Brethren about their heritage. Many thanks to this wonderful team of coworkers who eased the burden over several few years.

I also thank the faculty and staff of Ashland Theological Seminary for offering me a home for continued study, teaching and community as Assistant Professor of Historical Theology. Dean John Byron has used much of my research to assist the seminary in better articulating its Brethren ethos. I'm grateful to him and my many colleagues for taking mere ideas of this dissertation, incarnating them on a regular basis, and encouraging me to get it published.

Appreciation is also extended to Wipf & Stock for working with me on this project. Their willingness to publish this book is a testament to their commitment to make scholarship widely available. Special thanks to both

George Callihan and Emily Callihan for their patience, kindness, continued support, and keen insights.

I must also recognize my family. My wife, Allison, our two children, Miles and Clementine, and our miniature dachshund, Golly, have dealt with many moments where I was not mentally present because I was thinking about, or working on, the original dissertation. Allison has especially felt the burden of this endeavor. She has been patient and encouraging throughout it all.

Lastly, I submit this entire work with enormous gratitude for the lives of both J. Allen and Clara Worst Miller. They have become role models for me. I am amazed at their courage, intellect, faith, and leadership. They were an incomparable pair. The Brethren Church *is* better because of their leadership. I believe the Brethren Church *will be* better with renewed attention given to their lives and witness.

Introduction

WHY PROPOSE THAT A particular individual, in this case J. Allen Miller (1866–1935), is important to any path forward for the Ashland Brethren amid American evangelicalism? Viewing Miller as a central theologian for the Ashland Brethren, then and now, takes a starting point from James McClendon's *Biography as Theology: How Life Stories Can Remake Today's Theology* (2002).[1] McClendon proposes that biography is essential to theology because

> by recognizing that Christian beliefs are not so many "propositions" to be catalogued or juggled like truth-functions in a computer, but are living convictions which give shape to actual lives and actual communities, we open ourselves to the possibility that the only relevant critical examination of Christian beliefs may be one that begins by attending to lived lives. Theology must be at least biography. If by attending to those lives, we find ways of reforming our own theologies, making them truer, more faithful to our ancient vision, more adequate to the age now being born, then we will be justified in that arduous inquiry. Biography at its best will be theology.[2]

Miller remains an exemplar for the Ashland Brethren as they seek to live out their distinct witness in their communities, their churches, and especially

---

1. See McClendon, *Biography as Theology*. McClendon uses the biographical sketches of Dag Hammarskjöld, Martin Luther King Jr., Clarence Leonard Jordan, and Charles Edward Ives to discern how biography assists in deepening one's appreciation for each of these leaders' respective theologies and how their biographies assist us in moving from theology as an academic pursuit to, what McClendon's identifies as, a "theology of life."

2. McClendon, *Biography as Theology*, 22 (italics original).

in the classroom. He also serves as a helpful guide in Brethren engagement with American evangelicalism.

Since the mid-twentieth century, the Brethren have largely behaved as bystanders in evangelical developments. Aside from the role Ashland Theological Seminary has played within evangelical, theological education, the Brethren Church, as a denomination, has weathered numerous trends originating within evangelicalism. The Brethren have participated in developments from seeker-sensitive congregations to the church growth movement, from evangelistic renewal efforts to the latest missional church movement. But they have often failed to ask whether they should participate or what it means to be "Brethren" in such engagements.

This has changed over the past few decades as younger generations within the Brethren have responded to the research and scholarship of Brethren theologians to reclaim the distinct story the Brethren Church has to tell and to consider how such a narrative may assist them in a more self-conscious critical engagement with evangelicalism. Work by Ashland Brethren theologians like Dale Stoffer, Brenda Colijn, and Jerry Flora has laid a solid foundation on which thinkers and leaders of my generation can build. They have done the hard work of primary excavation.

It is also important to acknowledge the "pastor-theologians" of the Brethren Church who have assisted with the ongoing excavation of Brethren identity. Of note is the late Brian Moore (1943–2015) who called the larger Ashland Brethren family to reclaim their heritage in his small book, *A Brethren Witness for the 21st Century: A Search for Identity and Cultural Relevance* (2008). It was this book that reignited my personal journey into Brethren identity. Seven years later, my friend Bill Ludwig and I would feel called to take Brian's challenge seriously and commit our lives to making this distinctive heritage known within our denomination. Bill now pastors a local church in Ashland, Ohio, and is making the Brethren heritage tangible in that context. Much progress has been made. The Brethren Church National Office, our executive director, Steven Cole, and the Executive Board of the Brethren Church have a renewed interest in the heritage of the Brethren Church. This work materializes in a serendipitous moment for the Brethren.

From my time at Ashland Theological Seminary, I have been drawn to J. Allen Miller. His witness was one of loving obedience and trust in God, the Bible, and the Brethren way. As I explored his specific context, leading and teaching during the Fundamentalist-Modernist controversy of the early twentieth century, my appreciation for him grew as I discovered a thinker who rose above the anxiety that marked the two camps. Through conversations with Dale, I came to realize that Miller was assisting, and still assists, the Ashland Brethren with reclaiming their distinct heritage. In a way, Miller was helping the Brethren Church to think and behave as Brethren again. This is helpful to understand the flow of this research project.

Chapter 1 explores the theological streams of influence that constitute Brethren theology—Anabaptism and Radical Pietism—with particular focus given to key thinkers and leaders. It provides a high-altitude assessment of the theological antecedents that went into each and how the two streams of Anabaptism and Radical Pietism established the founding dialectic of Word and Spirit that marks Miller's, and the Brethren's, theology. So important was this founding dialectic, that central practices like believers' immersion baptism testify to it—inner and outer, individual and community.

Given the subsequent persecution of the early Brethren, chapter 2 traces their immigration to America and their assimilation into larger American society—first in Germantown, Pennsylvania, and then their western progression. Along the way, Brethren identity was tested, leading to schisms at the end of the nineteenth century that formed three expressions of Brethren—Old Order, Moderate, and Progressive. The Progressive camp became the Ashland Brethren who would experience further schism in the 1930s due to the Fundamentalist-Modernist controversy and its specific role in shaping the disagreement over the type of school that Ashland College, Ashland, Ohio, would be.

Chapter 3 inquires into the nuances of what came to be the American Fundamentalism and Protestant Liberalism of the late nineteenth and early twentieth century, which provide important context to the thought of Miller. Chapter 4 explores the distinct theological pilgrimage and witness of Miller. His biography and theology are explored to reveal the contributions that both conservative and progressive theologies of the period made. Special attention focuses upon Miller's theology of the atonement as it captures the blending of both conservative thought alongside an evangelical liberal influence.

Chapter 5 seeks to explore the theological epistemology and biblical hermeneutics of Miller. Miller's theology demonstrates sympathy with both poles of the theological spectrum mentioned above, he remains distinct as a thoughtful mediation between these two extremes. His theological approach, which will be identified as a "Word-Spirit Communal Revelationalism," consists in his particular theological epistemology and biblical hermeneutics—a centered set theological approach that keeps Christ at the center of biblical study and theological reflection.

Chapter 6 then brings Miller's theological witness into conversation with American evangelicalism and argues that this theological approach is helpful for the Ashland Brethren in their engagement with the contemporary

American evangelical landscape. Miller's witness can assist the Brethren in offering a corrective to several pathologies or distortions identified within American evangelicalism.

The hope of this project is that Brethren can develop a positive presence in their engagement with American evangelicalism. Over against the rationalism and scholasticism that underwrites much of Reformed, evangelical scholarship, the posture of Miller can reunite both doctrine and devotion in service of evangelical Christian scholarship. Miller can assist the Brethren in finding their voice in this context and can remind evangelical scholarship of both their Reformed and Pietist heritages.

1

The Confluence That Became the Schwarzenau Brethren

IN 1708, A NEW group emerged in the German village of Schwarzenau in the territory of Wittgenstein, that synthesized the theological views of Swiss-German Mennonites and Radical Pietism. In their theological outlook, they would end up creating a theology of Word and Spirit that provided balance to the two streams of thought that formed the burgeoning movement. They chose to call themselves "Brethren" after the Apostle Paul's name for his fellow believers in the various churches he addressed in his epistles. To the church leaders around them, they were known as the *Neu-Täufer*, "New Baptists of Schwarzenau," after their unique practice (and insistence upon) baptizing forward by trine immersion.[1] In his book *Another Way of Believing: A Brethren Theology*, Dale Brown captures the centrality of baptism to Brethren history and theology (albeit a little tongue in cheek):

> To baptize or be baptized was originally an act of civil disobedience, a stance that espoused religious freedom, separation of church and state, and voluntary acceptance of the faith. Unlike most of our history, early converts needed to count the cost of possible imprisonment, banishment as refugees, and suffering

---

1. This name distinguished them from the "Old Baptists," a term given to Mennonites.

even to death. In a safer nineteenth century, baptism at an earlier age seemed more feasible. A frequent historical caricature of Brethren preaching claims that whatever the text, the minister always managed to get around to the topic of baptism.[2]

The centrality of immersion baptism came from the growing sect's reading of the New Testament and a study of the early church, synthesized through the writings of Radical Pietist Gottfried Arnold.[3] In this practice they found a convergence of the inner change of heart described throughout Pietist literature and the outward form they believed Scripture and the early church required to indicate such a change. Baptism remains central for Brethren groups as a signifier of the central dialectics at the heart of our faith—inner and outer, individual and corporate, Word and Spirit.

The conversations that sustained the group that would become the "New Baptists" trace their origin to another Radical Pietist, Ernst Christoph Hochmann von Hochenau, a disciple of Arnold. Hochmann had a tremendous impact on Alexander Mack, considered the founder of the Brethren movement. If Arnold was the great teacher of the movement of Radical Pietism, then Hochmann was its chief evangelist. Hochmann's teachings provided the necessary catalyst to coalesce varied theological sentiments into the firm convictions that would serve as the foundation for the congregation in Schwarzenau. Mack did not blindly assent to Arnold's and Hochmann's views but drew upon insights gained in conversations with Swiss-German Mennonites in the region. Such an infusion of ideas helped form the historic dialectic that makes Brethrenism possible—Radical Pietism *and* Anabaptism.

Pietist and Anabaptist Challenges

Pietism

Pietism, especially the Radical Pietism that informed the early Brethren, is an important stream of thought in Brethren theology. If Anabaptism is the structure of the Brethren, then Pietism is the soul. Pietism is difficult to distill down to core tenets. The term first comes into vogue by a professor in Leipzig in 1689. "The name Pietist is known all over the city," he writes.

---

2. Brown, *Another Way*, 120.

3. Stoffer remarks, "Scriptural evidence for the threefold action has traditionally been found by the Brethren in the Trinitarian formula of the Great Commission. It has been held that the formula of Matthew 28:19 is elliptical in construction and therefore supports an action for each of the three names." See Stoffer, *Brethren Doctrines*, 263.

"What is a Pietist? One who studies God's word and leads a holy life. This is well done; indeed, it would be good for every Christian."[4] Though difficult to discern, Brian Moore has argued that four themes are common to this large umbrella movement. (1) The "fall" of the church, (2) a disassociation from fallen "Babel," a term applied to the fallen church, (3) an emphasis on new birth, the Holy Spirit, and personal holiness, and (4) an emphasis on an adult response to Jesus.[5] Roger Olson and Christian Collins-Winn further develop lists like Moore's and suggest that Pietism emphasized ten core tenets:

> (1) The embrace and acceptance of orthodox Protestant doctrine, broadly defined; (2) experiential, transformative Christianity; (3) conversion, the regeneration of the "inner man"; (4) conversional piety—a strong devotional life and a personal relationship with God through Jesus Christ crucified and risen; (5) visible Christianity—holy living and transformed character; (6) love of the Bible understood as a medium of an immediate relationship with God; (7) Christian life lived in community; (8) world transformation toward the kingdom of God; (9) ecumenical, irenic Christianity; and (10) the common priesthood of true believers.[6]

Pietism challenged the state religion to a more robust, vibrant expression of orthodoxy and discipleship. Born out of Lutheranism, Pietism differed in that "unlike the increasingly pessimistic and quietistic Luther, Pietists believed in the possibility of the active transformation of this world, the achievement of the kingdom of God on earth; and they believed . . . that it was their duty towards God, for the greater glory of God, to attempt to change conditions in the here and now."[7]

This Pietist challenge came in response to the systematizing of Luther's theology by the generation that followed the great Reformation thinker. Known by later scholars as "Verkonfessionalisierung," this development

> refers to the rigid confessionalizing of Lutheranism which was undertaken by its seventeenth-century theologians. The process was aided by the reappearance of Aristotelianism in German universities and gymnasia early during that century. The result was an unprecedented hardening of Lutheran doctrine. Not only did the guardians of orthodoxy endeavor to keep pure the

4. Durnbaugh, *Fruit of the Vine*, 8.
5. Brethren Encyclopedia Project, *Brethren Spirituality*, 69.
6. Olson and Collins-Winn, *Reclaiming Pietism*, 84–85.
7. Olson and Collins-Winn, *Reclaiming Pietism*, 101.

teachings of the communion but the truth had to be stated in accepted phrases. Any deviation in phraseology was immediately viewed with great suspicion. After John Gerhard, the various minutiae of the seventeenth-century systems of Lutheran theology had to be treated in proper order and sequence so as not to raise apprehensions of heresy. In this heavily dogmatic atmosphere, the essence of Christianity came to be regarded as consisting in a series of rationally ordered propositions. Faith had been largely re-defined so as to consist in personal assent to those propositions. Confessional theology and Christianity were regarded as almost synonymous.[8]

Brown is similarly critical in his evaluation of Lutheran Confessionalism, viewing it as a virtual reversal of the Reformation. Protestant Scholasticism became a sort of "intellectual Pelagianism" in which good works of the medieval church were traded for works of understanding. Justification by faith, a central belief to Luther, became a dogma to Luther's posterity. The pietistic source of dogma that marked the reformer's theology was lost by subsequent generations. The testimony of the Holy Spirit and the reading of the Bible were reduced down to "mere intellectual processes . . . to verify the creedal dogmas."[9]

What developed in light of this scholastic theology is what Stoeffler describes as "doctrinal nominalism." As a result, *fiducia* had become *assensus*, the liberty of the Christian man had given way to the tyranny of scholastic theology, and the Bible had once again become an arsenal of proof texts.[10]

The "liberty of the Christian" becomes front and center in the writings of Pietism. Lutheran confessionalism saw an unfortunate collapsing of faith into mental assent to Lutheran symbols and theology. Johann Arndt (1555–1621), considered the grandfather and precursor of Pietism, makes this criticism one of the central themes in his foundational book, *True Christianity*. "True Christianity," argues Arndt, "consists not in words or in external show, but in living faith, from which arise righteous fruits, and all manner of Christian virtues, as from Christ himself."[11] With these words, Pietism emerged as an impulse within Reformation theology.

These Pietist concerns, however, are not merely Christian humanism. Arndt writes later that "true Christianity" recognizes the need for an

---

8. Stoeffler, *Evangelical Pietism*, 182–83.
9. Brown, *Another Way*, 24.
10. Stoeffler, *Evangelical Pietism*, 183–84.
11. Arndt, *True Christianity*, 112.

experience of the divine. Faith is less intellectual assent and more a transforming experience of the transcendent.

> Note that faith consists in living, consoling trust and not in empty sounds and words. . . . This is true knowledge of God, which arises out of experience and consists in living faith. Therefore, the Epistle to the Hebrews calls faith a substance, a being, an undeniable witness (Heb. 11:1). This is a piece of the inner, spiritual worship, the knowledge of God, which consists in living faith, and faith is a spiritual, living, heavenly gift, light and power of God.[12]

Adding to this sentiment, Arndt writes, "In the living and working faith and in the following of the holy life of Christ, the true living knowledge of Christ consists."[13] Arndt's teaching inspired the central catalyst of Pietism, Philipp Jakob Spener (1635–1705).[14] As early as 1670 Spener was calling believers to meet in small groups. These small groups were known as "conventicles" and their central purpose was to take the Sunday sermon and discuss its application.[15] The seminal work of Pietism, *Pia Desideria* ("Pious Desires") was originally a foreword to one of Arndt's devotional works. In this work, Spener called for six reforms needed for the church to experience reform:

1. More thoroughly acquaint believers with Scripture by means of private readings and study groups in addition to preaching;
2. Increase the involvement of laity in all functions of the church;
3. Emphasize that believers put into practice their faith and knowledge of God;
4. Approach religious discussions with humility and love, avoiding controversy whenever possible;
5. Ensure that pastors are both well-educated and pious; and
6. Focus preaching on developing faith in ordinary believers.[16]

---

12. Arndt, *True Christianity*, 112.
13. Arndt, *True Christianity*, 277.
14. Spener's student, August Hermann Francke (1663–1727), would become the central theologian of Pietism and would serve on the faculty of the University of Halle, a center for Pietist theology in the late seventeenth and early eighteenth century.
15. The central impulse of Pietism lies in the individual, inner experience of God. As the movement developed, loosely organized fellowships (small groups) began to develop that Spener termed *ecclesiola in ecclesia*. Rarely did the *ecclesiola* separate from the established church. The Brethren were one of those separatist groups.
16. Spener, *Pia Desideria*, 1964. The orthodox *ordo salutis* of Spener's day was divine calling, illumination, repentance, saving faith, justification, and sanctification. The

Spener along with August Hermann Francke (1663–1727) would become central to one of two pietistic movements that sought to reform the church from within. Their particular branch of Pietism has been termed classical or churchly Pietism. In that spirit and pursuit of internal reformation, individuals like Spener and Francke became involved with the growing presence and teaching of Pietism at the University of Halle (*Universität Halle*) that was founded in 1694. In the late seventeenth and early eighteenth centuries,

---

first four were often subsumed under the heading of regeneration or conversion. Strong emphasis was placed on justification. See Stoeffler, *Evangelical Pietism*, 240–41. Though Spener and, subsequently, Francke follow this order, emphasis is moved from justification to regeneration, or "new birth." This shift will hold significant ramifications for Pietists. Pietists view forgiveness of sins as an aspect of new birth which was distinct from the orthodox understanding of forgiveness of sins being associated with justification. Reformers then derived their doctrine of assurance from forgiveness of sins rooted in justification. The Pietists connected assurance with regeneration and sanctification. Reformers, therefore, viewed assurance as an entirely divine gift that was forensically valid. For Pietists, this assurance came in the divine-human relationship in a cooperative understanding of sanctification. Therefore, an intrinsic dialectic developed for Pietist theology: an inner spiritual character deemed the "new birth" produced an outer expression of marks of obedience, good works, active faith, and love. See Stoffer, *Brethren Doctrines*, 252. The Brethren, however, depart even from Pietism and its language of sanctification and regeneration choosing, instead, a model of salvation marked by discipleship. Such a view is a product of the Anabaptist stream in Brethren theology. Menno Simons wrote a description of salvation, or the "new birth," that would have resonated with early Brethren:

> By this counsel we are all taught that we must hear Christ, believe in Christ, follow his footsteps, repent, be born from above; become as little children, not in understanding, but in malice; be of the same mind as Christ, walk as he did, deny ourselves, take up his cross and follow him; and that if we love father, mother, children, or life more than him, we are not worthy of him, nor are we his disciples. (See Wenger, *Complete Writings of Menno Simons*, 101)

Menno's connection between an inner experience of hearing Christ that is then manifested in a life of discipleship departs from a Pietist understanding of salvation that was more ethereal and inward in nature. Daniel Liechty remarks:

> The major strains of Protestantism stressed the absolute helplessness of the human individual before God to in any way affect salvation. . . . Anabaptists . . . stressed both the corporate character of salvation and the ability of the individual to cooperate with God's grace in the course of salvation. (See Liechty, *Early Anabaptist Spirituality*, 1)

Such a distinction, which would have resonated with the early Brethren, produced an inner and outer hermeneutic of Scripture in contrast to the mere external reforms of Protestants. "This 'inner' and 'outer' word was not an esoteric hermeneutic" but was an indictment of how the solely external reforms of the Reformation had failed to change moral conduct. For Anabaptists, "no spiritual experience of God or Christ could take place without it resulting in a marked betterment of life. A deepening spirituality meant a moral change in living habits." (See Liechty, *Early Anabaptist Spirituality*, 10.)

Halle became the intellectual center of Pietism. Spener encouraged Francke to teach at Halle where, for the remainder of his life, Francke both pastored and taught theology. Francke would add significant theological basis for Spener's ideas.[17]

The other camp found the institutional church too corrupt and separated entirely. This branch, known as Radical Pietism, was never satisfied with merely reforming the church. The Radical Pietists argued that the true church had been lost through centuries of complicity with the empire dating back to the "fall of the church" under the Emperor Constantine. Encouraged by the writings of the mystic Jakob Boehme (1575–1624), these *Radical* Pietists called for a full separation from the institutional church. Boehme's writings had a strong underground influence on this blossoming movement detailing illuminations of the "deep mysteries of life and cosmos" via a school of thought known as "theosophy."[18] His most famous works were *Aurora*[19] (1612), which detailed visions he had received in 1600, and *Weg zu Christo* (The Way to Christ) (1622), which was a collection of several short works. Boehme's writings were influential on the Radical Pietist Gottfried Arnold.

Gottfried Arnold (1666–1714) studied at the University of Wittenberg, considered the citadel of Lutheran orthodoxy, where he focused his studies on the thought of the early church. While at Wittenberg he was influenced by Spener. Arnold, like other Radical Pietists, struggled with Spener's reform when contrasted with the vision of the early church that Arnold discovered in his studies. Therefore, in 1696, his first work, *Die erste Liebe zu Christo, oder, Wahre Abbildung der ersten Christen: nach ihrem lebendigen Glauben und heiligen Leben* (The First Love for Christ, or, True Illustrations of the Early Christians according to Their Living Faith and Holy Life),

---

17. See Kurian et al., *Encyclopedia of Christianity*, loc. 26715. Kurian, Lamport, and Marty discuss the pietistic and renewal traditions of continental Europe that would shape American Christianity. Of significance for later developments in this project is Francke's student, Nikolaus Ludwig Count von Zinzendorf (1700–1760). Zinzendorf's Pietism made its way to England via the Moravian community, who would have a great impact on the life, preaching, writings, and witness of John Wesley (1703–1791) and the Methodist movement.

18. Durnbaugh, *Fruit of the Vine*, 10. "Theosophy," or nature wisdom, is a hypermystical form of theology in which nature is seen as the penultimate expression of divine wisdom and truth. Knowledge of divine truth "must be found in 'the heart of God' [mystical union with God] from whence nature proceeds, and only the pure in heart can see God. Hence it requires a strenuous spiritual discipline." See Ensign, "Radical German Pietism," 30–31.

19. The book was originally entitled "*Die Morgenroete im Aufgang*" (The Rising of the Dawn). The book was never finished. The work was considered heretical and Boehme was threatened with exile. This forced his subsequent works to go underground.

depicted the first three hundred years of church life in an attempt to capture the primitive church's understanding of the faith and the necessity of a life changing, loving relationship with Christ.[20] In this first work, Arnold began to make his defense of immersion baptism based on the example of the early church.[21] This mode of baptism became a signifier of his quest for a larger retrieval of the witness of the New Testament church.

In 1699, Arnold published his largest work, *Unparteiische Kirchen- und Ketzer-historie* (Impartial History of the Church and of Heresy), the first work to describe church history from the dissenters' point of view (many of whom were deemed "heretics"). Arnold's thesis was cutting: "Heretical movements had actually perpetuated the true church, while the orthodox church that had persecuted them was, in reality, the anti-church."[22] His critique of the established churches sounds quite similar to that of the Anabaptists:

> The church has always flowered best under the cross; it was never the majority and the persecutor but rather the minority and the persecuted. The anti-Christian false church has always found its work and its holiness in outward things, symbols, shadows, sacraments, manners, and ceremonies.[23]

This project, consisting of two large volumes, led to accusations by established church leaders that Arnold showed more sympathy toward heretics than established churches or their clergy.[24] Yet it was this last work that solidified Arnold's classification as a Radical Pietist. Arnold argued that works were deemed "heretical" by those in positions of empire in the conflated existence of church and empire. This produced an accommodated church. When faith and empire were at odds, Arnold claimed, empire always defeated a true understanding and presentation of the faith. What remained was an accommodated church devoid of the true gospel.

With this distortion came an accommodated understanding of baptism. Where the early church employed baptism by immersion as a sign of a believer's commitment to a life of regeneration and discipleship, the accommodated, established churches promoted infant baptism. "Arnold . . .

---

20. The work was reprinted five times before 1732, revealing its larger appeal. Arnold cites men such as Origen, Pelagius, Vigilantius, Eutyches, and Nestorius as "witnesses of the truth." See Arnold, *Abildung*, 8, 23.

21. Arnold argues that the Holy Spirit is received prior to baptism. See Arnold, *Abildung*, 2, 14, 19.

22. Durnbaugh, *Fruit of the Vine*, 12.

23. Durnbaugh, *Fruit of the Vine*, 12.

24. Stoffer, *Brethren Doctrines*, 23.

holds that the introduction of infant baptism, for which he sees no historical evidence prior to the third century, tends to distort the connection between baptism and faith."[25] Stoffer continues, "[Arnold] insisted that early Christianity involved first of all a true, vibrant, living faith; and that secondly it involved pious behavior which is inseparably related to faith."[26]

Bringing together the examples of the early church, the writings of Arndt and Spener, and patristic sources, Arnold becomes the first Pietist to advocate for immersion baptism. Such a practice captures Arnold's rediscovery of the witness of the true church since the true church was not known by its orthodoxy (correct doctrine) but by its orthopraxis (true life/behavior).[27] Stoffer captures the importance of water baptism for Arnold (and eventually the early Brethren):

> Arnold understands baptism as a sign of an already commenced conversion and rebirth; by virtue of this rite, one is received into community. For Arnold baptism is integrally tied to the active faith which must follow repentance. . . . Because [the water of] baptism effects nothing, it realizes its true meaning only through conversion and a change of character. Thus, renewal of the heart and daily repentance are necessary aspects of every Christian life.[28]

By viewing baptism as a sign of the new birth and a pledge to live a new holy life, Arnold maintained a close connection between regeneration and baptism without baptismal regeneration. Counter to baptismal regeneration that posits that the act of baptism is a mediation of grace, Arnold held that the original connection between regeneration and baptism, found in the thought of the early church, was immersion baptism conveying the visible fruit of the grace of God, namely conversion. The water does not save nor does the act of baptism. Baptism is the outward expression of an inner change. In obedience to the witness of Scripture and the early church, the inner working of the Spirit is publicly expressed with the outer witness of immersion baptism that is evidenced in the New Testament. This insistence on the outward form of baptism put Arnold at odds with other Radical Pietists, including his disciple Ernst Christoph Hochmann von Hochenau (1670–1721), who would influence Alexander Mack.[29]

25. Stoffer, *Brethren Doctrines*, 33.
26. Stoffer, *Brethren Doctrines*, 41.
27. Durnbaugh, *Fruit of the Vine*, 12.
28. Stoffer, *Brethren Doctrines*, 33.

29. There is disagreement as to when Hochmann first met Arnold. Some believe that one of the "two companions" present with Dippel at Geissen in 1697 was

The early Brethren are heavily indebted to the Pietist witness for their desire to have a lived faith, to lead a devotional life, and to model a transformative witness to the world. The absence of any sort of structure to Christianity, as several Radical Pietists espoused, created friction between the early Brethren and other Radical Pietists. The early Brethren disagreed with other Radical Pietists who held that the way to restore the primitive church was to abandon external symbols altogether. Brethren advocated, instead, a "blessed middle way." Stoffer remarks, "One of the hermeneutical principles that guided the Brethren was a harmonizing approach to Scripture [and theology] which sought to give due consideration to all the biblical data."[30] With practices like immersion baptism, the inner experience of the faith demanded by Radical Pietism was balanced with the need for an external witness and structure advocated by Anabaptist piety.[31] For this structure, the early Brethren looked to Anabaptism.

Anabaptism

Three important groups for the early Brethren were the scattered Radical Pietists, Dutch and North German Mennonites, named after the Anabaptist churchman Menno Simons (1496–1561), and the Swiss Brethren.[32] The Brethren wholeheartedly affirmed the Pietist concern regarding the fallen nature of the church. If the Radical Pietists gave the Brethren an awareness of the fallen nature of the church, the Mennonites and Swiss Brethren gave them a rationale for establishing a "true church" and a blueprint for its structure.

The early Brethren would have agreed with Menno's famous document "Why I Do Not Cease Teaching and Writing":

Hochmann. For further exploration, see Ensign, "Radical German Pietism," 150. Also see Renkewitz, *Hochmann von Hochenau*, 43. Renkewitz provides the only biography of Hochmann. The question of water baptism had been raised by Hochmann's followers in 1703 and 1706. See Willoughby, *Counting the Cost*, 48–49.

30. Stoffer, *Lord's Supper*, 159.

31. It is important to note that many Anabaptist/Mennonite groups (up to the present day) do not agree with the mode of baptism the early Brethren employed.

32. The Swiss Brethren had come to the Palatinate during the second half of the seventeenth century due to persecution in Zürich and Bern—two Swiss cantons where Anabaptism still survived. Stoffer remarks, "It should [be noted] that the Swiss and South German Anabaptists had already agreed at the Council of Schleitheim on the essentials which Mennonites came to adopt . . . and which the German Baptist Brethren took over nearly two centuries later." See Stoffer, *Brethren Doctrines*, 258.

> Behold, beloved reader, in this way true faith or true knowledge begets love, and love begets obedience to the commandments of God. Therefore, Christ Jesus says he that believes on him is not condemned. Again, at another place, Verily, verily, I say unto you, he that hears my word, and believes on him that sent me, has everlasting life, and shall not come into condemnation; but is passed from death unto life (John 5:24). *For true evangelical faith* is of such nature that it cannot lie dormant, but manifests itself in all righteousness and works of love; it dies unto the flesh and blood; it destroys all forbidden lusts and desires; it seeks and serves and fears God; it clothes the naked; it feeds the hungry; it comforts the sorrowful; it shelters the destitute; it aids and consoles the sad; it returns good for evil; it serves those that harm it; it prays for those that persecute it; teaches, admonishes, and reproves with the Word of the Lord; it seeks that which is lost; it binds up that which is wounded; it heals that which is diseased and it saves that which is sound; it has become all things to all people. The persecution, suffering, and anguish which befall it for the sake of the truth of the Lord are to it a glorious joy and consolation.[33]

Menno's writings reflect the importance of the communal witness of the church. The church is to be a community of regenerate individuals who together provide an alternative witness to the ways of the world. This witness was centered in the christocentric hope which informed their hermeneutic as "all Scripture [pointed] to Jesus and proper interpretation [began] with understanding Jesus as the key to understanding Scripture."[34]

The existential character of the Mennonite witness with its simple coherency was attractive to the early Brethren. The emphases of a

> view of Christ as the Example of the new life, the straightforward approach to the Word which emphasized the Gospels rather than the more theological Pauline corpus, a conception of soteriology which saw all the aspects of the conversion experience pointing to the actualization of the new life in Christ, the prominent kerygmatic quality of the ordinances, the mild realized eschatology of the visible church all played a part in making Mennonite doctrine life-oriented.[35]

Such emphases were evident in the central Anabaptist texts of the period that were formative for the early Brethren. One of those texts was

---

33. Wenger, *Complete Writings of Menno Simons*, 307.
34. Brethren Encyclopedia Project, *Brethren Spirituality*, 71.
35. Stoffer, *Brethren Doctrines*, 56.

the *Martyrs Mirror* (1660).[36] Providing a detailed martyrology of seventeen centuries, *Martyrs Mirror* advocated distinction from the world, which was a formative posture to the Anabaptist, and stressed piety and obedience.[37] Early Brethren would have read *Martyrs Mirror* alongside the Swiss Brethren text *Guldene Aepffel in silbern Schalen* (Golden Apples in Silver Bowls: The Rediscovery of Redeeming Love) published in 1702.[38] The Swiss Brethren, recovering from a 1693 schism with the newly formed Amish sect, found a willing and open dialogue partner with the early Brethren, in their shared desire for an Anabaptist piety.[39] Unlike the Swiss Brethren, however, who began with an Anabaptist foundation and were later influenced by Pietism, the Brethren began with a Radical Pietist perspective that was modified in the direction of Anabaptism. This pursuit of both inward piety *and* outward structure was a needed corrective for the early Brethren from the mysticism of Radical Pietism. Brian Moore notes:

> Whereas Radical Pietism emphasized personal and individual spirituality, [Anabaptism] provided an emphasis on an outward and corporate spirituality. The Brethren would seek to wed these two emphases, but always with Jesus as the focus of life and practice. . . . The Brethren would overlap both Anabaptist and Radical Pietist thought with their emphases on obedience to Jesus and following him as example in life.[40]

With their emphasis on obedience to Jesus as both Lord and exemplar, the early Brethren embodied a christocentric unity revealed through both Word and Spirit.

This inner and outer life of piety and obedience is captured well in trine immersion baptism which remains a central practice of Brethren theology. The discussion of this dialectic through baptism is transmitted, ironically, through Hochmann who struggled with the need for immersion baptism. To his interactions with the early Brethren we will turn shortly.

---

36. Van Braght, *Martyrs Mirror*, 1938.

37. *Martyrs Mirror* is actually divided into two sections—the first traces the development of baptism and the second catalogs Christian martyrs.

38. *Golden Apples in Silver Bowls* served as one of the foundational books arising out of seventeenth-century Swiss Anabaptist spirituality. Published in 1702 in Basel, Switzerland, this wide-ranging compilation of texts drew from varied genres such as martyr testimonies—Michael Sattler, Thomas von Imbrioch, Matthias Cervaes, and Konrad Koch, a formal confession of faith, prayers, instructions for singing, and devotional admonitions.

39. Gross, *Golden Apples*. See also Stoffer's comments on a "pietized Anabaptism" in Longenecker, *Anabaptist Piety*, 35–46.

40. Brethren Encyclopedia Project, *Brethren Spirituality*, 71.

Before a discussion on the influences of both Hochmann and German Mennonites on the early Brethren, especially Alexander Mack, it is imperative to understand the social and religious milieu that was the German Palatinate and the Wittgenstein territory of the early eighteenth century.

The Eighteenth-Century German Palatinate & Wittgenstein Territories

Germany was ravaged by the Thirty Years' War. Though the Treaty of Westphalia (1648) had ceased the warring between the rival factions, it had two consequences for dissenting groups that affected the early Brethren. First, while the treaty ended violence among the three major churches—Catholic, Lutheran, Reformed—dissenters were not tolerated. Anabaptists and Pietists alike were viewed with great suspicion and, in some territories, sought out and punished with imprisonment, torture, or death. Such condemnation only bolstered the Anabaptist view that the true church entailed a sharp distinction from the world. *Martyrs Mirror* solidified this distinction as the text was a popular devotional tool of Anabaptist families. Meanwhile, sermons in Lutheran and Reformed churches were often "violent attacks against other faiths," which only served to reinforce a disdain for dissent.[41]

Secondly, the treaty made the religion of the territory that of the leader. This was captured well by the popular slogan of the period, "As the prince, so the religion." Prior to the treaty, the religious identity of the German Palatinate, specifically, went from Lutheran (1546) to Reformed (1560) and then flip-flopped four more times before 1648. Over 150 years the region switched religious identification six times, meaning one could literally go to bed in a Lutheran territory and wake up in a Reformed one.[42]

In 1706, the noble in power in the region of Wittgenstein, the adjacent region north of the Palatinate, in which the village of Schwarzenau was located, was Count Heinrich Albrecht (1658–1723). Albrecht was favorable to all refugees for two reasons. First, because of the Thirty Years' War, there was great economic need in the region—many religious dissenters were glad to settle and find work in the territory in exchange for the right to practice their distinctive faith beliefs. Second, Albrecht had an affinity for Pietism.[43] As Hochmann's disciples were forced to leave Schriesheim, in the Palatinate, they landed in Schwarzenau in the Wittgenstein territory under

---

41. Durnbaugh, *Fruit of the Vine*, 6.
42. Durnbaugh, *Fruit of the Vine*, 7.
43. See Moore, *Brethren Witness*.

Albrecht's jurisdiction.[44] The Imperial Cameral Court of 1708 found the region to be a place of refuge for "vagabonds, Pietists, Anabaptists, Quakers and Mennonites."[45] To that group of "vagabonds" we now turn.

Ernst Christoph Hochmann von Hochenau, German Mennonites, and the "New Baptists of Schwarzenau"

Hochmann von Hochenau was originally planning on going into law. While at the University of Halle, he found himself converted by the teachings of August Hermann Francke (1663–1727), a disciple of Spener, to Pietism. Hochmann's theology quickly became radicalized by the thought of Gottfried Arnold, whom he met in 1697. With Arnold, Hochmann found no "iota of an express command in Scripture for [baptizing infants]."[46] Later in his life, while imprisoned at the Castle of Detmold, Hochmann produced one of the first Radical Pietist statements of faith in which his rejection of infant baptism is detailed. This quest became elaborated in the subsequent preaching themes that animated his itinerant ministry:

1. He [Hochmann] had been called by Christ to preach the gospel.

2. There is a spiritual church (that often stands in contrast to the visible church of the day).

3. The kingdom of Christ is at hand.[47]

---

44. Schriesheim held a policy of religious toleration for close to forty years under the leadership of elector Karl Ludwig (ruled from 1648–1680). Ludwig permitted a limited number of Mennonites to settle in the region to help with the rebuilding necessary following the Thirty Years' War. In 1685 the family line ended and a new elector, Johann Wilhelm, ruled from 1690–1716. Wilhelm was pro-Catholic and even though churches were to be shared by the three faiths, Catholicism was given preference. Such a change in context forced those who would become the Schwarzenau Brethren to evacuate Schriesheim for Schwarzenau. See Durnbaugh, *European Origins*, 30–31.

45. Durnbaugh, *Fruit of the Vine*, 24.

46. Stoffer, *Brethren Doctrines*, 38.

47. Hochmann's three preaching themes are anchored in three streams he found in Christian mystical literature: (1) Christ must be formed in us; (2) he will unite himself with us if we surrender ourselves to him; and (3) we should follow Christ in our lives. As Stoffer notes, "this Christ-mysticism appears in Hochmann's thought much more frequently than the Boehmist-inspired Sophia speculation." See Stoffer, *Brethren Doctrines*, 258. Boehme speaks of Sophia in *The Way to Christ*. Sophia, "wisdom" in Greek, was the personification of the wisdom of God and is prevalent in Hellenistic religion. At times, Sophia is portrayed as a pure virgin spirit which emanates from God. The Sophia is seen as being expressed in all creation and the natural world as well as, for some of the Christian mystics like Boehme, integral to the spiritual well-being of humankind, the church, and the cosmos. Sophia is seen as outside creation but compassionately interceding on behalf of humanity

Alexander Mack (1679–1735), a miller in the village of Schriesheim in the Palatinate, met Hochmann around 1703 at which time Mack and his wife became involved with Radical Pietism. About 1705, they became devoted followers of Hochmann.[48] Their conversations quickly turned to baptism:

> A question much discussed in pietistic gatherings in Schwarzenau was the rite of baptism. For Mack, the New Testament clearly indicated that adult baptism was a necessary initiation into the body of Christ. Two "foreign brethren," probably Dutch Collegiants, who visited Schwarzenau in the summer of 1708, strongly urged the Mack group to practice adult baptism in spite of its illegality. . . . Hochmann replied immediately, expressing no opposition, providing baptism followed true repentance and faith. He cautioned them, however, to "count the cost" and avoid a sectarian spirit.[49]

Hochmann was uneasy about the need for an outward form of baptism, preferring a more spiritual understanding of the ordinance. Mack, influenced by Arnold and Swiss-German Mennonites, felt that the outward form was necessary for the witness of the church but was torn between his loyalties to the Scriptures, Hochmann, and the Mennonites with whom he had been in conversation.[50]

---

to alleviate its suffering by illuminating true spiritual seekers with wisdom and the love of God. Boehme's Sophia speculation influenced Jane Leade, the seventeenth-century Christian mystic and founder of the Philadelphian society that influenced numerous Radical Pietist groups.

48. Eberly, *Complete Writings*, 1. For more on Mack's family and life, see Donald Durnbaugh, "Brethren Beginnings." Also see Willoughby, *Counting the Cost*.

49. Eberly, *Complete Writings*, 3.

50. Notes in Mack's personal Bible reveal interaction with Anabaptist sources like *Golden Apples* along with a text known as the *Gospel of Nicodemus* in support of trine immersion. The *Gospel of Nicodemus*, also known as *Acts of Pilate*, is an apocryphal New Testament text claimed to have been derived from a Hebrew work written by Nicodemus, who appears in the Gospel of John (cf. 3:1–21). See Schneider, "Alexander Mack's Notes," 18–28. See also Meier, *Schwarzenau Brethren*. As Meier notes:

> Mack furthermore picks up those biblical passages that "distinctly and clearly" suggest the rite, and uses them to substantiate a symbolic understanding of water baptism: The expression "burial of sins" is found in Rom. 6:3; the passage at Eph 5:26 speaks of a "water bath"; according to John 3:5, the human being is reborn of "water and spirit." For Mack, immersion baptism points to a hidden truth: the "burial of sins." The "inner nature" of baptism shows itself in the outward performance of the rite or, the other way around, water baptism is significant of "what is inward." Mack fundamentally rejected the rite of pouring because of

Persecution erupted in the Palatinate forcing Mack and other disciples of Hochmann to flee to the neighboring territory of Wittgenstein. There they settled in the village of Schwarzenau. In this village, the first baptisms and formation of the first congregation took place.[51]

> After receiving Hochmann's letter, and after much Bible study, discussion, and prayer, eight persons chose to be baptized in the Eder River, which flows through Schwarzenau. In the first week of August 1708, those eight were baptized by trine immersion to establish what Alexander Mack, Jr., later called a "covenant of good conscience with God." An officiant chosen by lot baptized Mack, who then baptized the others. The once loosely organized group became a *Gemeinde*, or congregational community. They were called the New Baptists of Schwarzenau.[52]

Though early Brethren theology was greatly indebted to Hochmann on baptism, Mack and others felt that a break from Hochmann's spiritualized understanding was necessary. As Stoffer details:

> In many facets of their thought, Hochmann and Mack were in complete agreement. However, in the area of church organization and practice they had major differences. Hochmann's spiritualistic separatism undergirded his vision of an invisible church of the Spirit. . . . The outward sacraments were replaced by Spirit baptism and spiritual communion. . . . [Mack] supported the institution of an organized church along with the practice of such rites as baptism, the Lord's Supper, and discipline.[53]

Although many Radical Pietists would go on to reject outward religious practices entirely (in favor of a "spiritual" understanding of the

---

this parallel. Aspersion baptism also cannot make the "burial of sins" visible. Rather, it is alone the immersion under the water of the person baptized that reveals the deeper meaning of baptism to the believer. (See Meier, *Schwarzenau Brethren*, 123)

Stoffer further notes, "Though Hochmann and the Brethren shared the desire for the establishment of a visible community, their motivations for this desire had little in common. Hochmann's Spirit-impelled, eschatological fellowship belonged literally to a different world from the Brethren *Gemeinde* based on a desire to fulfill the New Testament commands and examples for baptism, communion, and discipline." See Stoffer, *Brethren Doctrines*, 258.

51. Willoughby has placed the date of the baptisms between August 5 and 8, see Willoughby, *Counting the Cost*, 58.

52. Eberly, *Complete Writings*. Six of the eight Brethren baptized were from the Reformed Church. The other two were Lutheran. See Willoughby, *Counting the Cost*, 58.

53. Stoffer, *Brethren Doctrines*, 66.

church), innovations in the outward form of baptism marked a significant divergence between Mack and Hochmann.

The truth implicit in Mack's understanding of baptism is that rather than being a mere spiritual symbol, as advocated by Hochmann, baptism communicated a personal faith commitment that was done publicly to reveal the work of regeneration already occurring in an individual of the community—it served as a rite of passage. The inner working of the Spirit must be embodied in compliance with the biblical witness of immersion baptism. The early Brethren would refer to this organic relationship as the inner word of the Spirit working alongside and in agreement with the outer word of Scripture. To the present day, the centrality of baptism by trine immersion baptism stands as a signifier of this Word-Spirit partnership at the heart of Brethren theology.[54]

A Dialectical Theology—Symbolized by Water Baptism Mack's Theological Synthesis of Hochmann, Arnold, and the German Mennonites

Mack's writings, while integrating multiple sources, are never systematic in nature. One of his writings is in an entirely conversational question and answer format and often a response to criticism received from other religious groups or from a territorial ruler. Several of Mack's writings reveal his interactions with territorial rulers. One example is a letter to Count Charles August, the eventual prince of the territory of Nassau-Weilburg from 1719–1753. Written on September 5, 1711, the letter details how Mack, contrary to the orders of Count Charles August, baptized the daughter of

---

54. While Anabaptist and Radical Pietist sources account for the derivation of practice and thought of the early Brethren, there is research that reveals a third source, the Polish Brethren (Socinians), as having an influence on Mack and others. Mack notes: "The Greek word for the command to *baptize* actually means to immerse . . . [as is] translated by most translators." The binding of Mack's writings in German—third (1799) and fourth (1822) editions—with Felbinger's *Christian Handbook* (*Christliches Hand-Büchlein*), shows the importance of Felbinger's thought on Mack. Felbinger's *Christian Handbook* served as a source for his own thought and practice. See Felbinger, *Christliches Hand-Büchlein*. The *Christian Handbook* is divided into seven sections: "(1) the creation of man, his fall, and his restoration; (2) the reception of innocent children into the Lord's visible church; (3) holy baptism; (4) church discipline; (5) holy feetwashing; (6) holy communion; and (7) the prohibition of the swearing of oaths." See Stoffer, *Brethren Doctrines*, 58–59. Felbinger begins his exposition on baptism as follows: "To baptize and to immerse are one and the same." See Felbinger, *Christliches Hand-Büchlein*, 37. Felbinger cites that baptisms in the New Testament occur at sites with much water therefore, in his interpretation, ruling out sprinkling as a mode of true baptism.

Eva Elizabeth Hoffman on August 21, 1711. Mack and the widow were expelled from the territory, prompting Mack to respond with an exposition on a Brethren understanding of baptism. This is the only known letter written by Mack and it emphasizes radical obedience to Jesus—even to the point of suffering. Mack writes:

> If . . . true baptism brought no cross with it, but rather a good life, honor, and comfort as does infant baptism, the learned theologians would undoubtedly know how to support the Holy Scriptures. As, however, true baptism brings with it all sorts of contempt, and one cannot be a friend of the world at the same time, they say, against their own consciences, that it is an outward work not essential for salvation. Meanwhile, they allow the poor Christians to proceed under great difficulty, while they follow along living very comfortably with a doctrine which indeed keeps them from and avoids the cross.[55]

Notable in this letter is Mack's connection of baptism with obedience, not salvation. This is a product of both Radical Pietism and Anabaptism. While the former group did not adhere to the need for an outward religious practice, it disagreed with the connection of salvation and baptism with the latter group. Just as Jesus' earthly baptism precipitated great suffering, so it will also be for his followers.

With the same emphasis of obedience in the need for the outward symbol of immersion baptism, Mack, in his book, *Basic Questions* (1713) answers forty questions submitted by Eberhard Louis Gruber, who would become one of the main leaders of the Inspirationists.[56] Written in a simple question-and-answer format, *Basic Questions* details the first responses to "outsiders" by Alexander Mack.

> QUESTION 1: Do you maintain that for over one thousand years there has been no true and genuine baptism, and, consequently, no true church on earth?
> ANSWER: We maintain and believe that at all times God has had His church which observed the true baptism and ordinances. This was, however, always hidden from the unbelievers and often consisted of but few members. Despite this, the gates

---

55. Eberly, *Complete Writings*, 19.

56. The Community of True Inspiration, or Inspirationists, had their origins in German Pietism, though they rejected the dogmatism of Lutheran Christianity. Their belief in contemporary divine inspiration, through certain chosen "instruments" (*Werkzeuge*), distinguished them from other German Pietist groups. Their original communities were in Hesse. After emigrating to the United States, the group became the Amana colonies now located in southeastern Iowa. See Hoehnle, *Inspirationists*.

of hell could never prevail against the church of the Lord Jesus. It can also be proved from the histories that God has caused His ordinances to be revealed as a witness to the unbelievers at all times.[57]

Mack presents the questions in a Socratic manner throughout the text giving the reader a mental picture of both Gruber and Mack having a conversation around a table. Reaffirming an earlier answer to Gruber, Mack responds to the need for water (read "immersion") baptism:

> QUESTION 11: Is water baptism necessary?
> ANSWER: [After comparing to Abraham's faithfulness—even to sacrificing his son if need be] . . . we believe that if a man lives in a holy and perfect way, and his life is affected by true faith in Christ, it will indeed be easier for him to have faith to be obedient to water baptism than it was for Abraham to sacrifice his son.[58]

Basic Questions captures the centrality of the distinctive practice of trine immersion baptism and the dual nature of inward change leading to an outward proclamation in the act of trine immersion baptism as an act of obedience to Christ's example. Mack was convinced that immersion baptism was the practice of the early church which the Brethren sought to model.[59]

Mack trusted the reading of the early church by theologians like Arnold. Coupled with his own readings of Scripture and Arnold, Mack utilized Anabaptist sources like *Golden Apples* to justify the three forward actions in Brethren baptism. His reading of the sources, including the *Gospel of Nicodemus*, secured the Brethren's distinct mode of baptism.

---

57. Eberly, *Complete Writings*, 22.
58. Eberly, *Complete Writings*, 27.
59. Schneider, *German Radical Pietism*, 109. Schneider notes:

> The motif of the imitation of Christ was brought to bear here in a two-fold manner. The New Baptists [Brethren] sought "to take the commanded testimony of Jesus Christ according to its true intent in faith" and "to bear all commands of Jesus Christ as gentle yoke." They also wanted to take the life of the earthly Jesus as a model in the outward expression of their lives, following in his footsteps. A concrete example of this was to have themselves baptized as adults through immersion, just as he had done. The practice of baptism corresponded to "the example of the first and best Christians." They saw themselves as standing in agreement with the early Christians, which was the goal of the entire Pietist movement. It can be plainly seen that the New Baptists were profoundly influenced from their reading of Gottfried Arnold.

Because of these sources, when Gruber asked the following question, Mack not only defends the early Brethren mode of baptism but connects it with obedience and discipleship arguing that baptism was part of a process of transformation into the likeness of Jesus.[60]

> QUESTION 15: What about those who came after the early Christians and have not been baptized by water baptism?
> ANSWER: If they thought that their infant baptism was valid, then they were of course ignorant of the fundamentals of the Christian religion. They will probably have lived up to the fundamentals of Christianity to a small degree or not at all. They will scarcely have achieved the new creation which alone is acceptable before God. Still, we will not judge those who lived many years ago, but leave them to their God. However, similar ignorance of men today who perhaps oppose water baptism because of lack of knowledge will not help them at all on the Day of Revelation.[61]

Mack recognizes the ignorance of established churches of the past but calls his present-day community of faith to greater fidelity to both the New Testament and the example of the early church.

With Mack's acceptance of trine immersion baptism as the baptismal mode of the early church (and of the first three hundred years of church history), the schism between Mack and Hochmann developed. Hochmann feared that Mack's necessity of trine immersion baptism would make the group sectarian in spirit (a fear he felt knowing Mack's influence by Swiss-German Mennonites). Mack felt that baptism was a necessary symbol of Christian faith and obedience.[62] Subsequently, Mack's mode of baptism was criticized from three angles. First, Radical Pietists, like Hochmann, challenged the necessity of an outward form of baptism. Second, the Swiss-German Mennonites criticized the mode of baptism (trine immersion). Lastly, the established

---

60. Early Brethren believed that regeneration was found *through* baptism but not *by* it. Meier notes:

> Menno Simons described the nature of baptism in similar way. The forgiveness of sins does not occur because of baptism, but rather *in* baptism. The striking parallels between Menno Simons and Mack are to be explained by the frontline positions shared by both. Both stood in opposition to a spiritualization of baptism as well as to the understanding of baptism as a sacrament. The arguments found in the *Foundation of Christian Doctrine* and in the *Golden Apples* were well-known to Radical Pietists such as Mack." (Meier, *Schwarzenau Brethren*, 125)

61. Eberly, *Complete Writings*, 30.
62. Willoughby, *Counting the Cost*, 62.

churches vehemently opposed Mack's believer's baptism and rejection of infant baptism.[63]

Mack repeatedly leans on the inner-outer dialectic to support his mode of baptism. Whereas Hochmann stressed the former, Arnold was more balanced. Mack clearly takes his theological cues and balance from Arnold.[64] Again citing Arnold, Mack explains why infant baptism had been considered the norm before launching into an apology for immersion baptism:

> We find in Gottfried Arnold's *Portrayal of the First Christians* that infant baptism began to be practiced only at the end of the second century after Christ's birth. At first, they did it only upon request for those who desired it. Later, baptism was only at Easter. Finally, a certain pope issued an order that no child should die without being baptized. Thus, it has prevailed through long-continued custom until everyone now thinks that infant baptism was commanded by Christ.[65]

Therefore, as described in 1774 by Alexander Mack's son, Alexander Mack Jr., the first Brethren baptisms took place in 1708. Stressing the humility of the Mennonites and the impulse to return to the early church as promulgated by the Pietists, eight Brethren went down to the Eder River in Schwarzenau and committed their lives to Christ and one another.

> Certain details were deliberately omitted, for example, the name of the person who baptized the leader, Mack, before the latter baptized the others. They wished to avoid human error, such as honoring men rather than God. They were not interested in the acclaim or recognition of the world.[66]

What Mack and the early Brethren founded in Schwarzenau was a Word-Spirit movement that allowed both Bible and Spirit to shape their theological epistemology and subsequent hermeneutic. Such sources of authority allow for a propensity toward legalism as one's reading of Scripture and interpreting the movement of the Spirit can become quite subjective. Brenda Colijn notes that Mack's faith was saved from such legalism by several factors. First, the obedience demanded by the early Brethren was never to curry favor with God but was, instead, a loving and obedient

---

63. Stoffer, *Brethren Doctrines*, 78.

64. As has already been discussed, Mack found support for his mode of baptism not from Arnold but from other sources. However, his understanding of the dialectical symbolism of baptism does come from the writings of Arnold.

65. Willoughby, *Counting the Cost*, 79.

66. Durnbaugh, *European Origins*, 120.

response to the action of God in Christ. Second, the focus on obedience was never on the outer word of Scripture but, rather, the Living Word of Jesus. Third, obedience was to lead to transformation. The two form a symbiotic relationship—obedience conforms the will to produce transformation and transformation yields a response of loving obedience. Fourth, only obedience provides a peace of mind and assurance of salvation. Fifth, and final, obedience, as already mentioned, is not to be done legalistically but with an attitude and posture of love.[67] This ethic of obedience was safeguarded from legalism by the Word-Spirit relationship at the heart of Brethren theology. Mack in *Rights and Ordinances*, describing this relationship, regards them as outward and inward testimonies that always agree:

> Now the Scriptures are only an outward testimony of those things which were once taught and commanded by the Holy Spirit. . . . Since there is on Spirit and only one, then this holy and unique Spirit cannot will other than that which He willed for salvation many hundred years ago. That which the Holy Spirit ordained for the faithful was written outwardly. All believers are united in it, for the Holy Spirit teaches them inwardly just as the Scriptures teach then outwardly.[68]

Immersive, believer's baptism served as a signifier of this inner and outer relationship between Word and Spirit that produces a life of loving obedience in response. It was through practices like baptism that early Brethren believed they were living into the fulfillment of Jeremiah 31. "This law which is inwardly written by the Spirit of God," Mack writes, "is completely identical with that which is outwardly written in the New Testament."[69] In a hymn written by Mack entitled "Counting the Cost," that appeared in the 1720 Brethren hymnal, he poetically and devotionally details this dialectic at the heart of Brethren faith. In stanzas 1–2 he details how Jesus created the church through his Word. This provides an example for believers to live by. The Holy Spirit fills believers and brings them to maturity in Christ in stanza 4. In closing the hymn, it is the Word *and* Spirit that bring believers, in community, to the mind of Christ in stanza 13: "Arise, dear soul . . . , the time is now to stem the evil, for Christ himself goes into battle against those

---

67. Colijn, "Word and Spirit."
68. Mack, *Rights and Ordinances*, 43–106.
69. Prose translation by Durnbaugh, *German Hymnody of the Brethren*. Jeremiah 31:33 was an important messianic prophecy for the early Brethren detailing the Spirit's role in internalizing the law of Christ. It reads, "I will put my law in their mind and write it on their hearts" (NIV). This passage details a Word-Spirit hermeneutic as the law is internalized by the witness and influence of the Holy Spirit.

who will not listen to him in his outer and inner word. But those who do, have the mind of Christ."⁷⁰

Historical Implications

With the convergence of Radical Pietism and Anabaptism—signified in central practices like baptism—the early Brethren entrenched themselves in two meta-traditions in a manner that transcended both Radical Pietism and Anabaptism and received from both a call to found themselves on a Word-Spirit theological epistemology. The first comes out of the late W. R. Ward's research into early evangelicalism. Ward argues that much scholarship on evangelicalism begins too late and does not observe the roots of evangelical identity in German Pietism of the seventeenth and eighteenth centuries. When one explores this era of evangelicalism, Ward argues, an "evangelical hexagon" emerges that frames much of the later discussions of evangelical identity, though only five of the six characteristics are applicable to the early Brethren:⁷¹

1. A hostile view toward the scholasticism (Aristotelianism) that emerged in second-century Lutheranism;
2. A robust mystical theology to balance/correct the above scholastic distortions;
3. The centrality of the conversion experience as signifier for a regenerate life of discipleship;
4. An apocalyptic hope;
5. The creation and promulgation of small groups.⁷²

Ward's hexagon is helpful to begin to characterize a Brethren relationship with larger evangelicalism, specifically American evangelicalism. Not all of Ward's descriptions would fit the early Brethren.⁷³ Brethren do fit

---

70. Willoughby, *Counting the Cost*, 5.

71. Ward also includes the sixth characteristic of a mystical connection with nature as significant to his "evangelical hexagon." Ward seems to imply that early evangelicalism and mainstream Pietism are synonymous. The sixth characteristic of nature was quite evident in the thought of Arndt and Boehme. The five characteristics listed as relevant to the early Brethren, however, are more in line with the catalytic Pietist leader, Spener. See Ward, *Early Evangelicalism*, 4.

72. Ward, *Early Evangelicalism*, 4.

73. For more on Brethren and Ward's hexagon, see Kettering-Lane, "Evangelical from the Start?," 1–10.

Ward's first characteristic but their position would have been to reject what they deemed to be the elitism and the trappings of creeds, formulas, and confessions. There is an early impulse that pushes for a lived theology that encompasses both head and heart.

Ward's second characteristic is clearly present in the early Brethren. In reaction to the scholastic ethos that informed much of the established churches, the early Brethren were conversant with a number of mystical thinkers (Hochmann and Arnold mentioned already). This appreciation for mystical theology does not create the centrality of a "conversion experience" as denoted in Ward's third identifier. Instead, early Brethren argue for the centrality of baptism. As Denise Kettering-Lane notes:

> For the early Brethren, baptism was the primary marker of a change of life, not a story of conversion. Yet, there is a sense in which baptism marked the individual's move into the community of faith and the first step into obedience and reform of life. Thus, baptism marked the beginning of the reform of life.[74]

Baptism represents the inner/outer and individual/community nature of conversion for the early Brethren. A break between Hochmann and Mack, as already noted, occurred around the centrality of a visible witness of the church through practices like baptism. This witness, however, counter to Ward's fourth identifier, is not from an imminent eschatology or apocalyptic vision.[75]

---

74. Kettering-Lane, *Evangelical from the Start?*, 7. Kettering-Lane notes that among some Brethren there was particular interest in conversion experiences but it is not present in the writings of Alexander Mack. Kettering-Lane cites the autobiographical account of the conversion of Johann Lobach. See Durnbaugh, *European Origins*, 196.

75. Marcus Meier argues that Philadelphian eschatology was a coalescing factor for the early Brethren. His work is quite convincing and his command of research (much of it never before seen) is impressive and admirable. The intersection of Radical Pietism and Anabaptism is revealed to be much more complex than once thought. Utilizing city censuses, governmental documents, and correspondences from parallel movements of the period, Meier reveals the German Palatinate as a microcosm of the Radical Reformation. While Philadelphian eschatology (and more importantly, its failure to properly predict the end of time) served as a catalyst for several Radical Pietist sects of the period in their coalescence around structures, practices and governance, the ecclesiology of the Brethren was a product of Anabaptism, specifically Mennonite and Swiss Brethren (as has been shown). The telos of the Schwarzenau Brethren was less a failed Philadelphian eschatology and more a kingdom-minded people attempting to live out the separated life they found in the New Testament—in other words, the Schwarzenau Brethren were sectarian according to the vision they found of the church in the New Testament. Though the early Brethren would have held a premillennial eschatology from Pietism, they were not adherents of a Philadelphian eschatology as Meier insists. See Meier, *Schwarzenau Brethren*, 92–93. Stoffer further comments: "Mack also gave a

Lastly, and most notably for the early Brethren, Ward's fifth identifier of the presence of small groups rings true. Unlike Ward's description, however, the early Brethren separated from the established church. As Alexander Mack Jr. noted in his description of the Schwarzenau congregation:

> Here and there private meetings (in which the newly awakened souls sought their edification) were established alongside of the usual church organizations. However, because of the spiritual envy of the clergy, the hearts of the authorities were embittered, and persecution began to take place here and there.[76]

In light of these five identifiers, Kettering-Lane summarizes the role that Ward's research into early evangelicalism will have on projects such as this one:

> If Ward is right that early evangelicalism in Pietism . . . provided the roots from which evangelicalism today sprang, then it certainly makes sense that there continued to be some places of connection, *including an emphasis on Scripture and an interest in reformation of life*. Ward's argument provides a helpful lens through which we can see the involvement of early Brethren with evangelicalism as extending to an earlier period and connecting to some of the historical roots in Pietism (emphasis mine).[77]

An emphasis on Scripture and the ongoing reformation of life places the Brethren in a larger tradition that encompasses the movements of Radical Pietism and Anabaptism. This tradition has been termed the "Believers Church" tradition of which Donald Durnbaugh produced a masterful study.[78] Durnbaugh's research reveals seven characteristics of this larger tradition:

1. Voluntary membership
2. Separation of church and civil government

---

new foundation to other Radical Pietist emphases such as brotherly love, community, and the work of the Holy Spirit. Whereas these emphases were given an eschatological or spiritualist foundation in Radical circles, Mack concreted them in the life of the visible community. This preoccupation with giving visible expression to Jesus' teachings tended generally to weaken interest in eschatology." See Stoffer, *Brethren Doctrines*, 266.

76. Durnbaugh, *European Origins*, 37.

77. Kettering-Lane, *Evangelical from the Start?*, 9.

78. Durnbaugh provides a detailed historiography of this tradition, tracing its origin with the Waldensians, a separatist Medieval sect from the twelfth century. Spanning centuries, this tradition, according to Durnbaugh, encompasses the groups that are known as the Radical Reformation, of which Anabaptists, Radical Pietists, and eventually Brethren are a part. See Durnbaugh, *Believers' Church*.

3. Regenerate church
4. Church discipline as detailed in Matthew 18
5. Mutual aid
6. Believers' baptism
7. Centrality of both Word and Spirit[79]

It is in this tradition that the early Brethren most assuredly find a home. These seven identifiers will be essential in each generation of Brethren theological development and will produce points of tension and anxiety as Brethren interact with twentieth-century American evangelicalism. Durnbaugh's seventh characteristic, the dialectic of Word and Spirit, will anchor the other six in the Brethren witness. Pietism established the inward regeneration necessary for a covenanted community. Simultaneously, Anabaptism provided the discipline necessary for a regenerate community to exist counter to the fallenness of both established churches and imperial governments. For as Durnbaugh notes, "The Believers' Church . . . is the covenanted and disciplined community of those walking in the way of Jesus Christ. Where two or three such are gathered, willing to be scattered in the work of the Lord, there is the believing people."[80]

Concluding Observations

The Brethren view of baptism establishes a central Word-Spirit unity that captures the movement's theology on several fronts. First, this relationship of Word and Spirit reveals a desire to authentically describe the inward and then outward dimensions of the Christian journey. Second, it reveals a theology that is less a systematic, propositional understanding of truth and more a communal, lived out expression of Truth—seeing baptism as a relational following and obedience to Jesus who is the Truth (see John 14:6). Third, this unity places the Brethren in early evangelical streams of Pietism and Anabaptism into the larger tradition of the Believers' Church.

What develops with the genesis of the congregation in Schwarzenau, and is manifested in their understanding of baptism, is a fresh theological epistemology grounded in their new relationship with Jesus—inward regeneration expressed in a community of the regenerate. As Peter Rollins notes, this

---

79. Durnbaugh, *Believers' Church*, 32–33.
80. Durnbaugh, *Believers' Church*, 33.

view of truth is concerned with having a relationship with the Real (God) that results in us transforming reality. The emphasis is thus not on description but on transformation. This perspective completely short-circuits the long-redundant debate as to whether truth is subjective or objective, for here Truth is the ungraspable Real (objective) that transforms the individual (subjective).[81]

And in agreement with Rollins, Roger Olson argues that within Pietist groups, like the Brethren, the emphasis is on

> transformation, relationship, and activism . . . and less on . . . the importance of assent to propositions or participation in ceremonies and rituals. The keynote is inwardness with outward behavior flowing naturally from an inward transformation.[82]

This regeneration of the entire person, inner then outward, becomes centrally communicated in the Brethren understanding of baptism which serves as a blending of Radical Pietist and Anabaptist distinctives. Practices like baptism reveal a theology shaped by the interplay of Radical Pietist emphases of individuality and openness balanced by Anabaptist emphases of outward form, community and order.

This central interplay of Radical Pietism and Anabaptism and their shared call to a Word-Spirit centrality, informed the Brethren understanding of salvation and why they saw baptism intimately connected with discipleship. Salvation is a past, present and future tensed theological journey ("I was saved," "I am being saved," "I will be saved") between the believer, the church, and God. Brethren do not place an emphasis on *what* one knows. Instead, faith is a transformed life based on *who* the believing community (and individual believers) have come to know as real. This inner to outer and individual to community is captured by Stoffer:

> These governing principles give to the Brethren view of salvation and the Christian life their characteristic features: (1) enlightenment by the Word and Spirit as a necessary precondition to the salvation process; (2) repentance as a change of heart and mind which will bring forth fruits—a changed life; (3) faith as both confession of belief in Christ and commitment and surrender of one's life to Him; (4) obedience as a quality inherent in saving faith; (5) baptism as an integral part of the salvation process which looks backward as a response of obedient faith to

---

81. Rollins, *How (Not) to Speak of God*, 56.
82. Olson, "Pietism and Postmodernism," 376.

the gracious work of God and forward as a symbol of the new life . . . ; (6) God's gracious gifts to the repentant believer of forgiveness of sins, the Holy Spirit, justification, and adoption; (7) regeneration as the divine work of creating a new being in the believer; (8) union with God as a relational experience which acts as a catalyst for godly living; (9) the new life, denoted by obedient faith, as a loving response to a gracious Father; (10) sanctification as the progressive change of the believer into the character of Christ and the divine nature.[83]

Baptism is an inner and outer symbol—inner enlightenment, repentance, and regeneration moves outward toward a life of discipleship, faithfulness, obedience, and fruitfulness. With every baptism comes the response to Christ's call to count the cost. As Brown pointedly reminds his readers:

> For Mack, salvation was more than being saved to heaven when we die. Salvation is related to each meaning of baptism listed. A story that frequently circulates in Lancaster County, Pennsylvania, tells the same. A brother was saved in a revival that swept through the country over by the big river. The congregation he was joining gathered around the horse tank on one of the farms. After the third dip, he leaped out of the water waving his hands in the air and shouting, "It is finished! It is finished!" The elder grabbed the back of his shirt and looked straight into his eyes. "No, brother," he said, "it's just beginning."[84]

The Schwarzenau baptisms and subsequent congregation were just the beginning of the Brethren story. We now turn to the persecution and subsequent emigration to America that brings the Brethren story to the new world.

---

83. Stoffer, *Brethren Doctrines*, 245.
84. Brown, *Another Way*, 121.

2

Brethren in America

Schwarzenau, Germany, to Ashland, Ohio

In 1748, Alexander Mack Jr., known as "Sander," penned the following poem in response to the death of his dear friend Christopher Sauer II. Entitled "*Nun bricht der Hütten Haus entzwei*" ("Now breaks the cottage house in half"):

> Now breaks this house of earth in twain, now the body can decay;
> the pilgrimage is now over;
> now will my spirit recover;
> the soul has now won the fight;
> my Jesus has overcome the enemy.
> To Him alone be the honor.
>
> Now I will enter into Jesus who died for me.
> He has won through pain and death a refuge for my soul.
> He has prepared for me a better house in Heaven
> that I may praise Him in it forever and ever.[1]

Mack's poetry, even in moments of profound grief, reveals a "spiritual vision [of a] true homeland beyond the horizon of this world."[2] Dale Stoffer remarks on Mack as poet:

---

1. Heckman, *Religious Poetry*, 45.
2. Stoffer, "Alexander Mack Jr.," 16.

> Mack revealed a heart that dearly loved his Lord and that was filled with compassionate love for others.... Though not exhibiting a consistently highly polished style, his poems are characterized by spiritual depth and discernment.[3]

The depth and discernment that come from Mack's poetry reveal a simple (though not simplistic) faith rooted in his Brethren beliefs—shaped by streams of Anabaptism and Radical Pietism. Mack's writings reveal a deep sensitivity to Scripture and an awareness of the larger narrative arc of the Bible, along with a high view of the gathered church. These themes, informed by Radical Pietism and Anabaptism, are relayed in prose communicating meta-themes of discipleship, regeneration, and the vitality of the Holy Spirit.

This chapter will elucidate the historical development of the convergence of Anabaptism and Radical Pietism, that was signified in immersion baptism by first generation Brethren, as it takes root in American soil. This developing religious identity will be seen through biographical sketches that will serve to explicate not only the growing understanding of Brethrenism but also tension and crisis points of Brethren faith development in America. Two personalities will be especially important for this chapter—Sander Mack and nineteenth-century Brethren elder Peter Nead. These individuals highlight larger developments with Brethren of their periods respectively. Expansion moments for the Brethren occur with the presence of leadership that embody the synergy of both Radical Pietist and Anabaptist streams within Brethren thought.[4] Crisis moments, however, occur when the cooperation of these two parts of Brethren heritage weaken. The schisms at the end of the nineteenth century occurred because of the absence of such leadership. The Brethren were left fractured as the creative tension of the dialectic was lost. The closing of this chapter will detail the numerous factors that created the 1880s schisms of the fellowship and the subsequent schism within the Progressives in 1939.

European Persecution and Immigration to America

The newly formed Brethren experienced great disruption after the baptisms of 1708. Persecution caused sporadic flights to new regions in which to find asylum. The map below provides geographic context for Brethren

---

3. Stoffer, "Alexander Mack Jr.," 16.

4. The phrase "dialectical leadership" will be used to denote that manner of leadership in the Brethren that sought to balance both the Radical Pietist and Anabaptist contributions to Brethren thought and witness.

movement beyond Schwarzenau. The sect spread rapidly from Schwarzenau to other German areas, especially in the region around Büdingen, in the Palatinate, and into Krefeld. A brief mentioning of the significance of each will assist with tying the Brethren story to America.

- Büdingen: After 1711 the Schwarzenau Brethren established a daughter congregation here. Count Karl August (1667–1725) was tolerant of religious dissent but, in 1714, issued a ban on public religious activity not sponsored by the state church. The local Brethren left the area and settled in and around Krefeld. Nearby is the village of Düdelsheim, birthplace of Peter Becker.
- Heidelberg: During the late seventeenth and early eighteenth centuries, Heidelberg was the scene of much Pietistic activity, some centering around professors at the university. Conrad Beissel, the founder of the Ephrata Community, was born in 1690 at Eberbach on the Neckar River just east of the city. Nearby Ladenburg was the birthplace of Christopher Sauer I in 1695; his father was a Reformed pastor.
- Surhuisterveen: A Dutch refuge for the Brethren between 1720–1729.
- Basel: Pietist activity in Basel centered on the Boni family, who lived in the nearby village of Frenkendorf. Andrew Boni and his brother Martin were incarcerated in the Spalentor in 1706. Andrew Boni was expelled from the city in 1707 and became one of the first Brethren at Schwarzenau.
- Krefeld: In 1715 the Marienborn-area Brethren came here after being expelled from Büdingen and surrounding villages. Six Brethren from nearby Solingen were arrested in 1717 because of their baptism in the Wupper River.
- Berleburg: The site of the printing of the famous Pietist version of Scripture, the Berleburg Bible, between 1726 and 1742. It was also the location of an important letter from Christopher Sauer I to his friends in the area that prompted many to emigrate to America.
- Rotterdam: The port of exit for many Brethren who left for America in 1719, 1729, and 1733.

From Krefeld to the new world, the geographical journey of the Brethren was also a developing journey of identity and consciousness. The journey from Europe to America was a moment born out of necessity for the Brethren as they sought freedom for their religious expression. Born out of reaction to the reformation landscape of continental Europe, the migration to America granted the Brethren freedom to worship not afforded them in continental Europe. The Brethren immigration narrative, however, would be both productive and haunting to Brethren as they settled in their new home in colonial Pennsylvania. The new world was a welcome respite from persecution but they quickly recognized their outsider status in a new land.

The Beginning of a Brethren American Identity

Religious pressure and economic necessities combined to make migration to North America essential. Two large groups left, in 1719 and 1729, as well as several smaller parties between and after those years. By 1750 the Brethren had been transplanted to America. Those who came to Germantown in 1719 did not formally organize a congregation until Christmas Day, 1723, when they held their first baptisms and inaugural love feast, led by Peter Becker.

Peter Becker (1687–1758) served as a central connector of the European beginnings of the Brethren and their newfound home in America. Becker provided leadership to the first Brethren congregation in America—Germantown, Pennsylvania (outside present-day Philadelphia). Becker became interested in the Radical Pietist movement in Europe after growing frustration with the Reformed Church of his birth. With Mack Sr., he was attracted to the teachings of Hochmann von Hochenau. On May 15, 1714, he was baptized by the Brethren minister Johannes Naas in Dudelsheim.[5] Becker's oversight allowed not only for the formation of a congregation in the new world but also allowed it to flourish. It was Becker's evangelistic efforts that led to the formation of a second (Coventry) and third (Conestoga) Brethren congregation in colonial Pennsylvania.

Becker worked as a weaver and eventually apprenticed a Radical Pietist named Conrad Beissel who quickly became a leader of the Conestoga congregation. Beissel's Radical Pietist views, unchecked by Anabaptism, produced a division within the congregation in 1728. Finding the Anabaptist witness of the Brethren to be legalistic and oppressive to the Spirit, Beissel and his followers founded a communal society along the Cocalico Creek, a tributary of the Conestoga River in present day Lebanon and Lancaster counties of Pennsylvania. This society became known as the Ephrata Cloister, to which many Brethren were attracted. Ephrata championed unorthodox views that differed radically from the Brethren—including Sabbatarianism, celibacy, and monasticism. The central impulse of these views was the Radical Pietist slant that animated Beissel's faith. Becker and

---

5. Durnbaugh, *Fruit of Vine*, 36.

Mack Sr. attempted to reconcile with Beissel but the Ephrata community could not be reconciled to the perceived legalism of the Brethren (nor the Anabaptist structure of their witness).

Throughout the eighteenth century the Germantown congregation continued to play a leading role in Brethren life. In 1729, Mack Sr. led about 120 Brethren to America.[6] The leadership of Mack Sr., alongside capable leaders like Becker, Sander Mack, and Christopher Sauer II enabled the evangelistic zeal of the Brethren to spread their faith quickly in America, with congregations founded in Pennsylvania, New Jersey, Maryland, Virginia, and the Carolinas by 1770.[7] The Brethren became characterized by their practice of believer baptism by trine immersion and their observance of the Lord's Supper with its three parts: feetwashing, love feast, and communion. Their worship services had lively preaching and singing. Their congregations were led by unpaid or free ministers elected by the local church. Brethren sought to live a devout and Christ-like style of life and to maintain their principles of nonconformity, nonresistance, and nonswearing.

The Brethren, having recently emigrated from Krefeld, Germany, found themselves with Mennonite and Quaker groups in Germantown. The exemplar of this period was Alexander "Sander" Mack Jr. (1712–1802)—more specifically, his poetry. Jeff Bach describes Mack as "the most prolific Brethren poet in North America in the eighteenth century. His poetry opens an important window onto Brethren understandings of spirituality."[8]

Mack's poetry communicated themes of separation from the world, the pilgrimage of faith, and hope. As an alien in a foreign land, one that was often hostile, Mack remained steadfast in his hope. Throughout his poetry he references Pietist understandings of Christ who is the "Lamb of God," "the Bridegroom," and the "Good and Faithful Shepherd" and whose teachings are "sweet as sugar" and "sweeter than honey."[9]

---

6. Few Brethren remained in Europe. Those that did joined other Pietistic groups or the Mennonites. The Brethren had fully been transplanted to America by 1750.

7. Sauer and his father, Christopher Sauer I, were known for their printing establishment that served the German-speaking settlers in America. The Sauer Press published the three editions of the Sauer Bible, the first European-language Bible printed in America, along with almanacs, books, magazines, and newspapers. The Sauers used a specific typeface that was easier for German readers to read. Christopher Sauer II would suffer severely during the American Revolution when his press was confiscated and he was tortured for his unwillingness to support the revolutionary cause. Brethren of the period, by and large, did not support the revolutionary cause, believing they were to submit to the Crown according to the commands of Rom 13:1–7.

8. Bach, "Brethren Spirituality in the 18th Century," 3–24.

9. See Heckman, *Religious Poetry*.

Bach identifies the humanity that underlies Mack's prose. "Throughout Mack's poetic path of spirituality," he highlights, "is a deep, at times dark, awareness of the frailty and brevity of life and the wrong directions in which bodily desires can lead."[10] Samuel Heckman translated much of Mack's poetry from German into English and placed Mack's poems into two categories. The first were hymns and spiritual songs. The second were poems printed in Christopher Sauer's religious magazine between 1763 and 1772.[11]

Through these mediums—poems and hymns—Mack captures and communicates the Brethren immigration narrative as they reveal a transitional self-awareness. Brethren in colonial Pennsylvania were interacting with religious "others" in a new context. The tension of autonomy and communal identity, intrinsic to the archaic shift, reflects Brethren life of this period. Mack's writings reveal the creative tension of Anabaptism and Pietism as Brethren engage their new religious neighbors—German and English speaking alike.

Scott Holland reveals the Anabaptist theme of discipleship in Mack's poetry within what he terms the "poetics of Pietism":

> This linking of poetry to discipleship is intriguing. It of course speaks to the issue of the surpluses and excesses of meaning in religious language, always inviting further exploration and fresh articulation in the ongoing adventure of faith and following. However, it also speaks to matters of the heart. It is here, I would suggest, that the Pietist offers a helpful corrective to the Anabaptist.
>
> For the Anabaptist, discipleship is grounded very much in the clear and concrete exercise of *the will* to follow Jesus. In this sense it is a highly ethical and reasonable expression of faith and practice. The poetics of Pietism, however, emphasize the reasons of *the heart* which can be more touched by mystery, metaphor, wonder, love and transcendence in the romance of faith. . . . Mack writes very confessionally, emotionally and poetically.[12]

Holland's observation of a Pietist correction to the potential blind spots, namely the heart, of Anabaptism is quite similar to the translingual (and transcultural) reality of Brethren within colonial Pennsylvania. Poetry like Mack's would have assisted them in the exploration of their identity in the new world. There was a continual need for Brethren of the period to

---

10. Bach, *Brethren Spirituality*, 3–24.
11. Heckman, *Religious Poetry*, 151.
12. Holland, "Sander Mack," 108.

maintain the equilibrium of their Radical Pietist and Anabaptist heritage—a balance of individual and community, internal and external witness, head and heart, and, most importantly, the ongoing maintenance of the Word-Spirit organic relationship at the heart of their witness. Patrick Erben writes of two "iconic instances" of this translingual and transcultural reality for German groups like the Brethren.[13] The first he describes as the publishing of *Martyrs Mirror* by the Ephrata community in the 1740s and 1750s as its detailed stories of martyrdom were translated to the current political context "of a province rife with fears of war and mandatory armament." Secondly, the joint English Quaker–German sectarian participation in the Friendly Association for Regaining and Preserving Peace with the Indians during the Seven Years' War precipitated a revitalization of a common spiritual foundation among both groups, especially by stressing their common history of persecution and suffering.[14] These "iconic instances" would have marked Mack's life and the pilgrimage of the early Brethren in colonial America. Mack even participated in the translation of the *Martyrs' Mirror* at Ephrata and his life was marked by war. The threat of violence and division was always palpable in his world, yet his writings do not communicate anxiety. They speak to a peace, manifested through the medium of poetry, that in many ways accomplished the Philadelphian dream of transcendence.[15] Two specific examples of pilgrimage imagery in Mack's poetry are found in poems written on his birthday—a day that caused him to pause and reflect. The first is found in a 1779 birthday poem, "Once again a year is gone / O thou rock, eternity! / All my ardent longing goes far beyond this life / towards this true fatherland / for I'm a stranger here below."[16] The tension of true fatherland is evident in this poem. The eschatological hope of the colonial Brethren would have assisted their weathering of the many challenges and setbacks they experienced as a people.

The other example comes from a birthday poem from the following year (1780): "I can no more consider what happens in this world / For on these pilgrims' roads there shines for me a different light. . . . What brings me pain but helps me on, what brings me joy but holds me back / My true rest I find

---

13. Erben, *Harmony of the Spirits*, 245. While German Mennonites would have utilized Ephrata for publication of *Martyrs' Mirror*, they probably did so pragmatically—for financial reasons—as they would not identify with Philadelphia ideals. German Mennonites had the resources for such a printing and Ephrata accepted the task for economic reasons.

14. Erben, *Harmony of the Spirits*, 245.

15. Such a theme would have been consistent with Mack during his time at Ephrata. Philadelphian ideals are less present in Mack's later life.

16. Heckman, *Religious Poetry*, 152.

up yonder when my brief pilgrimage is done."[17] Amid the obstacles of colonial Pennsylvania, Mack and the early Brethren found peace in their eschatology. There premillennial eschatology would have shaped them to understand their current situation as in line with Scripture. It also reinforced their recognition of, involvement with, and care of other outsiders experiencing persecution—one only has to recall the plight of Native Americans and slaves. It's quite telling that in his final birthday entry (1803), at the age of ninety years, Mack refers to himself as "the poor pilgrim whom the mercy of God has sustained until he is ninety years old."[18] Pilgrimage, with the hills and valleys that mark the journey, was always near to Mack's heart because it was a frame of reference for how the early Brethren understood themselves in the new world.

Christian Bunner identifies eight themes central to Pietist literature of Mack's period. Pietist poetry and hymnody provided for

> the communication of religious assurance through individual experience of God; renewal and transformation of life through the Holy Spirit; the critique of dead, conformist church spirituality; the awakening of hope in an imminent eschatological kingdom of God; the transformation of believers by the divine Being; the formation of fellowship; the encouragement of active expressions of love; and the sharing of one's faith.[19]

These eight themes appear in Mack's poetry. One finds an ongoing travelogue of experiences of God coupled with the ongoing transformation of both person and perspective because of the activity of the Holy Spirit. There is a retelling of biblical stories and themes which allows for nuanced reflection on texts that had lost their impact because of established church polities. The theme of pilgrimage is animated by an eschatological hope which forms the witness of the church, and calls one to a generous spirituality with others on the journey. A tension of heart/emotion (Radical Pietism) and discipleship/community (Anabaptism) enliven his writings.

The strongest theme of Mack's writings is his christocentric hope. As the Pietist witness called Brethren to a new life in Christ, the Anabaptist witness anchored that conversion in the Bible for Mack. In these reflections, Mack would often translate biblical events into poetry. He details the passion of Christ in poetic prose in one journal entry. The following excerpt from a poem detailing Good Friday, captures Mack's ability to translate Scripture into a poem of personal application:

17. Heckman, *Religious Poetry*, 152.

18. Heckman, *Religious Poetry*, 152.

19. Heckman, *Religious Poetry*, 235–36. For more, see Bunner, *Lieder des Pietismus aus dem 17. and 18. Jahrhundert*.

Eight o'clock.
Dressed in white, Thou comest now
To Pilate once again,
For nothing 'gainst Thee can be found
Save only my guilt of sins.
Nine o'clock.
Wicked men are scourging Thee,
But the guilt I must confess
And in justice I should suffer
What the mad heathen do to Thee.

Ten o'clock.
The crown of thorns Jesus must wear,
The purple robe, the jeers and scorn,
All for me unworthy sinner,
And in addition He is beaten . . .

Three o'clock in the afternoon.
Now that all should be fulfilled
Which the Scriptures have foretold,
And that they might quench His thirst
They have a sponge filled with vinegar.

And the precious Lamb of God
Drinks it on the cross's beam,
Bows His head and suffers death
So that mercy I can receive.[20]

Though Mack firmly believed in the necessity of a life lived in accordance with Scripture he also held to the necessity of a vital, heartfelt inner life of the Spirit. Whereas Radical Pietism tended to elevate direct revelation over Scripture due to fear of legalism, Aaron Jerviss notes that

> the poetry of Alexander Mack Jr., however, seems to nicely balance the experiential and the external. Mack believes in a vital, Spirit-awakened relationship that still recognizes the written word of God in Scripture as a beneficial and necessary foundational document.[21]

Stoffer further details the elements of Radical Pietism, Pietism, and Anabaptism in Mack's poetry:

---

20. Heckman, *Religious Poetry*, 102–3.
21. Jerviss, "Spiritual Writings," 154.

Elements from Pietism and Radical Pietism

- Mild Christ mysticism, using the bride and bridegroom imagery drawn from Song of Solomon.
- The use of the term "Babel" to refer to established churches, especially because of their lack of discipline in the case of "unbelievers and despisers of the Divine Word."
- Belief in the thousand-year reign of Christ (the millennium).
- Universal restoration
- The recurring theme of love throughout his writings, a theme found in the thought of Jacob Boehme and many of the Radical Pietists.
- References to the kiss of peace or love as an expression of fraternal love.
- The creative spirit reflected in Mack's poetry and hymn writing; such creativity had disappeared for the most part among the Mennonites by this time.
- Hermeneutical emphases such as reading the part in light of the whole and comparing Scripture with Scripture.
- Spiritual Sensitivity

Elements Reflecting Anabaptist Thought and Practices

- A high view of the visible church, the gathered community of the disciples of Christ.
- Consensus decision making, as reflected in great meetings or annual meetings attended by Mack.
- A commitment to discipline.
- The theology of baptism.
- Belief that children are in a state of innocence and are covered by the salvific work of Christ; they therefore do not need to be baptized.
- View of communion as a memorial of Jesus' suffering and death.
- Reference to the "shadow" of the law and the "essence of the new covenant."

Elements Derived from Both Pietism/Radical Pietism and Anabaptism

- Nonresistance.
- A strong appeal for regeneration, a new life conformed to Christ.
- Understanding the Christian life in terms of discipleship to Christ or following him.
- The vital role of the Holy Spirit in all aspects of the Christian life.
- Reference to the inner and outer Words to refer to the Spirit and Scripture respectively.
- Following the example of the early Christians.
- Commitment to serve the "least of these."
- Humble yieldedness toward God.[22]

Stoffer further remarks from Mack's poetry and other writings, "Mack is inwardly and spiritually a Pietist, and outwardly and practically an Anabaptist."[23]

Mack's christocentric hope was a fusion of both his Radical Pietist and Anabaptist moorings. Poetry became a vehicle to detail his spiritual reading of Scripture. Almost as a corrective to the externalism of his father's faith, Mack concludes that when externals are given absolute authority over the internal witness of the Spirit "misery and division" are created as people take a stand on one passage while rejecting others (passages and people) that seem to contradict it. He instead calls for the church to utilize "spiritual eyes" so that such contradictions can be harmonized. Mack Jr. reveals a theologian with a deep appreciation for and application of the Holy Spirit. Since the Spirit is the original author of the text, only it can create and preserve unity. Furthermore, the Spirit's influence will be marked by love: "[Above] all preserve love, for thus one preserves light. The good God, who is the pure impartial love, can and will supply gradually where insight is lacking here or there."[24] Hope, unity and love serve as the indicators of the true church. Whether in times of celebration or crisis, these outward signs communicated the inner commitments to both Word and Spirit for the Brethren. The nineteenth century would prove to be a great challenge for the Brethren on exactly this front.

22. Stoffer, "Alexander Mack Jr.," 18.
23. Stoffer, "Alexander Mack Jr.," 18.
24. Mack, "Letter concerning Feetwashing," 444–45.

The Brethren Expansion

Brethren of the nineteenth century would begin transitioning from a German-speaking people on the fringe of the American mainstream to a people speaking English and developing dialogue with the larger society.[25] During the antebellum period the Brethren entered a period of introspection and reflection on their identity amid migration beyond the borders of Pennsylvania. A tendency for dogmatism and a strong push for order in theology began to appear and is manifested in the theological writings of the period as the Brethren wrestled with the larger questions of assimilation. Steven Nolt, while not writing about Brethren of the period but rather German Reformed and Lutherans of Pennsylvania, maintains that German religious groups (of which the Brethren were one) were America's first groups to experience a phenomenon that he characterizes as "ethnicization-as-Americanization."[26]

By the 1780s, Pennsylvania Germans had taken very few steps toward assimilation into the larger Anglophone society of the early Republic.[27] The United States was constitutionally a land demographically dominated by "British stock" residents.[28] Those who had started the Revolution were now the sole ones debating its legacy and such an Anglophone society was at odds with those of German stock. The resulting tension became one of ethnicity in early America.

> Ethnicity rested on a conscious acceptance and perpetuation of culture—the interrelated collection of symbols, folkways, institutions, and ideals that defined and gave meaning to the good life and the accepted way of living it. . . . But ethnicity . . . was always more than attachment to a particular language or collection of distinctive folkways. At its heart were values and ideals that gave meaning to ordinary activities and relationships.[29]

These ethnic "values and ideals," according to Stephen Longenecker, experienced at minimum four "revolutions" during the early nineteenth century. Studying those deemed "religious outsiders" rather than "mainstream" in the Virginia backcountry, Longenecker defines the revolutions as American, Methodist, market, and Southern—though these revolutions impacted

---

25. During this period, the Brethren were officially known as the German Baptist Brethren and informally as the Brethren. Another designation in scholarship on the period is "Dunker."
26. Nolt, *Foreigners in Their Own Land*, 3.
27. Nolt, *Foreigners in Their Own Land*, 3.
28. Nolt, *Foreigners in Their Own Land*, 22.
29. Nolt, *Foreigners in Their Own Land*, 29–30.

Brethren beyond the Shenandoah Valley. In Longenecker's assessment, what developed during this period was a tension not just between outsiders and mainstream but, rather, a tension over what "outsiderness" meant.

"[Outsiderness]," Longenecker asserts, was an indicator that "[prevented] separation from the world from being empty rhetoric." Such definition increased the likelihood "that the group [would] resist the mainstream."[30] The "mainstream" consisted of those in power who made the division from the cultural mainstream distant. "Outsiders" were those nonconformists who saw the division from the societal mainstream as being much more local and thus demanding clear ethnic borders with the world.

While both mainstream and outsiders claimed nonconformity, Longenecker argues that the four revolutions that swept through the nineteenth-century Shenandoah Valley specifically, and larger America generally, identified the authentic nonconformists as those who faced persecution for their beliefs. The dialectical challenge presented to Brethren of the period was how to simultaneously be in the world but not of it (cf. John 17:14–19).

The first revolution was the impact of the American Revolution on outsiderness. Brethren developed specific practices that informed their otherness to the mainstream, regardless of who was in charge. Practices like nonresistance forged an identity boundary amid a country at war.

Another seismic cultural shift came with the Methodist Revolution of the nineteenth century with the impact of revivalism, especially, on outsiders and mainstream religion. The Methodist revolution occurred as a "new wave of revivalism and emotional worship [throughout] Protestantism in the early nineteenth century."[31] Accentuating the role of personal experience in worship and the importance of evangelism and civic duty, revivalism "brought enough change and so successfully overwhelmed its competition and captured the soul of America that it constituted a revolution."[32] Brethren rejected revivalism finding it to be a distortion of the dialectic of Radical Pietism over against Anabaptism by skewing faith to a hyper-individualistic experience. Brethren maintained inspiring worship as a communal witness around the growing presence of meetinghouses.

The third revolution occurred in the market—a revolution that "reconstructed the economy, transforming a localized, subsistence, handicraft process into a market-oriented, cash and debt, industrialized system."[33] Those who had once been able to categorize extravagance like fashion as

30. Longenecker, *Shenandoah Religion*, 12.
31. Longenecker, *Shenandoah Religion*, 7–8.
32. Longenecker, *Shenandoah Religion*, 59.
33. Longenecker, *Shenandoah Religion*, 80.

"sinful" were now confronted with the "world." Brethren of the period still remained separate from this revolution but this boundary line would create great angst in the late nineteenth century as a faction known as the "Progressives" demanded greater engagement with society.

The final revolution arose from the secession of southern states from the Union and the problem of slavery. "As the Valley's majority increasingly fell into step with slaveholders," Longenecker asserts, "Brethren ... occupied the opposite pole by tagging this popular institution as part of the sinful world."[34] This became a part of their outsiderness. With this outsider identification came great persecution that Longenecker identifies as "unionism."[35]

> Unionism's emergence as a marker of outsiderness shows that sometimes one firmly held boundary against the world can unexpectedly lead to another; determined anti-slavery resulted in opposition to Confederate nationalism. Secondly, boundaries of little notice can quickly become critical in new circumstances; nonviolence in peacetime was a little-noticed marker, but it brought persecution when the nation-state desperately struggled for life.[36]

Whereas Methodists and Presbyterians witnessed assimilation into the mainstream in the wake of the American and market revolutions respectively, Brethren became the quintessential definition of "outsiders."

Polarization regarding identity emerged for the Brethren amid the ongoing "revolutions" and helps explain the divisions of the late nineteenth century. A dominant theme of nonconformity, and subsequent disagreement over the term, surfaced among the Brethren as it was central to understanding the true church. As various religious groups lost their "outsiderness," many simultaneously lost their witness. The second, but related theme was the tension of outsider and mainstream and how each fit in the process of what Nolt called "ethnicization-as-Americanization."[37] As outsiders assimilated to the mainstream a piece of their folk experience was lost. This "ethnicization" process demanded critical thinkers to assist the Brethren in navigating the turmoil of the period. Such a thinker and leader

---

34. Longenecker, *Shenandoah Religion*, 142.

35. While this would have been true only of Brethren in the South. "Unionism" does describe the backlash that nineteenth-century Brethren received with their response to the Civil War—the identifying meta-crisis of America in the nineteenth century. The Brethren stance against fighting and slavery put them against those who did not share such sentiments—often times against denominations with different theological outlooks on the conflict.

36. Longenecker, *Shenandoah Religion*, 181.

37. Nolt, *Foreigners in Their Own Land*, 3.

arose in Peter Nead (1796–1877), who was "a born Lutheran, a convinced Methodist, [and] a thrice-immersed Dunker."[38] Nead became for the Brethren a teacher, preacher, and writer.

Stoffer further contributes to the picture of Nead by opening his chapter on the theologian's life with the following introduction:

> Without doubt the most thorough and detailed exposition of Brethren thought during the nineteenth century comes from the pen of Peter Nead (1796–1877). In his two major works, *Theological Writings* and *Wisdom and Power of God*, Nead covers the major themes of systematic theology and considers at length the distinctive practices of the Brethren. His works received wide circulation among the Brethren and undoubtedly served to effect greater unity of thought throughout the Brotherhood. Albert Ronk pays tribute to Nead and his theological writing by observing that his "theology was so pungent and convincing, the minds of the people were so thoroughly settled as to the sacramental rites, that, in the disagreements which later caused three divisions among the Brethren, none of them arose over the Sacraments."[39]

Stoffer concludes: "For an in-depth understanding of the thought of the nineteenth-century Brethren mind, the investigation of thought of Peter Nead becomes mandatory."[40]

Nead was known as "the English Preacher" for his ability to serve in a bilingual capacity. Many Brethren ministers of the period still preached in German. A few were bilingual. As Fred Benedict notes, "Nead's great love for the Brethren's doctrines; his attachment to the church's traditions and his ability as a speaker which gave his arguments force and conviction certainly smoothed the transition to the new language."[41]

Nead's theological outlook stressed Scripture over the Spirit—a truncating of the dialectic that would prove detrimental to later Brethren of the nineteenth century. A legalistic tone develops in his writings which is why Nead can describe the Bible as "one law book" for the church.[42] Such a systematizing of thought led Nead to argue, for example, that "not only the mode [of baptism], but all that is connected with the institution [is] strictly

---

38. Durnbaugh, "Vindicator," 196.
39. Stoffer, *Brethren Doctrines*, 114.
40. Stoffer, *Brethren Doctrines*, 114.
41. Benedict, "Peter Nead," 66.
42. Stoffer, *Brethren Doctrines*, 119.

essential [and] willful omission in any one part of the institution," he notes, "would be an infringement upon the holy name of Jesus."[43]

The irony of the period is a series of articles Nead wrote in 1860 for the denominational magazine, the *Gospel Visitor*, wherein he strongly advocated that Brethren vote in political elections.[44] Nead's departure from a more traditionalist posture for the Brethren is intriguing as his rationale was radical for the Brethren of the period, "There was a time when we had our scruples about these things," Nead wrote, "but as subjects of the civil government we owe these duties to the government for the well-being of ourselves and fellow man."[45]

Nead received a reprimand from the Annual Conference and upon request through standing committee was made to publicly apologize remarking, "I am now tolerably far advanced in years—I have been a member of the church nearly forty years, but have not made that advancement in the knowledge of our Lord Jesus Christ as many others have done. To err is still too common with me."[46]

Nead's willingness to go out on a limb for Brethren voting reveals not just a nuanced understanding of the role of government and the church's interaction with the state but also a growing tension around the role of individual conscience and the witness of Annual Meeting. Nead's reprimand is a turning point as his later views will remain steadfastly in support of a growing group known as the Old Order who did not depart from traditional Brethren moorings of the period. In this instance, Nead reveals a progressive understanding of government different from the traditional Amish, conservative Mennonite, and conservative Brethren perspectives.

It's important to distinguish where Nead's thought nuances the traditional Brethren/Anabaptist perspective on government. In regards to the church's *involvement in* the government, Nead is quite orthodox by Brethren standards. In one of his more famous works, *Theological Writings*, he articulates the traditional Brethren view on church and world:

> To be strictly honest in all [the church's] dealings with all men: to speak the truth upon all occasions: to sue no person at law: not to resist evil, but to suffer: to do unto all men, as we would wish them to do unto us: love our enemies, consequently the

---

43. Stoffer, *Brethren Doctrines*, 119.

44. Further research needs to be done to see if Nead's advocacy for Brethren voting was in response to the slavery issue that was developing a North-South divide in the country.

45. Benedict, "Peter Nead," 70.

46. Benedict, "Peter Nead," 70.

members do not learn to go to war: to pay tribute to whom tribute is due.[47]

For Nead, the relationship of the church to civil government is determined by the Apostle Paul's words in Rom 13:1–7. In this passage, Paul argues that the role of government is to punish evildoers and protect the good of the land. All peoples, in response, pay taxes (or tribute in times of war) to the governing authorities.

Yet Nead's writings also reveal a struggle with answering the question of whether *all* governments are ordained by God.

> Thus, it is plain that our Saviour did not refuse to pay tribute, and if he did not I do not see why his disciples should. And the apostle Paul, in his letters to the Romans, treats this subject at large. In this chapter, he charges every soul to be subject unto the higher powers—that no one should rebel against the civil authorities, but to be obedient: "For there is no power but of God, the powers that be are ordained of God." Here it will not be amiss for me to remark that those powers which the apostle speaks of, as being ordained of God, cannot mean a base and corrupt government, or such powers as are in opposition to the Gospel of Jesus Christ: for if you admit, that all the powers that were, and are, in the world, have been ordained by God, then you must also admit, that it was the powers of God which put Jesus Christ, the apostles, and all the holy martyrs to death; which cannot be true, if the Gospel is from God. We must believe that all those powers which are ordained by God, are such as will not punish a righteous man, or one who feels it his duty to obey the Gospel. It is certain that all those powers which do oppose the precepts of the Gospel, are not from God; for God will never oppose himself.[48]

The telling distinction for Nead's understanding of civil government comes with this line: "For if you admit, that all the powers that were, and are, in the world, have been ordained by God, then you must also admit, that it was the powers of God which put Jesus Christ, the apostles, and all the holy martyrs to death; which cannot be true, if the Gospel is from God."[49]

---

47. Nead, *Theological Writings*, loc. 4906.
48. Nead, *Theological Writings*, loc. 1590.
49. Nead, *Theological Writings*, loc. 1590. If all governments are ordained by God, Nead argues, then God is complicit, even culpable, in the death of his son and the apostles. Governments that rule as a "terror to good works," Nead writes, are not ordained by God. See Nead, *Theological Writings*, loc. 1595.

Nead's rationale for the church to abstain from the patterns of the world is patience, obedience, and hope—Anabaptist and Pietist postures also evidenced in the writings of Sander Mack. The irony is that while Brethren of the period were not to be involved with civil government, beyond paying the tribute, their witness put them in direct confrontation with the Civil War as rumors of secession grew. With the South's secession from the Union, Nead's words became haunting to Brethren. Unfolding before them was the embodiment of Nead's good and corrupt governments. The patient, obedient and hopeful witness of the church was a continual reminder of the new kingdom followers of Christ lived in after their baptism. It is the Word-Spirit testimony, constitutive of a Brethren epistemology, that assured the church of its salvation and sanctified it for mission. Nead writes, "The believer, by examining the Gospel, finds, that he has proceeded agreeably to the word; and, in examining his heart he perceives that he is operated upon by a Spirit which precisely agrees with the Gospel."[50] Word and Spirit provided the assuring testimony needed amid crisis and conflict. The Word and Spirit called the church to look and behave differently from the rest of the world. The Word and Spirit enabled the church to resist temptation of all kinds. Even in conversations of voting, the Brethren were challenged by their perspective on a Word-Spirit, lived theology. The Word and Spirit was a reminder to Brethren of the nineteenth century, championed by leaders like Nead, to examine their biblical witness amid a society of simultaneous progress and disruption.

Such introspection and reflection were new for the Brethren. As a result, the Brethren brought increasing numbers of questions to Annual Meeting for deliberation.[51] With greater assimilation and the tumult of the antebellum South, Brethren faced several serious dilemmas. The first was a dilemma of faithfulness. What were the essentials of apostolic faith? Where was the line between timeless truth and cultural tradition? What changes in faith and practice were permissible? How could innovation and progress be reconciled with primitive Christianity? This dilemma was often expressed in a legalistic perspective regarding the ordinances—a quest for identity amid a sea of Christian denominations. This period, in some sense, became a struggle over Brethren dogma. Dogmatism arose among an Old Order faction that desired to retain the outward symbols of identity—plain dress, separation from the world, and distinct language.

50. Nead, *Theological Writings*, loc. 1206.

51. These yearly gatherings of Brethren from around the country began in the mid-1700s and served the dual role of maintaining fellowship among the scattered Brethren and developing unity on questions of faith and practice that were considered by the assembled Brethren.

Meanwhile, a progressive faction, the "Progressives" for their appreciation of progress, also known as the "fast element," sought to encourage localized engagement with society with a larger freedom/autonomy from Annual Meeting.[52]

A second dilemma arose regarding unity—how much unity of faith and practice was required? Where must it be preserved and where could variation be tolerated? Was unity of principle more important than unity of practice? Such a dilemma became expressed in varied interpretations of the purpose and authority of Annual Meeting.

The third dilemma was separation—how should Brethren remain distinct from other Christians and larger society? Where were the boundaries between true and nominal Christianity? Did Brethren possess a truer understanding of what it meant to follow Christ? This dilemma could be depicted as a calcification of Brethren practices. Instead, it was a quest for identity as the Brethren sought to differentiate themselves from other religious groups.

These three stressors—faithfulness, unity, separation—caused a crisis of authority within the Brethren. Annual Meeting wrestled with questions about its authority and was challenged on the scope of its oversight by the progressive wing. Questions before Annual Meeting reveal growing tension points: what means should be used to maintain unity and separation? Could Brethren be compelled or obligated to adopt certain practices? Which ones and how rigidly? What is the agent of enforcement and by what authority does it operate? How do Brethren—Old Order and Progressives—relate with America?

By the 1860s, these two opposing viewpoints had become entrenched within the church. The Progressives sought to encourage localized engagement with society with a larger freedom/autonomy from Annual Meeting, feeling the brotherhood should make full use of new methodologies like Sunday Schools, evangelism, higher education, and foreign missions to enable the church to spread its beliefs more widely and to more quickly move into the mainstream of American culture. The Old Order felt such innovations would move the church in the direction of worldly Christianity and away from the established faith of the church. During the 1870s, a third group, the main body of the church, the Conservatives, sought a mediating position between the two extremes. By the beginning of the 1880s, tensions among these factions had reached a breaking point. This breaking point was exacerbated by seven streams of dissension:

---

52. It is fascinating to see how decisions of Annual Meeting became codified throughout this period to ironically produce a creed for Brethren behavior.

- Periodicals
- Education
- Evangelism
- Paid ministry
- Sunday Schools
- Dress
- Feetwashing[53]

For the purposes of this chapter, the streams of periodicals, education, feetwashing, and dress will suffice to capture the divergence arising among nineteenth-century Brethren.

Feetwashing—By What Mode?

A contentious issue dividing the two groups was the proper form of feetwashing. The Old Order practiced what was called the "double mode" of feetwashing in which one person washed the feet of several while another followed and dried them. This mode of feetwashing was generally practiced by Eastern Brethren churches. The Old Order desired uniformity on this practice. The Progressives sought freedom to practice the "single mode": each person both washes and dries the feet of their neighbor. This mode was practiced by the Far Western Brethren as well as the Germantown congregation. During the latter 1860s and throughout the 1870s this issue was bitterly contested in church periodicals and at Annual Meetings. Differences emerged between Far Western and Eastern Brethren.[54]

Periodicals—Who Speaks for the Brethren?

In 1851, Henry Kurtz (1796–1874), a leading Brethren elder in northeast Ohio, began the *Gospel Visitor* as a means of preserving the unity of the scattered church, resolving doctrinal and practical problems, and promoting the values and ideals of the Brethren. In 1865, Henry R. Holsinger (1833–1905) began

---

53. Stoffer offers detailed analysis of each of these streams of dissension in his chapter entitled "Issues Contributing to the Schism." See Stoffer, *Brethren Doctrines*, 133–44.

54. Of special note on this issue is the dialectical leadership of George Wolfe Jr., who held the far-western and eastern Brethren together in spite of their differences regarding proper mode of footwashing. Wolfe would later assist with the merger of the two groups in 1859. See Stoffer, *Brethren Doctrines*, 106.

the *Christian Family Companion* that advocated progressive ideals and utilized an open forum to encourage a full range of opinions on controversial issues.

In 1873, due to mounting criticism of his approach, Holsinger sold his paper to James Quinter (1816–1888), the editor of the *Gospel Visitor*. In 1878, Holsinger reentered the publishing business with the *Progressive Christian*, a strongly progressive paper. In 1870, the Old Order reluctantly entered the field with the *Vindicator*, a paper devoted to maintaining the old order cause. These periodicals and others kept attention focused on all the controversial issues facing the church and popularized the disputes concerning these issues.

Education—Is Higher Education Worldly?

James Quinter was a leading voice for the development of Brethren-related schools and colleges, arguing that such schools were needed in order to help train Brethren to meet the stricter standards for the teaching profession. Education, Quinter asserted, would allow for Brethren moral and religious convictions to be present in public-school education.

The Old Order were opposed to higher education because it was seen as a worldly pursuit that could lead to an educated and, in time, a professional ministry. Annual Meeting was initially opposed to higher education but reversed its stance in 1858. The first successful Brethren-related schools were Juniata College (1876), Ashland College (1878), and Mount Morris Seminary and Collegiate Institute (1879), which would merge with Manchester College in 1932.[55]

Dress—How Are We Separate from the World?

The Old Order felt that acceptance of traditional dress was an indication of a spirit of humility and modesty, feeling that uniformity of dress should be maintained by Annual Meeting. Progressives insisted that individual conscience should determine how one should apply the principle of nonconformity, feeling that mandatory uniformity destroyed the vital spirit of inner obedience that is at the heart of the Christian life.

By the end of the 1870s, three factions and their central arguments had coalesced. The Old Order wanted strict adherence to their perception of the established order. The Progressives advocated rapid movement into

---

55. For more on the development of Brethren higher education, see Sharp, *Educational History*.

the mainstream of American life. The Conservatives, the main body of the church, sought to mediate the two positions while maintaining the unity of the church.

Schisms—Different Visions of "Brethren"

In 1880 and 1881, after their "Miami Valley Petition" was rebuffed by Annual Meeting, the Old Order separated from the larger body.[56] Simultaneously, Holsinger's continued agitation for the Progressive cause led to a backlash against him and other Progressives. The 1881 Annual Meeting, held at Ashland College, appointed a committee to visit Holsinger in his home church in Berlin, Pennsylvania. This committee called for his expulsion which was upheld at the 1882 Annual Meeting. About six thousand Progressives joined what became the Brethren Church in 1883.

The Progressives held a convention in Ashland, Ohio, on June 29, 1882 that established plans for a new denomination, pending further efforts at reconciliation. When such efforts were not fruitful, the Progressives adopted the "Declaration of Principles," penned by Stephen Bashor, which maintained that in doctrinal matters there should be universal harmony, on

---

56. An earlier petition was drafted by the Old Order Brethren and presented to Annual Meeting in 1869. That petition expressed concern that the church had strayed, in many localities, from the "ancient order and practices." The petition, with a later amendment, expressed opposition to Sabbath schools, prayer meetings, social meetings, Bible classes, and protracted meetings—preaching geared toward conversion and baptism. The hope was that Annual Meeting would exercise its authority and quash such developments. When Annual Meeting did not respond authoritatively enough for the Old Order, a later petition, known as the "Miami Valley Petition," as it was drafted in the Miami Valley of Ohio, was drafted for presentation to the 1880 Annual Meeting. This petition had five key features: (1) the overriding concern was for unity and peace, (2) the "fast element" must be removed, (3) firm action must be taken against various innovations to protect the ancient order of the church, (4) the Old Order desired firm action—not the Conservative ethic of forbearance, and (5) the Old Order were concerned about their authority within the Brotherhood. See Stoffer, *Brethren Doctrines*, 146. The following response from Annual Meeting precipitated a departure of the Old Order:

> RESOLVED, . . . that while we declare ourselves conservative, in maintaining unchanged what may be considered the principles and peculiarities of our fraternity, we also believe in the propriety and necessity of so adapting our labor and our principles to the religious wants of the world as we render our labor and principles most efficient in promoting the reformation of the world, the edification of the church, and the glory of God. Hence, *while we are conservative we are also progressive.* (italics mine; see Holsinger, "Introductory," 2)

The Old Order, now the Old German Baptist Brethren, feeling rebuffed by the response of Annual Meeting, broke away in 1881.

questions of government and customs the church should observe congregational polity, and that the Conservatives were the ones who had departed from the historic principles of the church.[57] Thus the established and affirmed polity of the Brethren Church became "limited congregationalism":

> The apostolic idea of congregational church government relates alone to the incidental affairs of the local congregation, and not to doctrinal practices and tenets which must be general or universal—the same in all congregations, the doctrinal conditions of membership in one congregation shall be the doctrinal conditions in every other.[58]

The seven streams of dissension listed earlier leading up to the 1880s three-way split of the Old Order, Conservatives, and Progressives were like a flame to dry kindling.[59] Several of them have been explored already. The era was marked by macro stressors of technological and scientific development as industry created the modern cities of America, evolution was quickly replacing the creation narrative of human origins, and technological innovations like the telephone and light bulb were making American life more comfortable and connected. Coupled with these developments came a new movement of the period, revivalism, as mentioned earlier, that reframed the human-divine relationship and produced an evangelistic fervor. A strong emphasis on higher education arose among many denominational groups, progressive theological viewpoints in line with modern sensibilities were propagated.[60] These technological and scientific discoveries, coupled with revivalist impulses, applied pressure to how the Brethren understood their Christian engagement with the world. Through these macro trends, the dilemmas of unity, faithfulness and authority became translated to three factions each demanding, respectively, a witness of identity, unity or mission (see chart below).

Brethren Group	Identifying Issue
Old Order	Historic Identity
Conservatives	Ecclesial Unity
Progressives	Progressive Mission

57. For more on the 1880s schisms, see Stoffer, *Brethren Doctrines*, 145–56.

58. Stoffer, *Brethren Doctrines*, 166.

59. For the purposes of this chapter, "macro" will denote larger societal religious trends; "micro" will denote those internal trends among the various factions within the Brethren of the period.

60. Smith, *Revivalism and Social Reform*, 60, 98.

The battle lines were drawn regarding how to steward the core theological streams of Brethrenism—Anabaptism and Radical Pietism.[61]

The three camps each held a different central issue in the face of the larger assimilation dilemma for the Brethren. The Old Order carried the torch for historic identity as a boundary marker of true Brethrenism. The Conservatives (later Church of the Brethren) held that ecclesial unity was essential for maintaining Brethren identity. The Progressives, reacting to a perceived calcification of "Brethrenism," responded that Brethren faith must adapt to the modern world (see chart below). Within only a few years, the Conservatives, not favoring the Old Order's restorationist desires nor the Progressives' adaptation requests, had moved away from the Old Order and excommunicated the Progressives.[62]

Old Order	Conservative	Progressive
Outward Form	Balance	Inner Spirit
Uniformity	Balance	Personal Conscience
Community	Balance	Individual
Annual Meeting	Balance	Local Congregation

The Progressives, now the Ashland Brethren, emerged as a small remnant focused on Brethren engagement with the modern world eventually rallying around a struggling denominational college, Ashland College in Ashland, Ohio. This group would face further distress with the emerging Fundamentalist-Liberal controversy sweeping through the United States of the early twentieth century.[63] The missional impulse that had identified this

---

61. Stoffer explores many possibilities for the schisms of the 1880s. One of the theories entails that the streams of Anabaptism and Radical Pietism had become polarized from one another, which helps explain the posture of the Conservatives of the period who were seeking to keep both streams together. Other theories are explored but for the sake of this paper the separation of a Pietist and Anabaptist witness are used to help discern particular pathologies that developed in the respective camps—Old Order (Anabaptist pursuit of separation) to Progressives (Pietist pursuit of individuality and openness). It should be noted that it is an unfair caricature to believe that Pietism was absent from the Old Order or that Anabaptism did not influence the Progressives. See Stoffer, *Brethren Doctrines*, 145–56.

62. While more could be written on the three groups that came out of the 1880s divisions, this paper, for length and focus, will transition to the development of the Progressives.

63. The Fundamentalist-Liberal controversy was a late nineteenth- and early twentieth-century conflict around issues regarding the role of Christianity in society, the authority of Scripture, and the death, resurrection, and atoning sacrifice of Jesus. For more on these respective movements, see Marsden, *Fundamentalism*, and Dorrien, *Making of American Theology*.

group as "Progressive," for their appreciation of progress, would not dismiss the three central dilemmas of the nineteenth century—historic identity, ecclesial unity and progressive mission—though these impulses were nuanced for the period (see chart below).

Brethren Group	Identifying Issues	Desired Societal Engagement
Fundamentalist (Grace)	Dogmatic Identity, Prophetic Mission	Prophetic Separatism
Brethrenist (Ashland)	Ecclesial Unity, Engaged Mission	Cooperative Separatism

While both camps, Fundamentalist and Brethrenist, pursued missional engagement, the battle lines would be drawn around those seeking unity and mission (Brethrenist) and those arguing for a dogmatically entrenched theology more skeptical of the world—and especially liberal theology (Fundamentalist).[64]

On one side of the spectrum were the Fundamentalists. Fundamentalism combined a hyper-Reformed slant to theology with Keswick thought and dispensational eschatology.[65] Alongside these theological streams developed the Princeton Theology and the codification of their theology in *The Fundamentals* (1917). Though the name of this movement is known as Fundamentalism, a name with its origins in *The Fundamentals*, the Princeton theologians were not dispensational. Their posture, similar to that of dispensational eschatology, toward society became one

---

64. "Brethrenist" denotes the Brethren group that would form the Ashland Brethren after 1939. It is important to note that the 1939 split between the Ashland and Grace Brethren groups cannot be characterized as a Fundamentalist and Liberal split. Thinkers of the Ashland Brethren were not liberals and shared the concerns of Fundamentalists with the beliefs of Protestant Liberalism. Fundamentalists charged the Brethrenists with being "liberal" because, rather than dogmatically rejecting liberal theology, there was an openness to dialogue with it on issues like evolution and higher criticism of the Bible. "Skeptical" is a polite way of describing an often hostile posture to the world, especially liberal theology.

65. The main idea of Keswick theology, also known as the "Higher Life movement," is that one first experiences an initial conversion moment followed by a second work of God in their life. This work of God is called "entire sanctification," "the second blessing," "the second touch," "being filled with the Holy Spirit," and various other terms. Keswick teachers promoted the idea that Christians who had received this blessing from God could live a more holy life. In Keswick thought, one first experiences Christ as Savior and later as Lord, a separation that is antithetical to Brethren thought. Dispensationalism sought to address what were perceived as opposing theologies between the Old and New Testaments arguing that biblical history is best understood as a series of dispensations occurring in the Bible.

of withdrawal and aggressive criticism toward scientific and technological developments. A deep distrust of society, inspired by their reaction to American liberal and modernist theology, was apparent in their distinct stance to the surrounding world.

On the other side of the spectrum were those open to dialogue with liberal theology, though it is a caricature to believe the "Brethrenists" were liberals. The belief of this faction was that conversation was necessary with this new theology of the late nineteenth and early twentieth century.

It is to these two rival camps—fundamentalism and liberalism—that this work must now turn. These two camps have carved up much of the American religious landscape of not just the early twentieth century but also up to the present day.[66] Understanding the background of these two streams of thought helps us better understand the Brethren theologian J. Allen Miller (1866–1935).

Miller holds the fundamentalist and liberal factions of the Brethren denomination together during the first part of the twentieth century. In fact, present day Ashland Brethren live in the shadow cast by this pivotal theologian. He exhibits an inherent tension within Brethren known as the "conservative-progressive dialectic" arguing that truth is found in fundamentalism and liberalism and that the church must chart a unique third way between the two poles.[67] The secret to the resolution of the dialectic between conservative and progressive is Miller's understanding of the person of Jesus revealed by the Spirit. The Spirit's involvement with the church allows for an openness to new light. This new light, rather than contradicting the Bible allows for there to exist a continual refreshment to the Brethren hermeneutic all while remaining tethered to Scripture as central to the Brethren witness. The "proof" demanded by both conservatives and liberals is found in the Spirit's activity. In Miller, there is a retrieval of the central synergy of Brethrenism—Word and Spirit gifted from the dual heritages of Radical Pietism and Anabaptism—that had been greatly distorted and, often times, sorely missing, from Brethren of the late nineteenth century. It is this dialectic that animates Miller's thought as he holds the Brethren Church together amid a

---

66. The Fundamentalist-Modernist controversy was largely a crisis within white, American Protestantism. African American Protestants and Catholics were not affected.

67. Stoffer characterizes Miller's ability to remain tethered to Scripture (conservative) while remaining open to new developments in the world around us (progressive). The dialectic is apparent in that many conservatives embody a defensive posture of withdrawn and separation (Fundamentalism). Similarly, in the spirit of openness, many liberals separate from any understanding of transcendent truth opting, instead, for a rational ethic of naturalism. While both camps employ rationality it is only a posture like Miller's that allows for the resolution of dialectic tension in the person of Jesus revealed by the Holy Spirit.

turbulent period in American religious life—especially related to theological education at Ashland College. Before Miller's distinct theological witness and methodology can be explored, it is important to better understand the Fundamentalist-Modernist controversy that marked his era. Chapter 3 will explore what Dale Stoffer calls "the liberal controversy."[68]

---

68. It was liberalism that prompted the contentiousness in Brethren life of the early twentieth century and offers a helpful backdrop to the thought of J. Allen Miller. Consequently, Stoffer identifies this as "the liberal controversy" that impacted the campuses of Ashland College and Ashland Theological Seminary. See Stoffer, *Brethren Doctrines*, 180ff.

3

The Liberal Controversy

According to historian Ernest Sandeen, "America in the early nineteenth century was drunk on the millennium. Whether in support of optimism or pessimism, radicalism or conservatism, Americans seemed unable to avoid—seemed bound to utilize—the vocabulary of Christian eschatology."[1] The eschatology of Protestants, reflecting the era's optimism and hope, was expressed as a blending of millennialism and American nationalism that stemmed from a Puritan conviction that the colonists were a chosen people. Such beliefs were only reinforced by the Revolutionary War coupled with the vast western migration.[2] One response was the burgeoning liberal theology movement that sought to engage the scientific, technological and philosophical currents of the era. By the end of the nineteenth and into the early twentieth century, however, a new movement, that eventually took the name of "Fundamentalism," would emerge in reaction to liberal theology. These two movements would collide around developing fault lines within American Christianity that remain to the present day.

The creation of these two movements finds its origin in the denominationalism of American Protestantism. In detailing this new polity, Sidney Mead notes that the soul of America was held in tension between

---

1. Sandeen, *Roots of Fundamentalism*, 42.
2. Sandeen, *Roots of Fundamentalism*, 43.

rationalists on one side and a combination of a "pietist sectarianism" and traditionalist churches on the other in the "lively experiment" that was and is religious freedom in America.³ The working out of this experiment was a spiritual reaction that formed American denominations over against rationalistic, deistic interpretations of the faith. It is in this development that Mead details six traits that came to characterize denominations during the nineteenth century.

The first was a sectarian tendency for each denomination to justify its existence by tying itself back to the early church. This resulted in an ahistorical bias that undercut tradition-based ecclesial authorities. Sectarian voices saw these tradition-based churches as a distortion of the true church, grounding their assessment in a common appeal to "no creed but the Bible" and the right of "private judgment," under grace, in its interpretation.⁴

The second trait was "voluntaryism" in which the church moved from a traditional ecclesial body to a voluntary association that required persuasion, not force or coercion, to gather.⁵ This voluntary zeal led to a third trait, a missionary impulse enterprise. Missions was a central impulse to American denominationalism, shaped primarily by the influence of Pietism. What began as winning converts to Jesus with the betterment of society as a byproduct of that work, became, by the last quarter of the nineteenth century, a conception of the work of the church as addressing the deplorable economic and social conditions of America. This new thrust would be referred to as the "new theology" or "social gospel" (to be discussed later).⁶

This voluntary zeal was strengthened by a fourth trait, revivalism, that saw persuasion and popular appeal as the primary tools of a voluntary church—revivalism soon emerged as the accepted method of such churches. Mead notes several results of this revivalist fervor. A simplified gospel message developed as the central appeal of revivalism that sought to appeal to common people in their language. A shift from Calvinism to Arminianism emerged with an emphasis on human initiative, or "getting religion."⁷ Such an emphasis stressed tangible results (numbers) that led to

---

3. The "lively experiment" is a play on Thomas Jefferson's description of the religious freedom in the early republic as a "fair experiment" in a new world.

4. Mead, *Lively Experiment*, 113.

5. Mead, *Lively Experiment*, 113–15.

6. Mead, *Lively Experiment*, 115–21.

7. This shift is not indicative of all American Christianity of the period. Groups like Methodists, Lutherans, and Brethren would never have identified as Calvinist. Mead's point is indicative of more prominent evangelicals of the period, especially those of New England (though this shift was occurring in all parts of the country). A notable shift began to occur in the nineteenth century away from divine sovereignty toward

utilitarian methodologies. Such methodologies prized revivalists who were close to people and could rouse their emotions.[8]

A fifth trait emerged with a subsequent flight from reason as churches rejected the rationalism of the Enlightenment. Post-Revolutionary-era evangelical Protestantism[9] parted ways with the intellectual trends of society as an ever-growing chasm developed between religion and reason. Revivalism, ironically, employed rationalism. Scottish Common-Sense Realism, a highly rational philosophical worldview, was applied to scriptural exegesis. Just as the physical universe is governed by logical, reasonable laws, so also, it was argued, the spiritual realm is governed by logical, reasonable laws of God's Word. This developed into a "plain reading" of the Bible.[10] This plain reading, however, came with difficulty as a plurality of perspectives on the "plain Bible" emerged.[11] With this plurality of appeals to the New Testament church came the sixth, and final, trait of American denominationalism, a competition among denominations to justify minor distinctive points of the growing web of denominations.[12]

The developing denominational polity of American Protestantism coupled with the post-Revolutionary War belief in the divine destiny of America created a socio-spiritual expectation within the young republic that Nathan Hatch has identified as a "civil millennialism."[13] Such an expectation was shaped by postmillennialism, the dominant eschatological view in America at the beginning of the nineteenth century.[14] Adding to this fervor were two great awakenings (1725–1760, 1787–1825) that played a key

---

human activity and capability. This would pave the way for revivalism. Methodism, as already mentioned, played a significant role in this shift as well.

8. Mead, *Lively Experiment*, 121–27.

9. "Evangelical" here denotes those Christians committed to the core of Christian orthodoxy, often in reaction to the Unitarianism of the rationalists of early America. It is important to differentiate this evangelicalism from that of neo-evangelicals that emerges in the 1940s. For a brief differentiation of these two camps, see Grenz et al., "Evangelical," in *Pocket Dictionary*, 47–48.

10. Mead, *Lively Experiment*, 127–29.

11. This is not simply a historic phenomenon around the Bible. A sociological examination of this present reality is explored by sociologist Christian Smith. Smith, *Bible Made Impossible*, 3–54.

12. Mead, *Lively Experiment*, 129–33.

13. See Hatch, *Democratization of American Christianity*, 162. Hatch details the populist impulse prevalent in American Christianity from the founding of the republic to the present. Hatch, "Origins of Civil Millennialism," 407–30.

14. Postmillennialism asserts that Christ will return after the millennium (Rev 19–22) and will be ushered in by a period of societal reform. This eschatological view differs from the more pessimistic view of premillennialism which believes the return of Christ will be forecasted by societal decay.

role in developing a more optimistic eschatology. Simultaneously, Christian missions were excelling and expanding due, in part, to the missionary spirit of revivalism. Postmillennialism would remain strong throughout the rest of the nineteenth century due to the activism, optimism, frontier mentality, and progress ingrained into American society and would remain quite evangelical for the duration of the period.[15]

Another view developed that did not share the optimistic sentiments of postmillennialism. A growing disillusionment appeared as missions and evangelism had not yet brought the millennium and subsequent regeneration of the world. These failures led others to doubt postmillennial sentiments. Latent frustration coalesced into a premillennial eschatological view with growing convictions of end time events being fulfilled in spite of the church's efforts.[16]

An increase in premillennialism produced a growing interest in prophecy. William Miller (1782–1849), for example, took a commonsense approach to prophecy in one of America's first well-known prophetic ventures. Viewing prophecy study as analogous to the study of nature, Miller made calculations that led him to claim that 1843 would be the year of the Lord's return. From the early 1830s onward, he crisscrossed the North proselytizing with his message. When the year came and went without the Lord's return, a period known as the "Great Disappointment," his followers, known as "Millerites," arrived at October 22, 1844, as the new date. To their dismay, great disappointment accompanied the intended day.[17] This is an important event as it marks a shift from a historicist expression of premillennialism to a futurist expression.[18] The Millerites would bolster dispensationalism

15. Stoffer, "Nineteenth Century Background."

16. One such instance was the French Revolution that ended papal power in France. In 1798 French troops marched on Rome, established a republic, and sent the pope into banishment. This affirmed the eschatology of a select group of American Protestants who viewed the papacy as the Antichrist. These events were seen as a fulfillment of Rev 13:3 concerning the "deadly wound" received by the beast.

17. "The Millerites rank as the largest and most influential early nineteenth-century American premillennial group, and in their emphasis upon the exact year of the second advent they did give unusual prominence to one aspect of millenarian expectations. . . . The main thrust of Miller's teaching was that Christ would return, the wicked be judged, and the world cleansed by fire about 1843. . . . Prophecies of the Bible were always literally fulfilled and that chronological sequences in the apocalyptic books should be interpreted according to the year-day theory." See Sandeen, *Roots of Fundamentalism*, 44, 51.

18. Historicist premillennialists believe that scriptural prophecy, especially the passages in Daniel and Revelation, give the entire history of the church in symbolic form. Thus, they look into the church's past and present to find prophetic fulfillment and to discern location in God's prophetic timetable. In contrast, futurist premillennialism,

that had developed earlier in the century through John Nelson Darby (to be discussed later in the chapter). Dispensationalism developed around a futurist approach to prophecy and the Great Disappointment of the Millerites reinforced this approach over against the historicist one. This shift from historicist to futurist made dispensationalism the dominant premillennial eschatology of the late nineteenth and early twentieth centuries.

Another movement, already mentioned, that was constitutive of American Protestantism of the period was revivalism. Revivalism of the nineteenth century was energized by seismic shifts in theology. As dominant American theological belief shifted away from Calvinism to Arminianism, revivals, which early progenitors like Jonathan Edwards would declare occurred due to God's mysterious workings, were increasingly interpreted as being dependent on various human methods. As a result, nineteenth-century revivalism divorced itself from the dominant Calvinist foundations of earlier revivals. The quintessential American revivalist, Charles Finney (1792–1875), though a licensed Presbyterian minister, quickly distanced himself from Calvinist thought by advocating the use of "new measures" such as the anxious bench from which derived the modern practice of "coming forward" at an altar call to make a decision for Christ. Finney was hyper-pragmatic with revivals. In his *Lectures in Revivalism* (1835) he wrote that "a revival is not a miracle, or dependent on a miracle in any sense. It is purely philosophical [read 'scientific'] result of the right use of the constituted means."[19]

Revivalism introduced questions that were indicative of the social, political and philosophical milieu of American Christianity in the nineteenth century. Robert W. Caldwell III has classified these concerns as follows:

First, there were issues related to what ministers are to do while preaching the gospel. Numerous questions surfaced here:

- Is preaching *the moral law* (the Ten Commandments) a necessary prelude to preaching the gospel?
- Are ministers to direct sinners to use the *means of grace* (such as praying, reading the Scriptures, attending preaching services) as they seek God's salvation in Christ?
- How do the doctrines of *election* and *spiritual inability*, if true, practically translate into evangelistic method?

---

evident in a dispensational theory of premillennialism, ascribes biblical significance to almost every new development in current world events. The shift from historicist to futurist shifted many Christians of the period away from a posture of curiosity and engagement to one of prediction and separation.

19. Finney, *Lectures on Revivals*, 12.

- Should ministers call sinners to *repent immediately*, or should they direct sinners to *wait to discern certain signs of genuine faith* in the heart before calling them to repentance and faith?
- Should ministers employ a method, such as an *anxious bench* or *altar call*, to call anxious souls to come forward publicly and receive spiritual counsel, or should they leave it up to individuals themselves to seek the counsel of spiritual advisers after a revival service?

Second, there were questions related to the spiritual experiences that individuals were expected to pass through in their journeys through the conversion process. The questions included the following:

- Is it necessary that individuals pass through a period of spiritual distress known as *conviction of sin* before they are ready for faith in Christ? If so, how much conviction is necessary?
- Is conversion a *lengthy process*, or does it normally occur in a *short period of time*?
- What, specifically, are sinners to *do* to be saved? Do individuals *wait for God* to create in them a new heart, or are there *steps they can take* that render salvation more probable?
- What are the *essential marks of salvation*? How do individuals *truly know* that they love God and believe in Christ?
- Should converts experience an *assurance* of salvation *immediately* at the moment of belief, or is assurance the *fruit of Christian maturity*?[20]

Caldwell concludes that the theologies of nineteenth-century revivalists "focused on the interplay of . . . three themes—their theologies of salvation, the ways they practically preached the gospel, and the conversion experiences they expected from those experiencing salvation."[21] These themes will come to be central to later conversations in twentieth and twenty-first-century American evangelicalism.

Timothy L. Smith identifies three further "fundamental changes in the inner life of American Protestantism" that were spawned by the mid-century revivals. They witnessed greater lay participation, a concern for inter-denominational cooperation and unity, and an increased ethical sensitivity.[22]

The Civil War congealed these shifts as the end of the tragedy with its victory over slavery was seen by many to signal an imminent triumph of

---

20. Caldwell, *American Revivalists*, 6–7.
21. Caldwell, *American Revivalists*, 7.
22. Smith, *Revivalism & Social Reform*, 80.

the kingdom over personal and social evils, bolstering the resolve of many denominations in their work for the kingdom's coming. Such views were important stepping stones to two significant traits of the Protestant liberalism of the late nineteenth and early twentieth centuries. First, millennial expectations were beginning to coalesce into what was called the "social gospel." Second, the presentation of postmillennialism was expressed in terms of progress and evolution.[23] By the end of the nineteenth century, American liberal theology, fueled by an era of great scientific, philosophical and technological progress, was in full swing.

Protestant Liberalism

American liberal theology of the late nineteenth and early twentieth centuries was a theological system of beliefs that "flowed out of the Enlightenment and laid the enduring conceptual foundations of modern critical scholarship by appealing to the authority of critical rationality and religious experience."[24] Central theological developments were an emphasis on continuity in contrast to discontinuity in the world (stressing God's immanence against the transcendence stressed by traditional theology), the autonomy of human reason and experience (against a sole emphasis on revelation), and an understanding of the nature of life and the world as dynamic rather than static (progress over against unchanging propositional truths).[25]

Continuity

During the nineteenth century, modern science described the world as a closed system of cause and effect. This closed system was signified by evolution. As the Enlightenment championed reason over revelation, any understanding of divine special creation was dismissed.[26]

Simultaneously, the absolute idealism of German philosopher Georg Wilhelm Friedrich Hegel (1770–1831) lent itself to a pantheistic identification of God and the world in his unfolding dialectical process of thesis, antithesis, and synthesis. Combined with the central claim of Romanticism

---

23. Smith, *Revivalism & Social Reform*, 236. The progress and evolution experienced were less from a Darwinian teleology and more from the nearness people felt to God by mid-century revivals.

24. Dorrien, *Making of American Theology*, xvi.

25. Cauthen, *American Religious Liberalism*, 5.

26. Cauthen, *American Religious Liberalism*, 7.

that the presence of God was in humanity and nature, God was seen not as the aloof deity of deism but the very spirit and soul of the world.[27]

Coupled with these scientific and philosophical innovations, several developments were occurring in religion. A historical-critical study of the Bible emerged that sought to understand the Bible not as special revelation or authority but in its original context. A burgeoning science of comparative religions led to a questioning of the uniqueness of the Christian faith which prompted the dream of a universal religion.[28] In conjunction with the religious developments listed above, revivalism, already mentioned, made God more approachable by stressing God's immanence over against transcendence as God was seen as working in the evolutionary process.[29]

There were several implications to this understanding of continuity. First, the distinction between natural and supernatural was diminished as the importance of revelation and miracles disappeared. Second, objective revelation was replaced by reason and experience. Third, the goodness of humanity was affirmed over inherent sinfulness. Fourth, the Jesus of history, not the supernatural Christ, was affirmed. Fifth, individual salvation gave way to social salvation as an interest in the life hereafter was replaced by an ethical demand on the present day moral and spiritual development of humanity. Furthermore, a belief in the twofold destiny of humanity—saved and lost—was replaced by a belief in the ultimate salvation of all. Sixth, and final, a distinction between church and society gave way to the transformation of all society into the kingdom of God.[30]

Autonomy

Along with a belief in God's nearness came an affirmation of the autonomy of reason and experience via scientific inquiry, speculative reason, and inner experience. The Enlightenment enthroned reason and rejected other authorities. Immanuel Kant (1724–1804) had earlier laid the foundation of attaining metaphysical truth about God, soul, and world through reason alone.

Several sources displaced the authority of Scripture. Scientific discoveries had demonstrated the falsity of the worldview of the Bible, creating a scientific worldview that, in turn, made theology an empirical science. This conflation of theology and science was a product of the seventeenth century

---

27. Cauthen, *American Religious Liberalism*, 8.
28. Cauthen, *American Religious Liberalism*, 8–9.
29. Cauthen, *American Religious Liberalism*, 8–9.
30. Stoffer, "Prelude to the Controversy."

as the world came to be seen in mechanistic and materialistic ways—God was simply the creator (deism).[31]

Romanticism reacted to this mechanistic view of the world by stressing God's immanence. True religion was not external religious authority but one's inner sense of duty/obligation with an emphasis on an ethical action of religion. This posture was bolstered by revivalism that emphasized personal experience over dogmatic, propositional truth.[32]

In this vein, two men are of significance. Friedrich Schleiermacher (1768–1834) grounded religion in the affective—an absolute dependence on God—making theology a systematic presentation of religious experience. In contrast to Schleiermacher's more inward approach, Albrecht Ritschl (1822–1889), like Kant, grounded faith in practical religion eliminating the transcendence of tradition and revelation and prizing an ethical and imminent religious expression.[33]

With the perception of and quest for autonomous reason came several implications. First, religion was grounded in religious experience and theology became secondary to, and dependent upon, religious experience. Second, reason was made equal to, or dominant over, revelation, and theology became a practical, not speculative, discipline. Third, and final, placing experience over dogma reduced doctrinal disputes and served as a foundation for the church unity favored by liberals.[34]

Dynamism

As theology shifted from God's transcendence to immanence and reason became enthroned over revelation, a shift from static, unchanging, propositional truths of faith to the dynamic, progressive realities of liberalism occurred. The Enlightenment espoused a dogma of social progress—based in reason and science and signified by evolution. Hegel's idealism saw history as a process of evolution by which the Absolute realizes itself in time.[35] Such

---

31. Cauthen, *American Religious Liberalism*, 14–15.

32. Cauthen, *American Religious Liberalism*, 15.

33. Cauthen, *American Religious Liberalism*, 19–20. Ritschl held that Schleiermacher, like Hegel, opened the door to mysticism rather than, like Kant, grounding religion in its ethical expression. Schleiermacher grounded religion too far in the affective for Ritschl, making religion too subjective.

34. Stoffer, "Prelude to the Controversy."

35. Hegel developed a dialectical schema that emphasized the progress of history and ideas from thesis to antithesis and then to a synthesis. Hegel's dialectic has most often been characterized as a three-step process, "thesis, antithesis, synthesis"; namely, that a "thesis" would cause the creation of its "antithesis" and would eventually result in a

an evolutionary philosophy shaped a historical study of Scripture that saw the Bible as a progressive record of experiences of humanity's discovery of God.[36]

The implications of this dynamism are numerous. First, theological formulations were held tentatively as ideas were always changing. Second, salvation of society, what was termed "social salvation," trumped appeals to individual conversion. Third, evolution created skepticism over the revelatory narrative of the creation of the world. Fourth, a dynamic view of the world reinforced God's immanence as God was brought into the evolutionary development of nature. Fifth, all religions were seen as evolving from lower to higher stages/consciousness as reason and religious experience were given priority over revelation. Sixth, individual and general eschatology were rewritten with an implicit universalism and a long progressive view of ushering in the kingdom of God. Seventh, and finally, a historical interest set in play the search for the historical Jesus who became the focal point of liberal Christianity.[37]

These three streams—continuity, autonomy, dynamism—make liberalism less a monolith and more a multifaceted, multi-perspectival theological construct optimistically in line with the technological, philosophical and scientific progress innate at the end of the nineteenth century. Kenneth Cauthen argues that to understand liberalism as a monolith is to misunderstand the movement entirely. "Wherever the combination of these three motifs became the determining principles of the thinking of late nineteenth- and early twentieth-century theologians in America, some type of liberal theology emerged."[38]

The intersection of these three motifs, Cauthen further notes, produced two dominant streams—evangelical liberalism and modernistic liberalism.[39] Almost all liberals, and modernistic liberals especially, believed

---

"synthesis." The "thesis-antithesis-synthesis" approach gives the sense that things or ideas are contradicted or opposed by things that come from outside them. This approach to Hegel is perceived by many to be inaccurate today. Hegel only used it once and attributed it to Kant. The fundamental notion of Hegel's dialectic still remains, however, minus the "thesis, antithesis, synthesis" delineation. Namely, all things or ideas have internal contradictions. From Hegel's point of view, analysis or comprehension of a thing or idea reveals that underneath its apparently simple identity or unity is an underlying inner contradiction. This contradiction leads to the dissolution of the thing or idea in its present, simple form into a higher-level, more complex recognition of what Hegel terms the "Whole" (which is different from a "synthesis"). See Hegel, *Phenomenology of the Spirit*.

36. Cauthen, *American Religious Liberalism*, 22–23.
37. Stoffer, "Prelude to the Controversy," lecture notes.
38. Cauthen, *American Religious Liberalism*, 25.
39. Cauthen, *American Religious Liberalism*, 26ff.

in the potential of autonomous reason. Into this debate was an attempted mediation between a modern outlook and a historic faith. Citing Cauthen, Stoffer expounds on evangelical liberalism:

> Evangelical liberalism was denoted by a desire to maintain fidelity to the historic doctrinal and ecclesiastical traditions of Christianity except insofar as modern circumstances required adjustment or change.[40]

Liberals in this camp—such as William Newton Clarke (1841–1912), William Adams Brown (1865–1943), Harry Emerson Fosdick (1878–1969), and Walter Rauschenbusch (1861–1918)—were thoroughly christocentric, viewing Christ as God's chief revelation of moral and religious truth. God's revelation, however, was seen as in direct continuity with human reason and experience. As Cauthen explains, the Bible was not appealed to because of its authority but its truth validated itself "in experience by virtue of its own inherent reasonableness and practical value."[41] Michael Langford lays out eleven typical characteristics of this evangelical stream in liberal theology that mark it up to the present:

1. A use of the Bible that is not always literal
2. Reason and revelation in harmony
3. A non-legalist account of redemption
4. The possibility of salvation outside a narrow path
5. Toleration
6. Original sin, but not original guilt
7. Belief in free will
8. A view of providence that respects the integrity of the natural order
9. The joint need of faith and works
10. A minimal number of basic teachings
11. A range of acceptable lifestyles[42]

Modernistic liberalism, on the other hand, was more concerned with a modern outlook than historic faith. Such liberals took the "scientific method,

---

40. Stoffer, *Brethren Doctrines*, 180.

41. Cauthen, *American Religious Liberalism*, 28.

42. See Langford, *Liberal Theology*. Langford characterizes all liberal thought into a single list. Instead, using Cauthen's terminology, I find Langford's characteristics to best apply to the *evangelical* stream of Protestant liberalism.

scholarly discipline, empirical fact, and prevailing forms of contemporary philosophy as their point of departure."[43] They therefore "approached religion as a human phenomenon, the Bible as one great religious document among others, and the Christian faith as one major religious-ethical tradition among others."[44] This viewpoint thrived at the University of Chicago in the late nineteenth and early twentieth centuries under theologians like Shailer Mathews (1863–1941), Shirley Jackson Case (1872–1947), E. S. Ames (1870–1958), and Henry Nielson Wieman (1884–1975).[45] Fundamentalists, in response to such a rationalistic outlook, would develop their own rational system to defend the Bible's authority.

Fundamentalism

If liberal theology was the accommodating response to modernity, the growing conviction that would become Fundamentalism took a different stance but was animated similarly to liberalism by rationality.[46] Four streams shaped this reactionary movement. First was a new premillennialism shaped by futurism and dispensational thought—of note is the thought of John Nelson Darby (1800–1882). Second were Bible and prophecy conferences and institutes that networked across America. Third was the Keswick view of salvation and sanctification. Fourth was the codification of what would become Fundamentalist thought with the writing of *The Fundamentals* from 1910–1915 (and published in 1917).

John Nelson Darby and the Premillennial/Dispensational Movement

Dispensationalism originated with John Nelson Darby, a leader of the Plymouth Brethren. The Plymouth Brethren began as a sect out of Anglicanism in Dublin, Ireland, in the late 1820s. Darby propagated dispensationalism in America between 1862–1877. Dispensational thought contained a futurist approach to premillennialism. The first evidence of a Darbyite view of premillennialism is found in American periodical literature in the 1860s

43. Ahlstrom, *Religious History*, 782–83.
44. Ahlstrom, *Religious History*, 782–83.
45. Stoffer, *Brethren Doctrines*, 180.
46. It's important to note that Fundamentalism as a name does not appear until the publication of *The Fundamentals* (1917). Prior to this label, the "fundamentalist" cause was a vast network of Bible and prophecy conferences and a prevailing premillennial eschatology.

with a strong reception among Calvinistic denominations—specifically Northern Baptists and Presbyterians. Throughout the 1870s and 1880s, the popularity of pretribulationist premillennialism grew.[47] The premillennialism of dispensationalism was pretribulational arguing that Jesus will return to take up Christians into heaven by means of a rapture immediately before a seven-year worldwide tribulation. They anchored this belief in the Apostle Paul's remarks in 1 Thess 4:16–17: "For the Lord himself will come down from heaven, with a loud command, with the voice of the archangel and with the trumpet call of God, and the dead in Christ will rise first. After that, we who are still alive and are left will be caught up together with them in the clouds to meet the Lord in the air" (NIV). This "rapture," as it came to be known, preceded a seven-year period of tribulation that dispensationalists pieced together from apocalyptic passages in Scripture. This eschatology became highly antagonistic toward the postmillennial optimism of the period.[48]

Futurism, the competing eschatology of numerous millenarians and the Plymouth Brethren, became dominant among American millenarianism after the 1840s, eventually commanding the adherence of a great part of British and United States millenarians.[49] Darby taught two "second comings." The church is first taken secretly from the earth and, at a later time, Christ would return in a public second appearance described in Matthew 24 revealing Darby's view of history as a "progressive revelation."

Darby's system sought to explain the stages in God's redemptive plan for the universe. There was nothing especially radical about dividing history into periods. What separated Darby's dispensationalism was his method of biblical interpretation, which consisted of a strict literalism, the absolute separation of Israel and the church into two distinct peoples of God, and the separation of the rapture (the "catching away" of the church) from Christ's

---

47. George Marsden notes that Darby's reception among Calvinist churches happened because, like Calvin, he placed a great stress on the sovereignty of God and minimized the importance of human ability. See Marsden, *Fundamentalism*, 46.

48. Later in history, both World Wars would shatter postmillennial optimism and ensconce this form of premillennialism as a dominant eschatology among conservative evangelicals.

49. Sandeen, *Roots of Fundamentalism*, 60. Sandeen sees, among the many streams that shaped later Fundamentalism, an obsession with the millennium—namely, a premillennial eschatology, as being the dominant stream in the movement. Some scholars have questioned Sandeen's heavy emphasis on the millennium to Fundamentalism claiming that Sandeen almost makes millenarianism and Fundamentalism synonymous. It is difficult to tell the story of Fundamentalism without a premillennial, dispensational theology. Therefore, Sandeen's writing will be utilized often for this chapter.

second coming. At the rapture, Christ would come *for* his saints. At the second coming, he would come *with* his saints.[50]

Darby's ecclesiology is quite anemic as the church can become tangential to the plan of God. Darby's church appears almost as a parenthesis to God's plan, interrupting the prophetic timetable. As such, Darby believed the church was not revealed to the prophets of the Old Testament and had no intrinsic purpose in the return of Christ. "The church's joining Christ has nothing to do with Christ's appearing or coming to earth."[51] Darby wrote:

> It is this conviction, that the church is properly heavenly, in its calling and relationship with Christ, forming no part of the course of events of the earth, which makes its rapture so simple and clear.[52]

This created tension between Darby and American Christians. Belief that the true church could not be identified with any denominational system, but only exist as a spiritual fellowship, challenged denominational loyalties. Darby maintained that the consummation of this spiritual body would take place at the second coming of Christ when the members of the body of Christ, both living and dead, would be caught away to dwell with Christ in heaven. Though many struggled with the church as mere "spiritual fellowship," Darby's futuristic millennialism contrasted with historicist millenarians in two ways that are of great relevance to the later Fundamentalism-Modernist controversy.[53]

First, Darby taught that the second advent would be secret, an event sensible only to those who participated in it. Second, Darby taught that the secret rapture could occur at any moment—"often referred to as the doctrine of the any-moment coming."[54] Darby taught that the prophetic timetable had been interrupted at the founding of the church and that the unfulfilled biblical prophecies must all wait upon the rapture of the church.[55] This teaching of an imminent return of Christ became the greatest attraction to dispensational theology.[56]

Darby's ecclesiology seems to have acted as a catalyst for the rest of his beliefs as he advocated a church so spiritual that it almost seemed to exist

---

50. See Darby, *Collected Writings*.
51. Sandeen, *Roots of Fundamentalism*, 60.
52. Darby, *Collected Writings*, 11:156.
53. Sandeen, *Roots of Fundamentalism*, 62.
54. Sandeen, *Roots of Fundamentalism*, 63.
55. Sandeen, *Roots of Fundamentalism*, 63.
56. Sandeen, *Roots of Fundamentalism*, 64.

outside history. The church in his new dispensation of grace was a complete mystery and once it was raptured out of this world, God would return to the task of dealing with the earthly problems of Israel.[57]

Since for Darby the ministry of Jesus was divided into two parts (his early appeal to the Jews as earthly Messiah and his later role as founder of the church), the Gospels demanded careful exegesis to separate passages referring to Jewish promises and admonitions from ones directed to the church.[58] The task of the Bible teacher was, in a phrase that became the hallmark of dispensationalism, "rightly dividing the word of truth."[59]

His preoccupation with prophecy, with the second coming, and the restoration of the Jews to Palestine was shared by almost all participants in the millenarian revival.[60] Darby also shared with many non-millenarian thinkers of the nineteenth century "a philosophy of history which divided the past into a number of distinct eras in each of which the mode of God's operations, if not nature's, was unique. The eras were called dispensations."[61]

Darby had great difficulty in convincing Americans to accept all of his theology and he was least successful in convincing Americans that acceptance of his doctrine obligated them to abandon their denomination to meet with those "gathered only in the name of the Lord."[62]

Bible and Prophecy Conferences

The networks through which Darby broke onto the American religious scene were the interdenominational Bible and prophecy conferences of the nineteenth century. The main conference was the Niagara Bible Conference—the genesis of the many conferences that became a part of the movement. The Niagara Conference, from 1883–1897, met at Niagara-on-the-Lake, Ontario, where it acquired its name. It popularized futuristic premillennialism espoused by leaders like Darby.

Virtually every one of significance in American millenarianism attended the Niagara Conference.[63] A fourteen-point Niagara creed was au-

---

57. Sandeen, *Roots of Fundamentalism*, 66–67.
58. Sandeen, *Roots of Fundamentalism*, 66.
59. Sandeen, *Roots of Fundamentalism*, 67.
60. Sandeen, *Roots of Fundamentalism*, 67.
61. Sandeen, *Roots of Fundamentalism*, 68. Darby saw three distinct dispensations of religion—Patriarchal, Jewish, and Christian. Likewise, there are three high priesthoods—Melchizedek, Aaron, and Jesus.
62. Marsden, *Fundamentalism*, 31.
63. Sandeen, *Roots of Fundamentalism*, 134.

thored in 1878, primarily by James H. Brookes (1830–1897), a Presbyterian minister, who was the driving force behind the conference, and reveals the foundation for later Fundamentalism. Below is a simplified list of the main topics of the creed:

1. The verbal, plenary inspiration of the Scriptures in the original manuscripts
2. The Trinity
3. The creation of man, the fall into sin, and total depravity
4. The universal transmission of spiritual death from Adam
5. The necessity of the new birth
6. Redemption by the blood of Christ
7. Salvation by faith alone in Christ
8. The assurance of salvation
9. The centrality of Jesus Christ in the Scriptures
10. The constitution of the true church by genuine believers
11. The personality of the Holy Spirit
12. The believer's call to a holy life
13. The immediate passing of the souls of believers to be with Christ at death
14. The premillennial second coming of Christ[64]

The creed provides an index to the concerns of the millenarians. It is bracketed by the first article affirming the verbal inerrancy of the original autographs (art. 1) and the last affirming the premillennial second advent (art. 14). It affirms human depravity (arts. 3 and 4) and salvation by faith in the blood of Christ (arts. 5, 6, 7). It combines these articles with support of the church that departs from Darby's dispensational theology (art. 10).

All of the Bible, including the Old Testament, the creed affirmed, centers on Christ and all of it was designed to convey "practical instruction" to the reader (art. 9).[65] Articles 11 and 12 emphasized the personality of the Holy Spirit and the need for personal holiness. The millenarian article (14) is quite general and does not commit to any particular Darbyite or futurist position, but affirms that Christ will return personally and

---

64. For the full creed, see Sandeen, *Roots of Fundamentalism*, 273–77.
65. Sandeen, *Roots of Fundamentalism*, 134.

premillennially, and that Israel will be restored to Palestine.[66] The spirit of Niagara was best dominated by the quest for the manifestation of "the primitive, New Testament idea of an ecclesia."[67] The foundation was laid for a remnant theology that would come to animate later Fundamentalism.

Concurrently, Bible Institutes were starting in the 1880s with the purpose, as set forth by Dwight L. (D. L.) Moody (1837–1899), of fitting "laymen" for the "practical work" of "learning how to reach the masses."[68] Moody was active in Chicago working with the YMCA and founding Sunday schools in poor sections of the city.[69] He founded a Bible training institute in Chicago for lay workers that would later become Moody Bible Institute (founded in 1889). Moody also established a summer missions conference in 1887 that gave rise to the Student Volunteer Movement. This movement, and subsequent conferences, became a way of disseminating premillennial and Keswick teachings and shaped millenarians with Moody's Bible institutes.[70] Since the Bible institutes were interdenominational and tended to teach dispensationalism, they became the prime way to spread fundamentalism. They also taught Keswick teachings which were fast becoming the operating system of premillennial, dispensational theology.[71]

Keswick Movement

The Keswick movement began in England in 1875 and was brought to America by F. B. Meyer (1847–1929), who spoke at Moody's Northfield conference. Keswick doctrine won acceptance by those who might be identified as "mild-Calvinists" of the period, people like A. J. Gordon, C. I. Scofield, A. B. Simpson, and R. A. Torrey, who were also influential in dispensational

66. Sandeen, *Roots of Fundamentalism*, 141.

67. Sandeen, *Roots of Fundamentalism*, 144.

68. The first Bible institute was Nyack Missionary College in New York City, founded in 1882. Founded by A. B. Simpson (1843–1919), a former Presbyterian who founded the Christian and Missionary Alliance denomination. The more influential school, however, was the Moody Bible Institute. It was influential because of Moody and two others, Reuben A. Torrey (1856–1928) and James M. Gray (1851–1935). Torrey helped Moody build the Chicago Evangelization Society (now Moody Bible Institute) starting in 1889. In 1894 he became the pastor of the Chicago Avenue Church (now Moody Bible Church). He also served as the dean of the Bible Institute of Los Angeles (Biola) from 1912–1924. Gray served at the Moody Bible Institute from 1904–1934 (first as dean and then as president). See Marsden, *Fundamentalism*, 129, and Ahlstrom, *Religious History*, 812.

69. Noll, *History of Christianity*, 288.

70. Marsden, *Fundamentalism*, 129.

71. Sandeen, *Roots of Fundamentalism*, 181.

circles. Keswick teaching distinguished itself from Wesleyan and Oberlin perfectionism by teaching that sinful human nature, rather than being eradicated, is counteracted by the indwelling life of Christ in the believer. This "higher life" or "victorious life" movement stressed the importance of total surrender to Christ.

Keswick theology understood sanctification as a threefold activity: gift, crisis, process. Gift was the work of Christ on the cross for every believer. Crisis necessitated a conversion experience by which a person surrenders their life to Christ. Process, then, was the gradual development of the believer toward the life of Christ.[72] Douglas Frank, in describing the impact of Keswick theology on the period, writes:

> As with Scofield's popularization of dispensationalism in his Reference Bible, many evangelical Christians who imbibed the teachings of the Victorious Life had no idea that the version of Christianity being presented to them was a relatively recent, historically conditioned understanding of the Christian life. Essentially, it spoke to the spiritual agonies of a troubled Christian generation in its passage to modernity, and it offered that generation (and those who followed) an opportunity to transcend its agonies through the Spirit's power to indwell the Christian with a life of perfect victory.[73]

Not all premillennialists agreed with Keswick thought and its pursuit of the victorious life (or dispensationalism for that matter). Such disagreement prompted a codification of Fundamentalist theology via the thought of the Princeton School of Theology.

Princeton Theology

The Princeton theology, out of Princeton Seminary, viewed dispensationalism and Keswick thought with high suspicion and lamented the anti-intellectualism of both movements and the errors of revivalism. A bizarre alliance between followers of the Princeton theology and followers of dispensationalism emerged in their mutual cause against liberalism and modernism. Leaders of this era included Archibald Alexander Hodge (1823–1886), Benjamin B. Warfield (1851–1921), and, later, J. Gresham Machen (1881–1937). These theologians held to a commonsense approach to the Bible and believed in the ultimate harmony of Scripture and science.

---

72. Stoffer, "Prelude to the Controversy." See also Frank, *Less than Conquerors*, 115.
73. Frank, *Less than Conquerors*, 115.

The truths of both could be arrived at by a rational, objective, inductive approach. Charles Hodge (1797–1878), the father of A. A. Hodge, affirmed that "the Bible is to the theologian what nature is to the man of science."[74]

The New Theology of liberalism had been held back by more conservative theological institutions and leaders up through the 1870s. As the three major shock waves of the late nineteenth century—evolutionary naturalism, higher criticism of the Bible, and Idealistic philosophy—rattled the religious landscape, three positions on Scripture were identifiable by century's end. Some, influenced by German liberalism, rejected the infallibility of Scripture in favor of subjective means of verifying the truth of Scripture.[75] The majority still assumed the Bible was infallible in doctrine and without error in detail. Still others stood in a middle position.[76] A snapshot of this emerging fault line is seen regarding evolution and the "new geology" that challenged the veracity of the Genesis creation account. The two extremes took their stand. Charles Hodge of Princeton Seminary embodied this entrenchment in an 1874 work, *What Is Darwinism?* He answered: it is atheism.[77]

There emerged a group of scholars who sought middle ground on religion and science by upholding a conservative Christian faith and evolution, specifically. Notable are George Frederick Wright (1838–1921), professor of science and religion at Oberlin College, and Asa Gray (1810–1888) of Harvard. These men collaborated during the 1870s on how best to respond to Darwinism. Their response was framed in four points:

1. Deep respect for Darwin's contributions and a sharp criticism of the dogmatic repudiation of his thoughts on evolution.

2. A recognition that Darwin's theory lacked an explanation of variations.

3. An insistence that scientific investigation should continue without impediment.

4. A conviction that Darwinian theory did not contradict Christian doctrine.[78]

---

74. Noll, *History of Christianity*, 35.

75. This was the view of Scripture espoused by J. L. Gillin at Ashland College at the turn of the twentieth century.

76. Marsden, *Fundamentalism*, 105.

77. Ahlstrom, *Religious History*, 766ff.

78. C. W. Hodge (1870–1937), the son of A. A. Hodge and grandson of Charles Hodge, held a far more open attitude toward evolution than did his father. Charles Hodge wrote in 1880 that if the universe is the coherent plan of God, then the concept of "an ideal evolution, a providential unfolding of a general plan, in which general designs and methods converge in all directions to the ultimate end of the whole" is not incompatible with Christian theism. See Livingstone, *Darwin's Forgotten Defenders*, 113–14.

The two decades on either side of the new century provided sufficient evidence that conservative Christians were viewing developments like the New Theology, the growing social gospel awareness, and evolution with suspicion, concern, and fear. Initial skirmishes occurred within denominations—Northern Baptists and Presbyterians were particularly affected. A Baptist view of the church as a voluntary association of those who had experienced conversion, for example, was highly susceptible to liberalism. Controversies emerged over numerous perceived issues: questionable views on Genesis, lax positions on Scripture, and inadequate views on Christology—most notably a denial of the virgin birth.[79] Evolution, however, became the great signifier for the developing fundamentalist-liberal controversy.

War for the Bible: Crisis of Biblical Authority

A firm trust and belief in every word of the Bible in an age when skepticism was the rule and not the exception has been both the pride and scandal of Fundamentalism. Faith in an inerrant Bible as much as an expectation of the second advent of Christ has been the hallmark of this reactionary movement.[80] By the end of the nineteenth century, Christian faith no longer served as the necessary and inescapable cosmology of Western thought, and the Christian who hoped to remain faithful to the church found their faith more weakened by contemporary social and intellectual forces. It seemed that empirical investigation and reason provided a firmer foundation to knowledge than revelation, yet much of the Bible's loss of influence occurred because of the rise of science and not because of direct assaults upon the credibility of Scripture.[81]

> The church's answer to this onslaught was provided through a voluminous body of writing on Christian evidences, all aimed at demonstrating that the Bible was a trustworthy record of the workings of God among men.[82]

Most twentieth-century Fundamentalists and many twentieth-century historians have mistakenly assumed that Protestantism possessed a strong, fully integrated theology of biblical authority which was attacked by advocates of the higher criticism. No such theology ever existed. What did exist was a great deal of popular reverence for the Bible. A systematic theology

---

79. Marsden, *Fundamentalism*, 105.
80. Sandeen, *Roots of Fundamentalism*, 103.
81. Sandeen, *Roots of Fundamentalism*, 104.
82. Sandeen, *Roots of Fundamentalism*, 105.

of biblical authority, which defended the common evangelical faith in the infallibility of the Bible, had to be created in the midst of the nineteenth-century controversy. The formation of this theology in association with the growth of the millenarian movement determined the character of Fundamentalism.[83]

There is no evidence that the literalistic interpretation followed by the millenarians was grounded in any new understanding of the biblical text. This interpretation was dictated more by the success of key voices in matching prophetic and historical events, and by the popular belief that factual, empirical, and literal statements were more true than spiritual, allegorical, and figurative ones—a product of the Enlightenment.[84] The millenarians assumed that divine inspiration had so controlled the writing of the Bible that the resulting text was free of error or fallibility and that this freedom guaranteed them a divine, not a human, source of truth. More importantly, this secured an immediate and not a mediated revelation.

The millenarians built their movement upon a literalistic method of biblical interpretation to gain an apologetic advantage. As the swelling rolls of the millenarian ranks demonstrate, this appeal could be quite persuasive. But it was a most hazardous venture. It was hazardous, first, because its hermeneutical foundation was insecure. The millenarian utilized a literalistic approach to prophecy not because the author's intention was literalistic—but because the climate of opinion in that day offered more support for a literalist than a figurative interpretation. Second, it was hazardous because it tied the future of millenarianism to the maintenance of an inerrant and infallible text.[85] In this vein, the Princeton Theology was born. The theology was fathered by Archibald Alexander (1772–1851), a Presbyterian theologian and the first professor of the Princeton University, who was influenced by Scottish commonsense philosophers, and required his students to study the *Institutes of Elenctic Theology* of Frances Turretin (1623–1687), a Genevan theologian of the seventeenth century.[86]

---

83. Sandeen, *Roots of Fundamentalism*, 106.

84. Sandeen, *Roots of Fundamentalism*, 110.

85. Sandeen, *Roots of Fundamentalism*, 111.

86. Sandeen, *Roots of Fundamentalism*, 115. Turretin's *Institutio Theologiae Elencticae* (3 parts, Geneva, 1679–1685) was the culmination of Reformed scholasticism utilizing the scholastic method to dispute a number of controversial issues. In this three-volume work, Turretin defended the Bible as God's verbally inspired word, argued for infralapsarianism, and supported federal (covenantal) theology. The *Institutes* was widely used as a textbook up to its use at Princeton Theological Seminary by the Princeton theologians of the nineteenth century. It was replaced by Charles Hodge's *Systematic Theology* in the late nineteenth century. See Turretin, *Institutes of Elenctic Theology*.

Although the Princeton professors conceived of themselves as traditional Calvinist theologians, their fundamental assumptions about the theological task were derived from eighteenth-century models. They took their stand between two movements, deism and enthusiasm (or mysticism as they preferred to call it) and labored to demonstrate the insufficiency of natural religion against the deists, while convincing mystics that the Scriptures contained God's absolutely complete and final revelation.[87] In this land-between, B. B. Warfield argued:

> In the whole history of the church there have been but two movements of thought, tending to a lower conception of inspiration and authority of Scripture.... The first of these may be called the Rationalistic view.... The second of the lowered views of inspiration may be called the Mystical view.[88]

To such a view, Charles Hodge championed a rational approach to the Bible that sought scientific proof for biblical authority:

> If natural science be concerned with the facts and laws of nature, theology is concerned with the facts and the principles of the Bible. If the object of the one be to arrange and systematize the facts of the external world, and to ascertain the laws by which they are determined; the object of the other is to systematize the facts of the Bible and ascertain the principles or general truths which those facts involve.[89]

As is true of the whole Princeton Theology, the Princeton doctrine of inspiration was denoted by a strong focus upon external verifications to the neglect of the internal—this is notably different from the Westminster Confession of Faith (1647)—a Reformed confession of faith—that places the authority of Scripture internally with the work of the Holy Spirit.[90]

87. Sandeen, *Roots of Fundamentalism*, 116.

88. Warfield, *Inspiration*, 112–13.

89. Hodge, *Systematic Theology*, 1:18. It is also important to note that the work of Warfield and Hodge does not have the militant posture indicative of later Fundamentalism.

90. Sandeen, *Roots of Fundamentalism*, 118. The Confession insists that only the Holy Spirit can convince one that the Bible is the Word of God. Hodge prefers to argue that the Scriptures are the Word of God because they are inspired. John Calvin himself, not one to be seen as indifferent to the revelation of Scripture, wrote regarding the internal witness of the Spirit:

> God alone is a fit witness of himself in his Word, so also the Word will not find acceptance in men's hearts before it is sealed by the inward testimony of the Spirit.... Let this point therefore stand: that those whom the Holy Spirit has inwardly taught truly rest upon Scripture,

For the Fundamentalist understanding of inspiration, the Scriptures themselves were to be accepted because of the credibility of the apostles as teachers of doctrine. Ultimately this depended upon establishing the trustworthiness of the apostles. As Sandeen notes,

> When one recognizes that this apologetic took such a shape, in part at least, because of the pressures of higher criticism, the whole structure takes on an air of bravado. As doubts began to arise in the minds of many Christians concerning the accuracy of Biblical history, geography, or science, these Princeton theologians refused to retreat from the ramparts of an externally verified Bible to what they felt was the quagmire of inner light. The apologetic, however, was only the setting in which the Princeton scholars placed the jewel they called the biblical doctrine of inspiration.[91]

The Princeton theologians buttressed their biblical doctrine of inspiration first by claiming that "the inspiration of the Scriptures extends to the words."[92] Hodge, for instance, remarked that biblical writers "were controlled by Him in the words which they used."[93] Second, they argued that the Scriptures taught their own inerrancy.[94] When the challenge regarding translation emerged they, thirdly, emphasized belief in the inspiration of the "original autographs."[95] Verbal and inerrant inspiration was claimed not for the present Bible but for the books of the Bible as they came from the hands of the authors—the original autographs.[96]

---

and that Scripture indeed is self-authenticated; hence, it is not right to subject it to proof and reasoning. And the certainty it deserves with us, it attains by the testimony of the Spirit. For even if it wins reverence for itself by its own majesty, it seriously affects us only when it is sealed upon our hearts through the Spirit. Therefore, illumined by his power, we believe neither by our own nor by anyone else's judgment that Scripture is from God; but above human judgment we affirm with utter certainty (just as if we were gazing upon the majesty of God himself) that it has flowed to us from the very mouth of God by the ministry of men. We seek no proofs, no marks of genuineness upon which our judgment may lean; but we subject our judgment and wit to it as a thing far beyond any guesswork!

See Calvin, *Institutes of the Christian Religion*, 1.7.4–5.

91. Sandeen, *Roots of Fundamentalism*, 119.
92. Sandeen, *Roots of Fundamentalism*, 123.
93. Noll, *History of Christianity*, 39.
94. Noll, *History of Christianity*, 40.
95. Sandeen, *Roots of Fundamentalism*, 127.
96. Sandeen, *Roots of Fundamentalism*, 127.

Sandeen writes, "The gravest charge that can be leveled at the Princeton Theology is that it was not so much a theology as an apologetic, not so much an approach to be discussed as a position to be defended."[97] Continuing, Sandeen notes:

> It ought to be noticed that the effect of the Princeton doctrine of the Scriptures and the millenarian literalistic method of interpreting the Scriptures was very much the same. Both Princeton and the millenarians had staked their entire conception of Christianity upon a particular view of the Bible based ultimately upon eighteenth-century standards of rationality.[98]

Fundamentalist thought was ensconced in *The Fundamentals: A Testimony to the Truth* (generally referred to simply as *The Fundamentals*), a set of ninety essays written by sixty-four authors published between 1910 and 1915 by the Testimony Publishing Company of Chicago. It was initially published quarterly in twelve volumes, then republished in 1917 by the Bible Institute of Los Angeles as a four-volume set. According to its forward, the publication was designed to be "a new statement of the fundamentals of Christianity."[99] Central theological emphases were the following:

1. The verbal inspiration of the Bible "as originally given"
2. The deity of Christ
3. The vicarious death of Jesus
4. The personality of the Holy Spirit
5. The necessity of a personal infilling of the Spirit for victorious Christian living
6. The personal return of Christ
7. The urgency of speedy evangelization of the world[100]

A flag had been placed in the ground as Fundamentalism was born around this twelve-volume work. The repercussions of the above fault line in American Christianity were felt by all religious groups in America. Even the Brethren Church, headquartered in Ashland, Ohio, couldn't escape the tremors of these seismic shifts in theology.

---

97. Sandeen, *Roots of Fundamentalism*, 130.
98. Sandeen, *Roots of Fundamentalism*, 131.
99. Torrey and Feinberg, *Fundamentals*, 4.
100. Noll, *History of Christianity*, 10.

Brethren Engagement with Revivalism and Premillennialism

Before this chapter explores the "liberal controversy" at Ashland College, it is important to note that Brethren had engaged two dominant theological streams already mentioned—revivalism and premillennialism. The ensuing polarization of Fundamentalists and Liberals/Modernists emerged as a struggle for authority to name and defend Brethren identity.

Stoffer notes that "the movement which posed probably the greatest threat to the Brethren during this period was revivalism."[101] This is evidenced by the reaction against revivalism in the minutes of Annual Meetings in 1815 (art. 1), 1820 (arts. 1, 2), 1855 (art. 9), 1857 (art. 25), and 1859 (art. 3). Revivalist methodologies of protracted meetings and mourner's benches are noted in the minutes from 1842 (art. 2). Furthermore, what came to be known as "altar calls" and hymns call "mourners forward" are addressed in the minutes from 1855 (art. 21).[102]

It's important to also note that even though the Pietist and Anabaptist heritage of the Brethren caused them to view conversion as indispensable for the Christian life, "they were critical of the revivalist theology of groups like the Methodists and River Brethren and the 'new measures' of men like Charles Finney."[103] Stoffer further notes that what was

> especially disturbing to the Brethren was the teaching that forgiveness of sins, the new birth, reception of the Holy Spirit, and even complete sanctification should precede baptism . . . [as] such requirements prior to baptism are nowhere found in Scripture. Rather, Scripture links remission of sins, the gift of the Holy Ghost, and regeneration with baptism.[104]

The emotionalism of revivalism also bothered the Brethren. Singled out for "special criticism was the anxious bench, protracted meetings, emotional preaching, the telling of thrilling anecdotes, the use of singing to rouse the emotions, the production of 'animal magnetism' (hypnotism), and 'praying characters' offering their services to pray for sinners."[105] Such new measures, Brethren believed, were merely to stir emotions "to get the individual to believe that his sins are pardoned, and that he is born of God."[106]

---

101. Stoffer, *Brethren Doctrines*, 111.
102. Stoffer, *Brethren Doctrines*, 111.
103. Stoffer, *Brethren Doctrines*, 111.
104. Stoffer, *Brethren Doctrines*, 111.
105. Stoffer, *Brethren Doctrines*, 111.
106. Nead, *Theological Writings*, 249.

Since revivalist preaching "appeals to the feelings, but does not inform the mind," revivalism was seen as a failure in educating the believer "concerning the costly life of discipleship to which Christ calls his followers." John Kline, a Brethren elder and martyr of the nineteenth century, therefore protested against the sentiment found in the revival song:

> "Nothing, either great or small; nothing have I now to do:
> Jesus died and paid it all, Long time ago."
> This would surely be getting salvation at a cheap rate. There is in this no "trial of faith, more precious than gold," no "cleansing of the flesh and spirit, perfecting holiness in the fear of the Lord." This means receiving the crown without bearing the cross.[107]

The Brethren were not against "experimental religion" but maintained that a true change of heart must issue in a life of humble obedience and discipleship to Christ.

Throughout this period, the Brethren continued to hold a classical, premillennialist view of Christ's return—quite different than the premillennialism of Darby and other dispensationalist thinkers.[108] In general, Brethren of the period ordered the end events as: "the apostasy, the tribulation under the antichrist, the gathering of the elect at Christ's return, the Millennium, the general resurrection and judgment."[109] Stoffer makes several observations about the Brethren and eschatology during this period. First, the Brethren generally expected that Christ would return soon but were not "caught up in detailed speculations about the time He would return."[110] Second, Brethren literature during the period contains very little discussion of eschatology. Though it was part of the Brethren's Christian hope, the primary concern of the Brethren related to "the demonstration of the Christ-like life."[111] Like the Anabaptists, the Brethren possessed a realized,

---

107. Funk, *John Kline*, 334.

108. Classical premillennialism is called "historic" because many early church fathers (such as Irenaeus, Polycarp, and Justin Martyr) appear to have held it. This view holds that the second coming of Jesus Christ will occur prior to a thousand-year reign of the saints but subsequent to the great apostasy (and to any tribulation). A major difference between historic and dispensational premillennialism is the view of the church in relation to Israel. Historicists do not see so sharp a distinction between Israel and the church as the dispensationalists do, but instead view believers of all ages as part of one group, now revealed as the body of Christ. Thus, historic premillennialists see no issue with the church going through the Great Tribulation, and do not need a separate pretribulational rapture of some believers as the dispensational system requires.

109. Stoffer, *Brethren Doctrines*, 212.

110. Stoffer, *Brethren Doctrines*, 212.

111. Stoffer, *Brethren Doctrines*, 212.

or inaugurated, eschatology believing that the body of Christ was already being realized, by God's power, the life of the future kingdom.[112] Thus, returning to Brethren elder John Kline, the Brethren believed that

> the church, in its purest form and highest sense, is heaven begun on earth. . . . Since the church is the outward, visible form of God's kingdom on earth, it is of the utmost importance that the church give expression to and be a representative of the soul and spirit of the kingdom.[113]

The distortion of this eschatology and the great impact of movements like revivalism on American Protestant theology brought the aforementioned fault lines of premillennial-dispensational eschatology (later knows as "Fundamentalism") and tradition eschewing liberalism to Ashland College in the early twentieth century.

Brethren and the Liberal Controversy

The central figures in the liberal controversy of the 1910s can be divided into three groups: liberals, those trained in liberal circles that later rejected or modified their liberal perspective, and fundamentalists. The primary proponents of liberalism in the Brethren Church were John L. Gillin (1871–1958), Herbert L. Goughnour (b. 1893), and Charles E. Weidner (b. 1879). By the turn of the century, evolutionary concepts were being taught at Ashland College. The science professor at the college from 1899 until 1904 was C. Orville Witter, a firm advocate of theistic evolution.[114] Witter presented his beliefs in an article in the denominational magazine, the *Brethren Evangelist*, in which he wrote:

> Men are coming to see that the Bible cannot from the nature of things be an authority on questions of science and at the same time they see that in order to make a law that would evolve a human being from a protoplasmic cell [note he is working from this assumption], there must be a Being whose omnipotence and omni-science [sic] cannot be questioned. The scientist and theologian of this century will clasp hands and confess that the

---

112. This eschatology believes that the kingdom has already come in Jesus *but* still needs to be finalized and perfected.
113. Funk, *John Kline*, 299.
114. Stoffer, *Brethren Doctrines*, 182.

mind which formulated the book of nature and inspired the Word of God was one mind.[115]

Witter referred to evolution almost doctrinally. This view was buttressed by the presence of a modified form of evolution being accepted in the religion department of the college.[116]

There were other men who had been trained in liberal circles but completely rejected or modified their earlier liberal views. Significant in this regard were W. D. Furry (1874–1959) and George Ronk (1881–1964). Liberal sentiments are quite noticeable in Furry's thought during the first decade of the twentieth century. In 1901, he advanced the belief that both Testaments contained an evolutionary worldview. The ultimate goal, Furry claimed, was attaining the fullness of the stature of Jesus.[117] "It must thus be seen that Jesus Christ," he wrote, "is the typical man and that the end of creation is the making of a world of men like him."[118] The authority of the Bible was not found in a claim of inerrancy but in the experiences that are imitated in our lives. Furry notes:

> We have not placed sufficient stress upon the element of human experience in the interpretation of the Bible.... Since it is human to err we need not be surprised if we should find some errors in the Bible.... [The Bible] proves itself our book not because of any pretentious name or claim but because in the experiences of the men that wrote the book we find our own life—our own longings and desires expressed and satisfied. Eliminate the element of experience from the Bible and it will at once lose its hold upon men.[119]

Furry would later backtrack from some of his decidedly liberal viewpoints. In 1911, for example, when he became president of the college, he called for the church to "lay hold of the eternal deity of Jesus" and spoke of a "wholehearted and whole-minded devotion to the word of God."[120]

The third group in the liberal controversy were the Fundamentalist Brethren: J. C. Cassel (1849–1919), L. S. Bauman (1875–1950), and Alva J. McClain (1888–1968). Stoffer notes that the "roots of Fundamentalism in the Brethren Church are to be found in the Philadelphia First Brethren

---

115. Witter, "Message of Science," 8.
116. Stoffer, *Brethren Doctrines*, 182.
117. Stoffer, *Brethren Doctrines*, 183.
118. Furry, "End of Creation," 6.
119. Furry, "Higher Criticism," 9. See also Furry, "Our Father," 3.
120. Furry, "Church and Education," 3.

Church and in the person of J. C. Cassel particularly."[121] Christian and Missionary Alliance theology inspired the four main emphases in Cassel's thought—faith healing, foreign missions, a Keswick view of the Christian life, and premillennialism/dispensationalism. These emphases (minus faith healing) were held by the two main pastors of the Philadelphia church in the late nineteenth and early twentieth century, I. D. Bowman (1862–1953) and Louis S. Bauman.[122]

Bauman's interest in missions and premillennialism was bolstered by his attendance (at the urging of Cassel) at a Christian and Missionary Alliance convention, about which Bauman reports:

> I saw that according to the plain, unmistakable language of the Word of God, that my Savior's return was personal and premillennial, and that the time was drawing nigh, I was led further to see that the fulfilment [sic] of "the blessed hope" was vitally connected with the evangelization of the world.[123]

Prophetic study and lecturing would remain a central part of Bauman's ministry for the rest of his life.[124]

In 1913, Bauman became the founding pastor of the church in Long Beach, California, a position he would hold until 1947. This church became the center of dispensational and fundamentalist impulses in the Brethren Church.[125] "Bauman was active on the Bible Conference circuit and regularly submitted articles, especially on prophetic themes, to the *Evangelist*, the *Sunday School Times* (a Keswick-oriented periodical) and the *King's Business* (published by the Bible Institute of Los Angeles [Biola])."[126]

---

121. Stoffer, *Brethren Doctrines*, 184.

122. Stoffer, *Brethren Doctrines*, 184. Stoffer comments that "Cassel indirectly and directly mediated to L. S. Bauman the two themes about which Bauman's later life and ministry gravitated: foreign missions and prophecy."

123. Bauman, "Missions," 10. The death of Bauman's son, Glenn, in 1907 left Bauman with doubts concerning God's promises of the resurrection. This conference assured Bauman of the resurrection to which he noted almost a decade later:

> I opened the Book itself. I fell on my knees. I begged of the living God assurance—absolute evidence! And there in the old Book were the words: "Produce your cause, saith Jehovah; bring forth your strong reasons, saith the King of Jacob.... Declare the things that are to come hereafter, that we may know that ye are gods" (Isa. 41:01, 23, R.V.). (See Bauman, "Prophecy," 10)

124. Pearce, "Dr. Bauman's Life," 3.

125. Stoffer, *Brethren Doctrines*, 184.

126. Stoffer, *Brethren Doctrines*, 184.

Bauman was an exceptional mentor and discipled several men into the ministry. These men were known as "Bauman's boys." One of the more outstanding "boys" was Alva J. McClain (1888–1968). McClain attended the University of Washington, Biola (1911–1915), Antioch College, Xenia Theological Seminary (1915–1918, ThM 1925), and Occidental College (BA 1925). Xenia was Presbyterian Calvinist but premillennialism was the dominant view of eschatology.[127] McClain taught at Ashland Seminary (1930–1937, dean 1934–1937) and served as professor and president at Grace Theological Seminary (1937–1962).[128]

McClain's influence can be seen in the transformation of Bauman's "loose Biblical theology" (the traditional Brethren approach to Scripture) into a "logically consistent, systematic theology under McClain's guidance."[129] This new perspective emphasized "salvation by grace through faith, a corresponding view of salvation as punctiliar rather than as a process, the conception of baptism as a sign and seal of an inward grace rather than as a condition of salvation, stress on God's sovereignty, and eternal security for the believer (though Bauman did not accept this latter doctrine until the 1930s)."[130]

One of the earliest confrontations of the worldviews of liberalism and Fundamentalism is found in the first issue of the *Brethren Evangelist* in the twentieth century. The editor had solicited various denominational leaders to share with readers their visions for the new century. The contrasts are revealing. C. Orville Witter was quite optimistic, as was the pseudonymous contributor Quiet Observer, who wrote:

> It is painful to note the gloomy outlook that many good people are taking at the dawn of the twentieth century which I think has been ushered in with the most flattering prospects that ever attended the advent of any similar epoch. I do not understand how the pessimist brings himself to his sad beliefs. . . . After all, the

---

127. Stoffer, *Brethren Doctrines*, 185. McClain cites former Xenia Theological Seminary president William G. Moorehead (1836–1914) often in his writings. Moorehead was Reformed and premillennialist (an unusual combination for the period). He also served as one of six editors of the *Scofield Reference Bible* (1909). Moorehead had reservations regarding Scofield's teachings that are elucidated in a forty-four-page manuscript from Moorehead to Scofield in which Moorehead expresses serious reservation regarding Scofield's interpretation of the kingdom and the church.

128. Stoffer, *Brethren Doctrines*, 185.

129. Stoffer, *Brethren Doctrines*, 185.

130. Stoffer, *Brethren Doctrines*, 185.

world is growing better. Life is richer, fuller and sweeter than it was in the "good old times" to which the pessimists love to refer.[131]

J. C. Cassel's tone was entirely different.

> Humanly speaking I do not look for as great a proportionate advancement during the twentieth century over the nineteenth as there was during the nineteenth over the eighteenth. My reasons for this are twofold; first, because of physical limitations, and secondly, I believe that the dispensation will close and the Lord will come again before the century closes, and thus cut short the purely human genius and enterprise.[132]

This depressing vision of leaders like Cassel was eschatologically determined. Feeling that Christ's return was near, they looked for "the seduction, the deceptions, the heresies, the anti-Christ that the Word of God warns us with."[133] Further contention developed between the dispensationalists and those with a more moderate or liberal perspective around whether a literal or symbolic interpretation should be taken regarding certain biblical passages. In 1902, B. C. Moomaw began an exchange on the Genesis creation account by remarking that

> literalists used to believe that the world was created in six days of twenty-four hours each, which according to Bible chronology could not have been quite six thousand years ago. Science has shattered all this mistaken conception, and proved beyond cavil, not that the Bible account is wrong, but that our understanding of that narrative, our literal construction of it, is wrong.[134]

Answers from P. J. Brown and L. S. Bauman came quickly. Bauman faced the issue squarely: "Nothing is done more to subvert the truth, the authority, and the powers of God's Word today, than is the spiritualizing, idealizing, and allegorizing of Scriptures in which there is nowhere any intimation that they mean anything but exactly what they say."[135]

The controversy became ugly in 1915 when George T. Ronk and J. L. Gillin exchanged a series of "bitterly critical and sarcastic articles."[136] Ronk felt that the time had come to confront the dangers of liberalism.

---

131. Quiet Observer, untitled article, 23.
132. Cassel, "Forecast," 6.
133. Cassel, "Sermon," 4.
134. Moomaw, "Light," 2.
135. Bauman, "Literalization," 5.
136. Stoffer, *Brethren Doctrines*, 188. Ronk had been exposed to liberal thinking at Stanford University but had rejected it, by this time, for a conservative (even

The question involves the whole field of Biblical scholarship—theological training, interpretation, inspiration, eschatology, ministerial activities, church objectives. We do not hesitate to say the very foundation of Brethren faith is in the balance.[137]

In his five articles on "The Present Issue," Ronk addressed liberal emphases that he felt were contradictory to biblical and Brethren standards. In the first article, Ronk upheld the "right of each person to interpret Scripture for himself. Nevertheless, he maintained that this does not imply the church has no right to enforce correct teaching."[138] In the second article, he attacked the liberal view of the kingdom, maintaining the idea that kingdom would come through spiritual and moral evolution was based on the "authority of experience rather than the authority of Scripture and Jesus."[139] In his final article, Ronk noted that for the first time in the *Brethren Evangelist*, a church leader (Gillin) had proposed to "shelve the Bible as the inspired product of the Holy Ghost and substitute therefore [sic] experience, denying the primary authority of the Bible, asserting the infallibility of experience alone."[140]

Following Ronk's third article, Gillin responded by contending that there are only "four bases on which one could build his faith: an infallible church, an infallible creed, an infallible book, and an infallible experience."[141] In subsequent articles, Gillin addressed other issues related to Ronk's proposed corrective. In a second article he detailed that the "source of confidence" for Jesus was the "fact that he knew God."[142] The angst of these articles came to a head in late 1915 and 1916 with a debate between a premillennial/dispensational view of the kingdom versus an evolutionary/

---

fundamentalist) perspective. He would eventually become a moderate with the Brethrenists. His distancing with other Fundamentalists was in reaction to their developing militant posture.

137. Ronk, "Present Issue," 13.

138. Stoffer, *Brethren Doctrines*, 189.

139. Stoffer, *Brethren Doctrines*, 189. In this article and the next two, Ronk proposed a dispensational view of the kingdom.

140. Stoffer, *Brethren Doctrines*, 189. Ronk called upon liberalism to get rid of its intellectual superiority. His proposal is actually quite moderate for the period in regards to the authority of Scripture and makes no mention of inerrancy. He writes that "the Bible is the Word of God, infallible in all matters of doctrine, directly inspired by the Holy Spirit, each writer using his own vocabulary and background." This posture toward the Bible is why Ronk is placed in the middle camp since he had liberal training but came back to center. Gillin, like other liberals of the period, espoused the importance of "infallible experience."

141. Stoffer, *Brethren Doctrines*, 189.

142. Gillin, "Christian Faith," 4. Note that, for Gillin, Jesus is *not* God but simply *knew* God.

developmental view. Fascinatingly, and frustratingly, each side claimed support from Brethren heritage.[143]

The final act in the liberal controversy occurred in 1921. The previous year the National Ministerial Association had appointed a committee of twenty-five to draft a statement of faith which would be agreeable to the entire church. The committee was composed of men representing the theological spectrum of liberal to fundamental. The committee's finished product, "The Message of the Brethren Ministry," was actually the work of McClain, another unknown member, and a mediating voice in the theologian J. Allen Miller (1866–1935). It reads as follows:

> The Message which Brethren Ministers accept as a divine entrustment to be heralded to a lost world, finds its sole source and authority in the Bible. This message is one of hope for a lost world and speaks with finality and authority. Fidelity to the apostolic injunction to preach the Word demands our utmost endeavor of mind and heart. We, the members of the National Ministerial Association of The Brethren Church, hold that the essential and constituent elements of our message shall continue to be the following declarations:
>
> 1. Our motto: The Bible, the whole Bible and nothing but the Bible.
> 2. The authority and integrity of the Holy Scriptures.
> 3. The ministry of The Brethren Church desires to bear testimony to the belief that God's supreme revelation has been made through Jesus Christ, a complete and authentic record of which revelation is the New Testament and, to the belief that the Holy Scripture of the Old and New Testaments, as originally given, are the infallible record of the perfect, final and authoritative revelation of God's will, altogether sufficient in themselves as a rule of faith and practice.
> 4. We understand the basic content of our doctrinal preaching to be:
>   a. The Pre-Existence, Deity, and Incarnation by Virgin Birth of Jesus Christ, the Son of God;
>   b. The Fall of Man, his consequent spiritual death and utter sinfulness, and the necessity of his New Birth;
>   c. The Vicarious Atonement of the Lord Jesus Christ through the shedding of His own blood;

---

143. Stoffer, *Brethren Doctrines*, 190.

> d. The Resurrection of the Lord Jesus Christ in the body in which He suffered and died, and His subsequent glorification at the right hand of God;
>
> e. Justification by personal faith in the Lord Jesus Christ, of which obedience to the will of God, and works of righteousness, are the evidence and result; the resurrection of the dead, the judgment of the world, and the life everlasting of the just;
>
> f. The Personality and Deity of the Holy Spirit, who indwells the Christian and is his Comforter and Guide;
>
> g. The personal and visible return of our Lord Jesus Christ from heaven as King of kings and Lord of lords, the glorious goal for which we are taught to watch, wait and pray;
>
> h. The Christian should "be not conformed to this world, but be transformed by the renewing of the mind"; should not engage in carnal strife, and should "swear not at all";
>
> The Christian should observe, as his duty and privilege, the ordinances of our Lord Jesus Christ, among which are: (a) Baptism of Believers by Triune Immersion; (b) Confirmation; (c) the Lord's Supper; (d) the Communion of the Bread and Wine; (e) the Washing of the Saints' Feet; and (f) the Anointing of the Sick with Oil.

In this statement, "Miller's mark is seen in the Christocentric apologetic for the authority of Scripture and the triad of words describing the nature of this revelation—perfect, final, and authoritative."[144] McClain's thought is also evident in the document. It is

> evidenced in the Reformed view of salvation (justification by faith) and the characteristic emphases of Fundamentalism: the virgin birth, the utter sinfulness of man, the vicarious atonement, the resurrection of Christ, and the personality of the Holy Spirit. Noticeably missing is the traditional Brethren formulation of salvation: enlightenment, repentance, faith, baptism, remission of sins, and the gift of the Holy Spirit.[145]

---

144. Stoffer, *Brethren Doctrines*, 193.
145. Stoffer, *Brethren Doctrines*, 193.

Overall, the "Message" reveals the mediating nature of J. Allen Miller.[146] But, as Cassel had described a few years earlier, fault lines had developed between the "'old religion' and the new one built on evolutionary and scientific foundations."[147] For Cassel, and those like him, these fault lines produced a dichotomy between the following:

- Transcendence vs. immanence
- Divine salvation vs. culture and education
- Christ as Savior vs. Christ as exemplar
- Spiritual kingdom vs. earthly one[148]

To Cassel's credit, there was room to be concerned in the relationship of the Brethren to liberalism. Liberalism tended to distort the more positive anthropology of Brethren. The lack of a central creed made conversation and consensus apropos in an era when neither was consulted by the extreme voices. Furthermore, liberalism distorted the Progressives' desire for a more reasonable faith and the individual's right to interpret Scripture for her/himself but this was never to be irrespective of the faith of the community. Yet, contra liberalism, Brethren held that the primary problem with humanity was spiritual and that the solution necessitated a posture of transformation from the inside out within society rather than a version of the kingdom emphasized by modernistic liberals that was entirely earthly.

In the end, the liberals left the denomination and a growing tension developed between the moderate voices, the "Brethrenists" and the Fundamentalists. Stoffer describes each group as follows:

> The *Fundamentalist Brethren* were militant in their resistance to liberalism and the social gospel, viewing them as categorically

---

146. Shortly after the adoption of the "Message" by the Ministerial Association in 1921, Gillin chimed in with what was probably the overwhelming response of the liberal camp:

> I cannot but wonder what some of the old Brethren who in the early eighties fought their hard battle against man-made rules and definitions, and who decided that the New Testament is a "sufficient rule of faith and practice" on the ground that anything more is too much, anything less is too little, and anything "just the same" is superfluous, would think of this new endeavor to bind the consciences of the Brethren ministry. . . . It is much more difficult today than it was twenty years ago for a man to think for himself and interpret his "only creed, the Bible" in the way Paul interpreted his, viz., in the light of knowledge and experience and by the guidance of the Holy Spirit .(Gillin, "Red Cross," 14)

147. Cassel, "Religion," 3.

148. Stoffer, *Brethren Doctrines*, 193.

opposed to the Word of God. Their means of defending the fundamentals of the faith was direct confrontation and the development of statements of faith to be used as tests of orthodoxy. Those men whose faith was nurtured primarily within Brethren circles (*Brethrenists*) tended to be more irenic and emphasize the Brethren distinctives (the ordinances, peace principles) rather than closely reasoned theological formulations. It is true, however, that most Brethren leaders did receive *The Fundamentals* and that there is an inherent conservative bias built into the Brethren faith due to its emphasis on "the whole Gospel." Yet, even though the traditional Brethren leadership was willing to adopt statements of faith to clarify the Brethren position on controversial issues, this group refused to view these statements as creeds and use them as tests of fellowship.[149]

The 1939 split was already brewing as soon as the last drop of ink was spilled on the 1921 "Message of the Brethren Ministry." Though tensions were developing between the Fundamentalists and Brethrenists, the two camps remained as one because of the leadership of J. Allen Miller. In the tenuous dichotomy of Fundamentalism and liberalism, "Miller modeled a winsome Christocentric faith which touched the lives of countless students, professors, church leaders, and laity. [His] scholarship, leadership at the College and in the church, and devotional fervor made him [the] dominating figure in the church during the first third of the [twentieth century]."[150] It is to his witness and writings that we now must turn.

---

149. Stoffer, *Brethren Doctrines*, 194.
150. Stoffer, *Brethren Doctrines*, 195.

4

The Theological Pilgrimage and Witness of J. Allen Miller

ON MARCH 27, 1935, the campus of Ashland College was silent. The Brethren Church responded in disbelief as news spread across the country of Dr. J. Allen Miller's death. Dr. Miller's leadership, alongside that of his wife, Clara Worst Miller, had taken an institution on the brink of bankruptcy and closure and charted a new course for the college and its newly founded seminary almost thirty years prior.

William H. Beachler, a Brethren minister, shared in his eulogy of Miller what many knew about the man:

> As a teacher, Dr. Miller was human. By which I mean that his fine and broad learning never isolated him from the common run of us. Dr. Miller's life and bearing lent convincing proof that the highest educated can be simple, and at home, among the simple and common people. I shall remember Dr. Miller as a man who lived on earth among folks, and who kept his feet securely on the earth.
>
> He was not a "know it all" teacher. His fine modesty was always outstanding in his life and work as a teacher. I cannot recall that Dr. Miller ever impressed me as a man who had complete control and possession of all truth. Dr. Miller could concede to

those who even differed with him, some things, and it seemed possible for him to conceive of others being sincere even if they differed with him much. I like to remember just this about him. It was a proof of his broadmindedness, fairness, and courtesy, just as it was proof that in the presence of the endless fields to be explored, he considered that not one of us is more than a child. He was a humble, modest, unassuming teacher.[1]

Charles A. Bame, another Brethren minister, regarding the late Miller's qualities for leadership in both college and church, wrote in the *Brethren Evangelist* that Miller was

learned without pomposity; keen without being cutting; good without being sanctimonious; strong despite weakness; strict without being severe; different without being queer, he could love without palaver, disagree without bombast, oppose without quarreling. All this begat in him the great qualities of leadership we know he had.[2]

The Ashland newspaper, the *Times Gazette*, had a touching letter from the editor that concluded with a reminder of the witness Miller had in the community. The editor, Harry Horne, wrote: "Ashlanders will long remember the noble life and Christian character of Dr. Miller who demonstrated in his every day deeds and efforts that men are given the privilege of life so that they can be of service to their fellow-men."[3] The impact of Miller's life was grounded in his theological pilgrimage that revealed a distinct theological method with a pastoral posture to serve the world around him.

For the Brethren, Miller signifies the recovery of the balance of Anabaptist and Radical Pietist streams of theology. These streams converged in the Schwarzenau Brethren. This convergence produced a Word-Spirit unity that allowed the Brethren to embody a dialectic of inner/outer, individual/corporate, and head/heart. Yet the journey from Schwarzenau to Ashland marked a period of great American assimilation for the Brethren. As a result, the Brethren witness was greatly distorted during the nineteenth century. The resulting splits at the end of that century were primarily over demarcation lines regarding engagement with American society. The Progressives staked their future on engagement with the progress of society. In such engagement, the liberal controversy of the early twentieth

---

1. Beachler, "In Memoriam," 8.
2. Bame, "J. Allen Miller," 5.
3. Horne, "Dr. J. Allen Miller."

century revealed further struggles over demarcation as competing visions of Brethrenism emerged.[4]

Yet this fundamental both/and that had laid dormant was retrieved in the writings of Miller. The conservative-progressive dialectic that shaped his theological inquiry was one of his greatest gifts to the Brethren Church and evidences his Anabaptist-Pietist faith. As Stoffer remarks, this gift helped the Brethren rediscover their identity as "[Miller] brought to the fore several emphases that had been obscured [in the nineteenth century]: a better balance between the inward and outward aspects of the ordinances and a recognition of the truth that the Christian life must contain a mystical, spiritual relationship with God denoted by the desire to have the character of Christ informed in one's own life."[5] Miller's keen intellect and hospitable understanding of truth paved the way for generations of Brethren to understand the role of cultural engagement and the purpose of theological education in that pursuit.

J. Allen Miller's Biography

John Allen (J. Allen) Miller was born on August 20, 1866, near Rossville, Indiana. His father, William, was born in Lehigh County, Pennsylvania, in 1840. His mother, Mary, was a native of Lancaster County, Pennsylvania (born 1844). Although William spent his childhood on his family's farm, he secured an education and was a teacher in the schools of Lehigh County until 1857. It was then that he and Mary moved to Indiana and settled on a farm in Clinton County, where he became a prosperous farmer and spent the remainder of his life. He died in 1897, just three months after J. Allen's wedding. Mary died in 1879. Both are buried at Rossville, Indiana.[6]

William and Mary were the parents of five children, of whom John Allen was the oldest. They both held membership in the German Baptist Church, in which William officiated as a deacon. This German Baptist heritage is why Pennsylvania Dutch was said to always be in J. Allen's dialect. William filled numerous public offices in his community modeling the importance of service to his children. Through his father, J. Allen learned the values of hard work, education, community service, and a commitment to faith and church.[7]

---

4. Norris, "Cord of Many Strands," 156.

5. Stoffer, *Brethren Doctrines*, 227.

6. "History of North Central Ohio," lines 1–3.

7. "History of North Central Ohio." The other children born to William and Mary Miller were Sarah (b. 1869), William (b. 1871), also a minister in the Brethren Church,

The early life of J. Allen Miller started on his family's farm near Rossville, where he attended the district school. He was baptized by the great Brethren evangelist J. H. Swihart (1840–1923).[8] At age seventeen, Miller became a schoolteacher, following in his father's footsteps. He taught at the local school until matriculating at Ashland College in the fall of 1887 where he earned a bachelor of arts in 1890.[9]

Miller then attended Hillsdale College and Hiram College, earning both a bachelor of divinity and a master of arts from the latter institution.[10] During Miller's time at Hiram College (1894–1898), the college was intentionally reconnecting with its Disciples of Christ heritage under the leadership of E. V. Zollars (1847–1916).[11] Miller no doubt took note of the leadership of Zollars and others as Hiram reclaimed its denominational connection. Hiram proved a fruitful place for Miller to grow and develop as a thinker. In a written history of the college from the period, Miller is listed as a tutor of Latin, Algebra, German, and English.[12] He did further graduate work at the University of Chicago. In 1904 he was awarded a doctor of divinity degree from Ashland College recognizing his leadership and scholarship to both the college and the church.[13]

Miller served pastorates at Glenford, Ohio (1890–92) and Elkhart, Indiana (1892–94) before returning to Ashland. For many years, he pastored the Ashland church (now Park Street Brethren Church) in connection with his work at the college. It was in Ashland that he met and married the love of his life and his intellectual match, Clara Worst, the daughter of Dr. E. J. and Amanda Worst, natives of Wayne County. On December 22, 1896, Miller

---

Charles (b. 1874), and James (b. 1877), who died at the age of twenty. James was living at the Indiana School for Feeble-Minded Youth which opened its doors in 1890. James's obituary indicates a cause of death being "consumption," what would later be identified as tuberculosis.

8. Numerous men were called to the ministry through the efforts of Swihart.

9. Fascinatingly, an early constitution for the college, dated August 29, 1888, is in Miller's handwriting. This would make Miller both a student and a trustee of the college.

10. Miller briefly attended Hillsdale College for one academic year. Always one to grow where he was planted, in the *Manual of the Theadelphic Society of Hillsdale College*, Miller is listed as a member. The Theadelphic Society was a theological literary society that received as members "only those as were 'evangelical believers in Christ.'" Its work consisted "for the most part of essays, orations, speeches, short sermons, expositions of texts of Scripture, lectures, and impromptus." Organizations like this society would prove foundational for Miller's later life and ministry. See Hillsdale College, "Theadelphic Society."

11. Zollars also had a love of biblical scholarship. He wrote numerous texts on biblical study. His most famous were *The Great Salvation* (1895) and *The King of Kings* (1911).

12. *Hiram College*, 300.

13. Stoffer, *Brethren Doctrines*, 209.

and Clara Worst were married.[14] He and Clara Worst had three children: Caryl Elizabeth (b. 1900), John Allen (b. 1905), and Malcolm (b. 1911).[15] The Millers with their children would plant their family roots deep in the soil of Ashland, Ohio, and from there serve that community and their denomination.

In 1892, the General Conference of the Brethren Church requested a theology department at Ashland College to train Brethren ministers. This shift revealed the Progressives' new understanding of ministerial development.[16] Miller was designated by the board of trustees at their August 1894 meeting to serve as dean of the newly created theological department. This began Miller's tenure with theological education at Ashland College—a focus that would animate the rest of his life.

His presidential service at Ashland College began by stepping in as acting president after the failed attempts by prior administrations to secure a faculty from 1894–1896. From 1896–1898 the college was closed due to a lack of funding. Miller and Clara Worst were called upon to reopen the college in 1898. With a spirit of confidence in God's provision, they committed their lives to Ashland College. G. W. Rench, a friend and colleague of Miller, described their return to Ashland where they "parted the weeds and kneeling before the God of all grace, implored the eternal Throne to open up a way by which religious life might once more possess those fine buildings, and the glee of youth might vibrate within those walls."[17]

---

14. This paper will not explore the life of Clara Worst Miller (1876–1970). However, it must be noted that J. Allen and Clara Worst Miller were a formative couple for both the college, denomination, and larger Ashland community. Clara's intellectual prowess and love of academics made her the perfect spouse for Miller. She taught in several capacities in the life of the college and shared her husband's love of languages. She also coauthored a book on the history of the college to 1953. See Miller and Mason, *Short History of Ashland College*.

15. The influence of J. Allen and Clara Worst can be seen in the educational trajectory of their children. Caryl graduated from Ashland College in 1920 and did graduate work at the University of Wisconsin and the University of Chicago. She served as a teacher in the public schools of Evanston, Illinois, for four years before her marriage in 1928. John Allen was also a graduate of Ashland College, class of 1926. He did graduate work at Ohio State University, where he received a master of arts. In 1929, he married Gaynelle Heppard, also a graduate of Ashland College (class of 1927). Malcolm was also a student at Ashland College, class of 1929. He then entered the Ohio State University to take up the study of medicine. He later attended the University of Louisville, where he earned the degree of doctor of medicine. He married Marian Homewood in 1934. See database and digital images, http://www.ancestry.org, accessed November 20, 2018.

16. An August 24, 1893, motion by the Board of Trustees established a committee to draft a course of study for a theology department. See *National Convention*, 46.

17. Rench, "Church Leader," 5–6.

During his years as president of the college, Miller raised an endowment of $70,000 and installed the new college laboratory.[18] He was twice elected as moderator of the Brethren General Conference and served as president of its Board of Foreign Missions. He was also the chairman of the Board of the Hess Educational Foundation in Ashland and chairman of the Athletic Board of Ashland College.[19]

In addition to Miller's many denominational and community positions of leadership, Stoffer lists all the roles in which Miller served during his time at Ashland College and Seminary revealing the many research interests that would shape his distinct theological vision:

- Professor of History and English Literature (1887–88)
- Professor of History and Arithmetic (1888–89)
- Dean of the Theological Department (1894–96, 1898)
- President of Ashland College (1899–1906)
- Dean of the Theological Department (1906–13)
- Dean of Ashland Theological Seminary (1913–33)
- Professor of New Testament and Greek (1906–35)[20]

With all of his roles at the institution, Miller maintained a deep love of learning which made him a sought-after professor. He genuinely loved to learn alongside his students and peers. The community of scholarship around him was reflective of his ability to remain open to a myriad of views while always staying tethered to his core convictions.

Miller's Theological Conversation Partners

Miller's lecture notes, sermons, and *Evangelist* articles contain a fascinating cast of characters that reveal not only a well-read theologian but also an openness to an impressive spectrum of conservative to progressive theological influences. Below are brief biographical sketches on a few of the theologians and biblical scholars who appear more than once in Miller's notes:

---

18. Conservative calculation accounting for inflation would make this amount equivalent to close to $2,000,000 today. This was an astronomical feat that reveals Miller's commitment to the institution and his ability to cast a compelling vision to garner support from others.

19. "Tributes Are Paid to Dr. Miller," *Ashland Times Gazette*, March 27, 1935.

20. Stoffer, *"Gleam of Shining Hope,"* 353.

- *A. T. Pierson* (1837–1911) was a premillennialist and the leading spokesman for foreign missions. He was best known for his work *The Crisis of Missions* (1886).[21]
- *E. W. Kenyon* (1867–1948) was a radio preacher known for messages on faith and healing. Kenyon would influence the later Pentecostal faith movement.[22]
- *A. T. Robertson* (1863–1934) was the foremost Greek scholar of his day. A Southern Baptist, he was best known for his book *Grammar of the Greek New Testament in the Light of Historical Research* (1914).[23]
- *W. Robertson Smith* (1846–1894) was an Old Testament scholar, professor, and minister in the Free Church of Scotland. He served as an editor of the *Encyclopaedia Britannica* and contributed to the *Encyclopaedia Biblica*. Smith was well known for his book on the comparative study of religion, entitled *Religion of the Semites* (1899).[24]
- *S. R. Driver* (1846–1914) was a noted Bible scholar and Hebrew scholar. Driver's chief work, *An Introduction to the Literature of the Old Testament*, appeared in 1891. Among his early publications was *A Treatise on the Uses of the Tenses in Hebrew* (1874). Driver wrote in the spirit of the historical-critical method. He was one of the editors of the International Critical Commentary series of biblical books and contributed to commentaries on Deuteronomy (1895), Job (with G. B. Gray, 1905), Genesis (1911), Exodus (1911), Daniel (1900), and several other books of the Bible. He also participated in the compilation of *A Hebrew and English Lexicon of the Old Testament* (with F. Brown and C. A. Briggs, 1907), which remains in widespread use.[25]
- *Abraham Keunen* (1828–1891) was a Dutch theologian who became one of the main supporters of modern theology. His most notable work was a three-volume historical-critical introduction to the Old Testament published in 1865, entitled *Historisch-Kritisch Onderzoek naar het onstaan en de verzameling van de Boeken des Ouden Verbonds* (Historical-Critical Research into the Origin of the Books of the Old Testament).[26]

---

21. Streckert and Larson, "Pierson, Arthur Tappan," 1803.
22. Tennison, "Kenyon, Essek William," 1269.
23. Weaver, "Smith, William Robertson," 2143.
24. Johnstone, *William Robertson Smith*, 15–23.
25. Fitzgerald, "Brown, Francis," 339.
26. Wicksteed, "Abraham Kuenen," 571–605.

- *Julius Wellhausen* (1844–1918) was a German biblical scholar who contributed to the composition history of the Pentateuch and became a proponent of what came to be known as the "documentary hypothesis."[27]

- *Friedrich Delitzsch* (1850–1922) was a German Assyriologist who specialized in the study of ancient Middle Eastern languages and published numerous works on Assyrian language, history and culture. In a 1902 controversial lecture titled "Babel and Bible," Delitzsch maintained that many Old Testament writings were borrowed from ancient Babylonian tales, including the stories of creation and the flood from the book of Genesis.[28] In the early 1920s, Delitzsch completed *Die große Täuschung* (The Great Deception), which was a critical reading of several sections of the Old Testament, including the book of Psalms and the Prophets. For the remainder of his life, Delitzsch questioned the historical accuracy of the Hebrew Bible.[29]

- *Ralph Waldo Emerson* (1803–1882) was a transcendentalist essayist and poet who rejected the rationalism of Unitarianism (where he was a minister) and embraced European romanticism.[30]

- *B. B. Warfield* (1851–1921) was professor of theology at Princeton Seminary from 1887 to 1921 and was part of the conservative Princeton School. In 1881, Warfield wrote a joint article with A. A. Hodge (1823–1886) on the inspiration of the Bible. It drew attention because of its scholarly and forceful defense of the inerrancy of the Bible. In many of his writings, Warfield attempted to demonstrate that the doctrine of biblical inerrancy was simply Christian teaching and not merely a concept invented in the nineteenth century. His passion was to refute modernist influences within Presbyterianism and on Christianity at large.[31]

---

27. Wellhausen championed the documentary hypothesis of the Bible which is a view that the earliest writings of Israel's history were a compilation of multiple authors. There is some speculation as to whether Wellhausen was not simply a proponent of this hypothesis but one of its authors. Support for this claim comes from Wellhausen's best-known book, *Prolegomena zur Geschichte Israels* (Prolegomena to the History of Israel), published in 1878. In this work, he explored the development of the first five books of the Bible, the Pentateuch, and detailed their historical and social contexts. The resulting argument, called the documentary hypothesis, remains the dominant model among biblical scholars. There is scholarly debate as to whether Wellhausen authored this theory or whether he simply employed it in his work. Regardless, Wellhausen's presence in Miller's writings reveal that Miller himself would have been conversant with such a theory.

28. See Delitzsch, *Babel and Bible*.

29. Arnold and Weisberg, "Centennial Review," 441–57.

30. Lee, "Transcendentalism," 345.

31. Reid, "Warfield, Benjamin Breckenridge," 358.

- *George Barker Stevens* (1854–1906) was a Congregational and Presbyterian minister. He also served as a professor of New Testament Criticism at Yale Divinity School from 1886–1895 and then professor of Systematic Theology from 1895 until his death. Stevens' most popular works were *Theology of the New Testament* (1899) and *The Christian Doctrine of Salvation* (1906).[32]

While Miller doesn't heavily cite theologians, preferring to allow Scripture to speak for itself, the ones noted above reveal that he was not afraid to bring both liberal and conservative voices into conversation with the Bible.

One theologian not on this list, but used by Miller more than any other, was William Newton Clarke (1841–1912). Citations of Clarke's work span the various categories of Miller's thought. Clarke will prove helpful in elucidating Miller's distinct theological epistemological vision. Before consulting Clarke, a survey of Miller's theology will allow his writings to present his distinct, biblical hermeneutic.

J. Allen Miller—Brethren Systematic Theology

In the July 30, 1913, issue of the *Brethren Evangelist*, Miller penned what he called his "denominational conviction" in an article entitled "The Brethren Church: Why?"[33] The article was Miller's attempt to concisely define Brethren identity. In a three-tiered explanation—creedal, interpretive and doctrinal standards—Miller sought to elucidate the distinctiveness and significance of the Brethren way. "Our Credal [sic] standard is the New Testament," he wrote. "Aside from this we have no creed."[34] Unlike those who felt this timeless creedal standard was threatened by higher criticism, Miller shared no such antipathy toward this new approach to biblical studies.

> [The Bible] is a first Century Book recording the eternal principles and methods of the Kingdom of God. . . . Historical criticism is therefore of inestimable value when pursued within the bounds of its legitimate sphere. As a people we have nothing to fear and everything to gain by its help in the interpretation of our only CREED.[35]

---

32. Porter, "George Barker Stevens," 162, 167–75. Stevens will appear extensively in Miller's discussion of the atonement later (to be explored later in this chapter).

33. Miller, "Brethren Church," 1.

34. Miller, "Brethren Church," 1.

35. Miller, "Brethren Church," 1.

Rather than a threat, higher criticism was an opportune tool to better understand the central creedal affirmation of the Brethren.

The central tool of interpretation, the *interpretive standard*, of this timeless creed was simple and provocative. "Being [indicted] by the Spirit of the living God," Miller notes, "we hold with St. Paul that only the spiritually minded can ascertain its divine import. Its interpretation is not an intellectual feat."[36] He implored his readers that "a man born of the Spirit of God and led by the same Holy Spirit has a necessary qualification in understanding of the Spirit's message in the Book."[37] Rather than the rationalism that underwrote fundamentalist and liberal approaches to theology, Miller advocated for the Spirit. The goal of our interpretation is not knowledge but transformation by the illumination of the Holy Spirit.

Miller was adamant that these creedal and interpretive standards do not make one Brethren—other Christian groups believe in these affirmations. Instead, at the heart of Brethren identity were core behavioral commitments that embodied the center of Brethren existence—Jesus Christ.

1. Believers' Baptism: Miller noted that this practice was the "Apostolic form of Christian Baptism." While all Protestant Christians accepted the "validity" of this practice, the Brethren hold to the ongoing embodiment of this practice from the early church witness.

2. Communion Service: Aside from mentioning the Brethren distinctive of footwashing, Miller laid out a specific liturgical order indicating that the order of the service was footwashing, supper and, lastly, Eucharist or "Loaf and Cup."

3. Non-resistant Principles: Miller found the "bearing of arms and carnal warfare and the swearing of an oath, [as] utterly incompatible with and contrary to the Spirit of Jesus Christ."

4. Non-conforming Principles: It is here that Miller located an ecclesiological and eschatological witness for the Brethren. The church existed in contrast to what he identified as the "world-spirit" that was "dominated always and everywhere with the selfish and carnal, the satanic and lustful traits and qualities of the unregenerated life." Miller stressed that this witness "finds expression in several directions, the chief of which are those which guard the sacredness of the sexual and marital relations and those which lay stress upon the life of humility, simplicity, and service." While Fundamentalists would have been

---

36. Miller, "Brethren Church," 1.
37. Miller, "Brethren Church," 1.

staunch defenders of the former and liberals/modernists the latter, Miller pulled both into the nonconforming witness of the Brethren.[38]

It is striking that the distinctives of being Brethren, what Miller coined the "doctrinal standard," are more orthopraxical than doctrinal. At the heart of Brethren thought he found the need for embodiment. The evidence of true belief was in belief *and* behavior. It is also significant that Miller did not shy away from paradox in his theology. As Stoffer comments:

> He holds in dialectical tension the Word and Spirit, doctrine and life, conservatism and progressivism, conformity and exclusivism. Though Miller confessed his own inability to articulate the essence of Brethrenism, his own life and thought were an eloquent demonstration of the qualities which have typified the Brethren spirit.[39]

It is, therefore, unfortunate that Miller never authored a book. One can speculate to the reasons for such a conspicuous absence. Available to posterity are his theological reflections in the denominational magazine, the *Brethren Evangelist*, and in *Christian Doctrine: Lectures and Sermons* (1946), a book published posthumously that collected many of his sermons and lectures. From these two sources a systematic exploration of Miller's theology can be ascertained. The following systematic theology is not exhaustively Brethren nor is it exhaustive of Miller's work. Instead, it helps frame the distinct theological epistemology and biblical hermeneutic Miller maintained regarding theological exploration and ministry.

Doctrine of God & Revelation

During his time as a student at Hiram College, the young Miller wrote a series of articles for the *Brethren Evangelist* regarding the nature of divine self-revelation. One can only infer what precipitated such reflections. A number of liberal theologians were on Hiram's faculty who may have been offering

---

38. Miller, "Brethren Church," 1.

39. Stoffer, *Brethren Doctrines*, 229. Stoffer is alluding to an article written for the *Brethren Evangelist* in which Miller admitted:

> In seeking to characterize what I like to call the spirit and the genius of Brethrenism I always find myself at a loss for words. In the first place this is true because it is a LIFE that I am trying to depict. And what makes this all the more difficult at least for me is the fact that it is not the life of a particular man or woman but the life of a community that I am trying to describe. Yes, it is a life. To appreciate it one must really enter into it. (See Miller, "Brethren People," 3)

their own perspectives to this area of theology proper. It also could have been Miller's challenge for the Brethren to think beyond Jesus of Nazareth to the larger concept of God and God's personality. Regardless, Miller laid out his fundamental propositions regarding Divine self-revelation:

1. There is a God, all-powerful, all-wise, everywhere-present, and infinitely good.
2. Man is a rational, religious and responsible creature.
3. God has made a revelation of himself to man so that man can and does know him.
4. The Holy Scriptures of the Old and New Testament contain the Divine Revelation.[40]

Miller identified two distinct but essential aspects of God's revelation. First was a recognition of the *manifestation* of God as "the element in the act or process of Revelation in which the Divine truth or fact to be revealed is clearly, definitely and positively presented to the recipient of the Revelation; it is the communication to be made." But such a manifestation is not purposeful or personal unless humanity can receive such a communication. Therefore, *inspiration* served as "the element in the act or process of Revelation in which the chosen recipient is qualified to receive the manifestation of God. The *inspired man*, thus Divinely empowered, RECEIVES and COMMUNICATES what God discovered or manifested to him."[41] In human history, this divine revelation—the manifestation of God and the inspiration of humanity—has taken place in six doctrines:

1. Doctrine of creation: "Where reflection is directed to the *existence of the world*. The creation is the *word* of God wrought out. 'God said,' is the evidence of an utterance proceeding from a conscious and free divine act."
2. Doctrine of the preservation of the world: "There is indeed a *continuous creative* process presented to us in that God upholds by the might of His word the whole world every moment."
3. Doctrine of providence: "God has a care for the world and directs; it is not chance with Him."
4. Doctrine of government: "God governs, is the simple proposition affirmed by Revelation. All other wills are subservient to His will. The elements, animate nature, everything is ruled over by Him."

---

40. Miller, "Divine Self Revelation," 4.
41. Miller, "Divine Self Revelation," 4.

5. Doctrine of illumination: "In illumination there is presented to the intellect a knowledge of God's will. It pertains to the external or intellectual knowledge of the doctrines of God, especially as to man's spiritual nature, what he is and may be."

6. Doctrine of redemption: "The Bible declares man capable of being redeemed and presents the sublime teachings of God concerning redemption, from the first step as the expression of the Divine Being, mediation, and the eternal kingdom of God peopled with the redeemed and now holy souls of man."[42]

In these six doctrines of revelation, Miller maintained the purposeful and personal relationship of God to humanity. Counter to naturalism, that maintained a purposeful but not personal relationship, or Romanticism, that upheld a personal relationship absent purpose, Miller argued that God was both purposeful and personal. Using Clarke, Miller cited an excerpt from *An Outline of Christian Theology* in which Clarke outlined the animation of God's personality as love. Clarke writes, "Love is God's desire to impart Himself and all good to other beings and to possess them for his own in spiritual fellowship."[43] Love made God's revelation personal. Spiritual fellowship with creation makes the revelation purposeful. God wants to be known and this desire to be known is God's personality in revelation.

Miller simultaneously understood this revelation as that of a triune God—a threefold self-revelation of God. While affirming the biblical data for the Trinity, Miller states in a three-part explanation that Scripture does not describe three gods but one God in three persons: first, the unity (oneness) of God is taught exhaustively in Scripture; second, this unity is one of essence in three persons; and, third, the Trinity is a Revelation. Each of the members of the Trinity, innate to Miller's understanding of God, is revealed as personal, divine, and coequal.[44] Miller recognized that God's activity must be founded upon core characteristics of God's triune essence: "personality, life (independent existence), unity, eternity, incorruptibility, and immortality."[45] He offered special emphasis on personality which he considered foundational to the biblical conception of God. Such a conception of God distinguished Christianity from Monism and Pantheism. Furthermore, the very facts of an intelligible universe and the personal

---

42. Miller, "Work Divine Self Revelation," 2.
43. Clarke, *Christian Theology*, 88.
44. Miller, *Christian Doctrine*, 8–10.
45. Stoffer, *Brethren Doctrines*, 214.

constitution of human beings (who bears God's image) caused one to advance an intelligent Personality as Creator.[46]

With this understanding of God, Miller offered a working definition of God via a quote from Clarke: "God is the personal spirit, perfectly good, who in holy love, creates, sustains, and orders all."[47] From his study of Scripture, Miller deduced that the nature of God was that of Personal Spirit—"a living and active, a thinking, feeling and willing being who has personality." Hence God possessed every essential of personality in its perfection—revealed in a divine character that is perfectly good. The motive for God's personal, perfect, and purposeful relationship is embodied in the love of Jesus Christ. "The object—the One who makes Himself known to man [through] the Divine Self-Revelation—is GOD. . . . He became the objective Self of the revelation made."[48] The incarnation of Christ is paramount. While Romanticism emphasized revelation through nature, Miller is adamant that "nature at her best, her sublimest attempts, can only attest this knowledge. Indeed, the Divine Revelation is the one hand-book that gives the true interpretation to Nature's voice."[49]

Christ served as the intersection of God's eternal attributes and his moral qualities in relationship with humanity. Therefore, God's unique attributes remain: omnipresence, omniscience, and omnipotence, and immanence/transcendence. His moral qualities toward humanity are made known in holiness and love. Such holiness in God "describes that standard of being and conduct which is the norm for Himself and for His children."[50] This holiness included such aspects as righteousness, faithfulness, purity, justice, goodness, and wisdom embodied in a posture of love. Love thus became God's divine attitude of grace toward his children—the highest demonstration of divine love being the sacrificial death of Jesus Christ as it revealed God's love as just and merciful. This paradox of God's justice and love, essential to God's holiness, is indispensable to understanding Miller's doctrines of God and revelation—an absence of paradox and mystery

---

46. Miller, *Christian Doctrine*, 3–5.
47. Clarke, *Christian Theology*, 70.
48. Miller, "Object of Divine Self Revelation," 3.
49. Miller, "Object of Divine Self Revelation," 3. It should be noted that Miller would not take issue with general, or natural, revelation. Such revelation posits an intelligent designer. The faith of Christianity, however, is a specific revelation that culminates in the person of Jesus Christ. Nature will never attest to this specific revelation. Miller appears to hold a neoorthodox understanding of revelation as personal rather than propositional. While Miller would agree with Karl Barth (1886–1968) that nature does not reveal God, he would not hold the same antipathy toward general revelation as did Barth.
50. Miller, *Christian Doctrine*, 6.

distorts the nature of God. "Immanence without transcendence," love without holiness, "is pantheism and results in the denial of the personality of God. Transcendence without immanence," holiness minus love, "is deism and leads to the denial of the providence of God."[51] He wrote later in the same article:

> Man cannot find out or discover God unaided. It may be argued that God is revealed in nature, in the flowers, in mountains, in the boundless sea; or in the starry heavens, in the blazing sun, and in the thousand tongues of nature's visible and invisible forms. All these testify to, verify, what we know of God [through] Revelation. THESE THINGS DO NOT REVEAL.[52]

Indeed, humanity according to Miller, was hardwired for a revelation from God. He substantiated this with five reasons:

1. The necessity for a revelation from God is presupposed in man's finite nature.
2. The necessity for a revelation from God is evident from the fact that man has the capacity to receive such revelation.
3. The fact that the knowledge imparted to man in a revelation always lies beyond his ability to attain independently of such revelation is a ground for its necessity.
4. The necessity for a revelation from God is expressed in the soul's cry after God.
5. Both in history and experience, man's aspirations and his errors manifest the need for a revelation from God.[53]

Doctrine of Creation

Revelation was predicated on creation. Miller emphasized that God was the cause of creation who served as the sustainer and moral governor of the world but was neither absent or aloof. Instead, God was actively involved steering creation toward its intended end. God's primary eschatological tool was humanity. Even though sin had entered the world, God was using humanity to guide the world "toward the realization of an eternal and

---

51. Miller, *Christian Doctrine*, 7.
52. Miller, "Object of Divine Self Revelation," 3.
53. Miller, "Subject of Divine Self-Revelation," 2.

supreme purpose."[54] That ultimate goal was God's kingdom and its meaning was found in Jesus Christ who was "central in the plan of Creation, Providence and Redemption."[55] The eschatological telos of Christ's kingdom made creation meaningful and purposive. Humanity was the pinnacle of God's creation sharing likeness with God and serving as God's proxy in the world as God's image was imprinted on humanity's "self-conscious reason and freedom above all nature."[56] If humanity was made in God's image, then it followed that humanity shared aspects of God's personality. Those qualities of God's personality included a free and personal spirit, self-conscious reason, morality, and a religious and worshipful nature.[57]

Doctrine of Sin

With the fall, Miller saw a distortion of God's image, not a loss of it. Unlike earlier Anabaptist and Brethren thinkers, Miller was silent on the origin of sin, instead, focusing his discussion on the nature and consequences of sin in the world. Finding the motives of sin as self-will, self-interest, and self-preservation, Miller believed sin to be a narcissistic cancer that moved humanity's will away from the love revealed in Jesus Christ.

The flesh was a location of sin but never its origin in and of itself. While sin remained a debt that entailed a penalty of death, the death was not simply physical but, and Miller emphasized this point, also a spiritual death. It was the latter that led to loss of communion with God.[58]

His discussion of the imputation of sin provided another example of Miller's use of paradox in his theology. While his discussion of the nature and consequences of sin was quite conservative, he took what Stoffer calls a "liberal slant" regarding the imputation of sin, rejecting the notion that guilt

---

54. Miller, *Christian Doctrine*, 17.

55. Miller, *Christian Doctrine*, 17.

56. Miller, *Christian Doctrine*, 13. Such a position for humanity is satisfactory for Miller regarding the origin of humanity. He does not discuss speculation regarding evolutionary beginnings. Similarly, Miller is satisfied with the individual soul being a creative act of God without further speculation. Miller maintained a modified gap theory of creation believing that lower forms of life were the result of evolution. See Miller, *Christian Doctrine*, 13, 177. Regardless of his beliefs on evolution and creation, Miller would have agreed with E. E. Jacobs "that there is a world of difference between TEACHING evolution and TEACHING ABOUT evolution." See Jacobs, "Evolution," 6.

57. Miller, *Christian Doctrine*, 18.

58. Miller, *Christian Doctrine*, 19–20. Miller's writings speak often of life *with* God as the goal of the Christian journey. This devotional and pastoral approach to theology is a hallmark of Miller's theology.

was inherited or transmitted via original sin.[59] Instead, an original *tendency* to sin was heritable. "We begin with a predisposition toward sin," he noted. "A bias toward sin is [then] propagated. There is entailed upon each life a moral inheritance from all the past."[60] To break this bias toward sin, a high priest who not only is tempted in every way as we are but also serves as a sacrifice on our behalf is necessary (Heb 4:15).

Doctrines of Christology & Redemption[61]

The centrality of the Lordship of Christ was fundamental to Miller's entire theology. Jesus was both human *and* divine and was our high priest *and* sacrifice. Writing on the opening of John's Gospel, Miller deduced six essential truths regarding the divine identity of Jesus Christ:

1. Jesus Christ, the Son, is called the Logos;
2. He is eternal;
3. He existed in intimate union with God;
4. He was God;
5. He was Creator;
6. He is self-existent.[62]

The power of John's opening was that "the incarnation does not mean that the divine was changed into the human, becoming what it was not before; nor that it became commingled with the human becoming what it was not before." In paradoxical union, "The incarnate Word is no less divine than the pre-incarnate Word. In becoming flesh, he did not cease to be the Eternal Word."[63] Employing personality language, Miller, more so than earlier Brethren, emphasized the importance of the incarnation.

> Jesus Christ was a Perfect Man. His Humanity was real and complete. His Human nature was the same as that of other men. . . . He is the God-Man. He is Divine. He is Human. The union between God and man in the Person of Jesus Christ is a perfect and absolute union. He is a Divine-Human Personality.

---

59. Stoffer, *Brethren Doctrines*, 216. This would be liberal in circles that affirm an Augustinian and Calvinist understanding of original sin as original guilt.
60. Miller, "Sin (IV)," 7.
61. Specific study on Miller's view of the atonement will appear later in this chapter.
62. Miller, "Divinity," 6.
63. Miller, "Divinity," 6.

> No explanation of the personal life and character of Jesus Christ as set forth in the scriptures is so satisfactory as that which unites in him the Deity of God and the humanity of man by the incarnation.[64]

The divine humanity of Jesus laid the foundation for Miller to see "the whole life of Jesus on earth [as an] atoning life."[65] All of the reign of God was placed in the loving hands of Jesus Christ.[66] It's striking that Miller cited Clarke in this christological discussion revealing that he and the author shared agreement on Christ's divine and human identity:

> Jesus was not such a human being as human parents could bring into existence, but, by virtue of being divine, was the normal and ideal man; for surely God, coming into human personality, could constitute such a man. He was not only more divine but more human than any other; for the normal and ideal man is most human of all. This view shows why Jesus did not inherit human depravity, and was not born to human sinfulness. Instead of being produced out of the vitiated common stock, his humanity was divine, initiated by divine act, constituted by divine indwelling. It was a clean humanity because it was a divine humanity.[67]

In no uncertain terms, however, the humanity of Jesus, for Miller, does not indicate "that man [can] save himself. Jesus is the only Savior."[68] With this emphatic statement, he devoted considerable attention to justification

---

64. Miller, *Christian Doctrine*, 35.

65. Miller, *Christian Doctrine*, 35.

66. Miller, *Christian Doctrine*, 49. Miller cites Clarke again in this section. Quoting from Clarke, he writes: "The meaning is that Christ the word in humanity, having become to the world the expression of the saving heart of God, the one mediator between God and men, and the head of the new humanity, is therefore the administrator of the reign of God over men. All human interests are in the hands of him who has given himself for me." See Clarke, *Christian Theology*, 324.

67. Clarke, *Christian Theology*, 272. Miller cites Clarke in his discussion on the humanity of Jesus in his doctrinal statements. See, Miller, *Christian Doctrine*, 28. Both Miller and Clarke come close to the "celestial flesh" concept of Christ's identity found among Dutch Anabaptists. Menno Simons, for example, affirmed that Jesus was fully human and divine but that he did not receive his flesh from his mother Mary. Instead, God imparted to Jesus human flesh directly from heaven. In other words, Jesus shared human flesh with us but it was not flesh descended from Adam, like ours, but newly imported flesh from heaven. This is why it is sometimes called a "celestial flesh" Christology. The Dordrecht Confession of Faith (1632) refused to be too specific about the nature of Christ.

68. Clarke, *Christian Theology*, 272.

and sanctification, not found regularly in earlier Brethren literature.[69] While the life of Jesus models a life of discipleship for the regenerate community to emulate, salvation does not flow out of discipleship but only from the atoning work of Christ but is gradual and shaped by a life of discipleship. It is both an event *and* a process that "[holds] the inner and outer aspects of the faith in dialectical tension, upholding Christlikeness as the goal of the Christian life, and maintaining communion with God as an integral part of the salvation experience."[70]

By adhering to salvation as both event and process, Miller maintained traditional Brethren emphases regarding the *ordo salutis* (enlightenment, faith, repentance, obedience to the command of baptism). He did, however, employ a *liberal slant* against original sin, by arguing that guilt was not inherited but a tendency toward sin was—an *inherited depravity*. He did not accept the liberal notion of the perfectibility of humanity through moral and social development. Rather than the perfectibility of humanity, Miller notes that Jesus had sent his Spirit into the world to enliven his disciples to follow his example. Therefore, entrance into this kingdom of God "takes a new birth of the Spirit."[71] Miller saw this new birth as a multistage process of regeneration. The (1) new birth in the Spirit produced a (2) spiritual change and catalyst that allowed the Spirit to communicate through the Bible in a transformative way through (3) illumination. Illumination then aided believers in (4) a knowledge of God that resulted in a (5) friendship and fellowship with Christ. Such a fellowship allowed believers to (6) partake of the Divine nature that gradually made them a (7) new creature.[72] This new creature/creation by the power of the Spirit allowed for (8) believers to participate in the renewal of the world around them as they live in anticipation of, and witness to, (9) resurrection.[73] This new life entailed the incoming of the Spirit, forgiveness of sin, justification of the believer, mystical union with Christ, and adoption into the family of God. Miller saw all of these movements of the Spirit as occurring simultaneously and unable to be separated.[74]

---

69. Miller adopted the traditional Protestant approach to salvation rather than the earlier Brethren emphasis on regeneration and baptism.

70. Stoffer, *Brethren Doctrines*, 223.

71. Miller, *Christian Doctrine*, 69.

72. The idea of a gradual regeneration is Brethren and unlike the typical Protestant view that saw regeneration as the starting point of a believer's new life in Christ. Brethren, and Miller serves as an example, saw regeneration as a lifelong process of discipleship.

73. Miller, *Christian Doctrine*, 69.

74. Miller, *Christian Doctrine*, 79.

Almost sounding charismatic, Miller wrote that a believer "must first be baptized into the Spirit, that is, receive the Spirit. Communion with God is a spiritual exercise and possible through the likeness that is obtained between God and his Spirit-filled child."[75]

Doctrine of the Church

According to Miller, a community of "Spirit-filled children" constituted the church. As with all other prior major Brethren writers, Miller understood the church as having an indispensable role in the New Testament, maintaining that it was Jesus' intention early in His public ministry to "form a society into which he would gather his faithful disciples."[76] Miller found this "exemplified in [Christ's] choice of the twelve and His announcement of the founding of the church in Matthew 16:18. Hence, the faith founded by Jesus is to be conceived preeminently as a life to which there is a social-side—the Christian church."[77]

This new society served as an alternative witness to a fallen world. Where the world was formed by patterns of brokenness, violence and coercion, Christ had instituted a "Law of Love" for the church. Fascinatingly, though the church was distinct from the world, Miller felt this same law should exist for the state as well.[78] The church existed as a prophetic witness to the state by saying,

> "You *ought* to obey this law." The state and the municipality differ from the church in this, that where the church says "you ought," the municipality says "you must." The state itself comes within the sphere of the church, and it is her duty to see that the state obeys the moral law; she cannot coerce. She has and ought to have no authority over the state; but she has some and ought to have a thousand times more influence, and she ought to use this influence for morality. Every Christian ought to use his influence and his franchise so that as fast as possible the highest moral ideals for the individual may become the ideals for the state and the municipality.[79]

---

75. Miller, *Christian Doctrine*, 96.
76. Miller, *Christian Doctrine*, 103.
77. Stoffer, *Brethren Doctrines*, 223. See also Miller, *Christian Doctrine*, 103.
78. Miller, "Studies," 2.
79. Miller, "Studies," 2.

Miller departed from earlier Brethren in his willingness to engage larger society—even describing the church as a witness to the state. Rather than a blending of faith and government, Miller called for the church to embody a cooperative separatism—a distinct eschatological posture of the Ashland Brethren.[80]

For Miller, "the Kingdom is the goal or end toward which all of God's plans for this age point."[81] As such, the fullness of the kingdom remained in the future. Until the full realization of the kingdom, "the church stands related to the Kingdom as MEANS to an END."[82] The alternative witness of the church to the world was that of the kingdom. Eschatology was not prophetic speculation in Miller's writings but a theological outlook that constituted the posture of the church to the larger society. The church modeled the already/not yet paradox of the kingdom and contained faithful disciples who individually and collectively lived their Christian life publicly. The soul of the church was the creative tension of Word and Spirit that continually kept the love and mission of Christ central to its mission. The Spirit animates the text of the Bible to testify to the revelation of Jesus Christ. It was this revelation that makes the Bible authoritative and transforms the lives of its readers. The church is the tangible expression of this Word-Spirit paradox. Thus, this creative tension is lived out among a particular people to manifest a witness to the watching world. A world that is often founded on either/or thinking over against the both/and of God's kingdom. The eschatological telos of the kingdom shapes a people who live in the already/not yet.

Therefore, formation was imperative for such an ecclesial witness. In one of his earliest articles for the *Brethren Evangelist*, entitled "Steps of Indoctrinating the Young Convert," Miller outlines five practical ways for new converts to assimilate to the church and for the church to be properly receptive for the task of formation:

1. Church must believe sound doctrine. "If this church would make her converts strong doctrinally she must be the unflinching exponent of doctrine herself. . . . Lesser truths will adjust themselves in one's life if only the greater truth is well enthroned. I can give only one illustration. JESUS CHRIST IS THE SON OF GOD. The congregation which

---

80. Miller helps the Brethren recapture an ecclesial witness to the world that was largely absent from nineteenth-century Brethren, except John Kline. Miller's posture is reminiscent of Christopher Sauer I, II, and III. See chapter 3 for more on "cooperative separatism." This was a different eschatological approach from the "prophetic separatism" embodied by the later Grace/Fundamentalist faction.

81. Miller, *Christian Doctrine*, 163.

82. Miller, *Christian Doctrine*, 163.

believes this strenuously, maintains it and feels the logical force of all his teaching in the light of this foundational principle is destined to succeed."

2. Church must practice sound orthopraxy. "This involves the careful observance of the ordinances, rites and ceremonials of the primitive church, as instituted by Christ and his chosen Apostles under the Holy Spirit."

3. Centrality of sound preaching. "The pulpit is and must always be one of the most powerful molders of thought and life."

4. Private conversations—all members of the church share in this teaching.

5. Every young convert be made a reader of the *Brethren Evangelist*—"A congregation could make no better investment than to place the paper in the hands of every addition to her ranks."[83]

These very practical and formative steps helped assimilate a new believer into the distinct ecclesial vision of the Brethren.

Doctrine of Eschatology

Stoffer comments that "Miller's independence from any one theological viewpoint is most clearly manifested in his discussion of eschatology. He is critical of emphases in both liberal and fundamentalist views of eschatology in his desire to remain faithful to what he considers the Biblical teaching on the subject."[84] The kingdom of God remained essential to his eschatology as he found this theme in both the Old and New Testaments. In contrast

---

83. Miller, "Indoctrinate," 4.

84. Miller, *Christian Doctrines*, 225–26. For example, Miller shows surprising openness in acknowledging that the ultimate destiny of the wicked is a mystery that he does not find entirely revealed in Scripture. He sees three possible solutions to this problem:
  1. Universalism: which he does not find satisfying the necessity of eliminating the universe of sin's work
  2. Conditional immortality and annihilation: Miller finds this idea inconceivable because humanity, made in the image of an undying and eternal God, is somehow dissolved into nothingness
  3. Eternal hell: Miller finds the dualism inherent in the idea of an eternal hell in God's world at odds with God's nature. With this and the other possibilities, Miller admits his inability to find a conclusion and allows "the answers to unfold in God's own time." See Miller, *Christian Doctrine*, 295–96, 300.

to liberalism, Miller carefully distinguished the kingdom from societal initiatives. As mentioned earlier, he also distinguished the kingdom from the church—finding the church as the *means* by which God was working out his plans. The fullness of the kingdom was always in the future.[85] Even though the culmination of the kingdom would occur in the future, Miller did not speculate on the millennium, "not [finding it] in the didactic or narrative portions of Scripture."[86]

Counter to dispensational voices, Miller rejected any "fanciful divisions of time," or dispensations.[87] He saw only two divisions of time indicated in the New Testament: the present age, consummated in the kingdom of Heaven, and the Age to Come. The "last days" began with the birth of Jesus and Jesus' earthly ministry began the process which will culminate with his second coming.[88]

At Christ's return, evil will be overcome and God's eschatological project—the re-creation of the material order—will culminate in a new heaven and a new earth. Miller rejected the idea that the present earth will be completely destroyed with the establishment of the eternal kingdom of God."[89] The distinguishing marks of the coming kingdom, toward which all of the universe was directed, were detailed by Miller:

1. Jesus Christ will be King.
2. The kingdom will be universal.
3. The kingdom is not of the present order or world.
4. The kingdom will be the rule of the will of God.
5. The earth will be the domain of the kingdom.[90]

---

85. Miller, *Christian Doctrine* 163.

86. Miller, *Christian Doctrine* 226, 228, 242. Like many twentieth-century evangelical writers on hermeneutics, Miller confuses genre and purpose. Brenda Colijn, Brethren theologian, commenting on this excerpt from Miller, argues, "Didactic is a purpose; narrative is a genre. Narratives can certainly be didactic. [Miller] really means expository rather than didactic." See Brenda Colijn, interview by author, Ashland, OH, February 25, 2019.

87. Furthermore, he rejects certain key tenets of dispensationalism. He challenges the idea of a rapture prior to the tribulation as unbiblical. Instead, he believes the great tribulation mentioned in the apocalyptic writings referred to the overthrow of Jerusalem.

88. Miller, *Christian Doctrine*, 213–14, 217.

89. Stoffer, *Brethren Doctrines*, 227.

90. Miller, *Christian Doctrine*, 164.

With this kingdom vision, Miller found the endless prophetic speculation of his time to be missing the biblical conception of the kingdom. In his lecture notes he remarks: "The second coming of Jesus Christ [is] far more than an event at the end of this age. I believe the event at the end of this age is only the consummation of an age-long process now in progress."[91] This process included the witness of the church whose eschatological purpose was a larger mission to "not only [save] a few individuals from the wreck but to save the wreck itself."[92] Miller's eschatological vision rejected the pessimism of fundamentalism and, simultaneously, was opposed to the utopian conception of liberalism. The former ignored the role of humanity in the world. The latter disregarded the necessity of Christ's return to usher in the kingdom. The consummation (the New Jerusalem) that served as the culmination of the kingdom process begun at Christ's birth will "come to an end in the glorious manifestation of the personal presence of Jesus in the whole earth to bring to a consummation, an end, a finish, these world-wide age-long processes now in progress, and to set up the Kingdom of God."[93]

Theological Observations

Miller's lectures, sermons, and published articles, reveal a theological method that maintained a conservative tethering to Word and Spirit and was simultaneously progressive in its conversation with the theological developments of his day. This central dialectic of conservative and progressive is useful in understanding not only Miller's theology but also that of the Ashland Brethren.[94] This dialectic is quite evident in Miller's conversation on the atonement.

A Conservative-Progressive Approach to the Atonement

Miller's theology of the atonement, consistent with his other theological reflections, reveals conversation partners with both conservative and liberal theologians. His writing shows great consideration for a camp of thinkers described as "evangelical liberals"—especially Horace Bushnell (1802–1876) and Clarke.[95] Miller mentions only one theologian in his doctrinal writings

91. Miller, *Christian Doctrine*, 217.
92. Miller, *Christian Doctrine* 226.
93. Miller, *Christian Doctrine* 229.
94. See chapter 5 for a further description of this dialectic.
95. See the discussion of evangelical versus modernistic liberalism in chapter 3.

regarding the atonement—George Barker Stevens. Miller's reflections reveal his struggle with central tenets of both the penal substitutionary (PST) and satisfaction models of the atonement. While Stevens provides the groundwork for Miller's challenge to PST, it is the writings of Clarke (and Bushnell's influence on Clarke) that heavily influenced Miller's proposed alternative. Ironically, Miller will follow Bushnell and Clarke to a point they reject—expiation, the belief that Christ took away our guilt through the payment of a penalty or the offering of an atonement. What Bushnell and Clarke find repugnant, Miller reinterprets and conveys as central to a biblical atonement model. Here, "atonement" describes the entirety of theological conversation regarding Christ's death. A central component of atonement conversations, alongside *expiation* mentioned earlier, is "propitiation" which conveys the role of Christ's blood to appease God. Miller and Bushnell will nuance these terms better than Clarke or Stevens. To better understand why Bushnell and Clarke disagreed with expiation, one has to better understand their respective views regarding the atonement.

There is a myriad of views on the atonement. For the purposes of this chapter, the contrast between moral government and classical penal substitutionary views will be discussed. Some confusion can occur when discussing the atonement because the terms used sometimes have differing meanings depending on the contexts in which they are used. For example, "substitutionary atonement" is often used to refer to penal substitution alone when the term has a broader sense including other atonement models that are not penal.[96] Penal substitution is also sometimes described as a type of satisfaction, but the term "satisfaction atonement" refers particularly to Anselm's theory known as the "satisfaction theory." In this picture, humanity owes a debt to God himself. God's sovereignty has been dishonored by humanity's fallen nature. Anselm argued that the insult given to God is so great that only a perfect sacrifice could satisfy. Jesus, being both God and man, was this perfect sacrifice. Other pertinent theories, not detailed here, include the ransom theory in which Christ's death is a ransom sacrifice and the recapitulation theory in which Christ is seen as the new Adam who undoes the wrong done by the first Adam. Each of these theories include an understanding of Christ as substitute.

"Substitution," as well as referring to specific theories of the atonement (e.g., penal substitution), is also used in a less technical way—for example, when inferring a broad meaning that Jesus, through his death, did for us that which we can never do for ourselves. In this way, and relevant to the

---

96. "Many assume that 'substitutionary atonement' is merely a shorthand way to refer to 'penal substitutionary atonement.' . . . Substitution is a broad term that one can use with reference to a variety of metaphors." See Baker, *Proclaiming*, 5.

atonement conversation of this chapter, the phrase "vicarious atonement" is often used as a broad way of describing Christ's work on our behalf—his substitution for us. The conversation that follows is an attempt to locate each of the respective theologians in their respective context and understand their particular slant on the adjective "vicarious." The multiple streams of this conversation demand great care to understand what is being referred to by different theologians in varying contexts.[97]

Another view of the atonement, and one that became popular among New Haven theologians of the nineteenth century, was the moral government, or subjective theory. This view is typically taught within a paradigm of salvation that focuses on positive moral change as the core of Christianity. God is depicted as concerned with whether a person's inner character is good or evil (where "good" refers primarily to unselfish love toward others). In this system, Jesus' martyrdom and subsequent resurrection affects positive moral change within the hearts of individuals and to transform societies to become more loving. The inspiring power of Jesus' martyrdom and subsequent resurrection is often cited as catalysts for moral change.

The moral influence view of the atonement was originally advocated and taught by medieval theologians Peter Abelard (1076–1142) and Peter Lombard (1100–1160). By the nineteenth century there was a blending of this view with the moral government theory of atonement espoused by Hugo Grotius (1583–1645), who theorized that Jesus' sacrificial death occurred in order for the Father to forgive while still maintaining his just rule over the universe. The blending of these theologies with the influences of the Enlightenment, Romanticism, and revivalism created a liberal theological system that emphasized Jesus in the following roles, over against his divinity:

---

97. For example, in article regarding the church fathers and their understanding of atonement, theologian Derek Flood challenges readers to interpret "substitution" in a way that honors their respective understanding. He notes:

> It is not enough to simply identify *substitutionary* or even *penal* themes in the writings of the church fathers, and assume that this is an endorsement of the Reformed understanding of penal substitution. Instead, one must look at how a patristic author is using these concepts within their own understanding of the atonement and ask: what salvific purpose does Christ bearing our suffering, sin, and death have for this author? Rather than simply "proof-texting" we need to seek to understand how these statements fit into the larger thought-world of an author. In short, it is a matter of context. The main task of this essay, therefore, is to explore the context in which the church fathers understood substitutionary atonement. (See Flood, "Substitutionary Atonement," 144)

- Teacher—a majority of the Gospel accounts focus on Jesus' teachings. These teachings focus largely on individual and social morality, and encourage love.
- Example—many New Testament passages speak of imitating Christ and following his example. The Gospel accounts provide a rich body of material from which early Christians drew examples.
- Founder and Leader—the Church movement has a large role in the moral influence view, as its purpose is to continue to morally transform individuals and societies.
- Martyr—Jesus' crucifixion is viewed as a martyrdom, in which he was killed as a consequence of his activity to bring moral transformation.

Advocates of the moral influence theory over the centuries have ranged from those who fully affirm the orthodox doctrine of the Trinity and divinity of Christ to those who claim that Jesus was fully human but not divine, revealing that the model does not necessarily constitute a heretical approach to the nature of Christ.[98] Language of substitution, propitiation and expiation are not normally found in this conversation. The argument could be made, however, that Christ's death as example produces a positive change that serves as expiation.

A contrast to the moral government view is a classical understanding of penal substitutionary theory which argues that Christ, by his own choice, was punished in the place of sinners (substitution), thus satisfying the demands of God's justice (propitiation) so God can justly forgive sins (expiation). It serves as a specific understanding of substitutionary atonement that can make atonement and punishment synonymous. Counter to moral influence, a penal substitutionary paradigm denies the saving value of human moral change. It focuses on faith in Christ and his death on our behalf, leading to a positive final judgment based on what Christ has done for us—not on any positive moral qualities that we possess ourselves. As a result of these conflicts, a strong division has remained between liberal Protestants (who typically adopt a moral influence view) and conservative Protestants (who typically adopt a penal substitutionary view). While atonement theologies have marked conversations within the church from the apostolic period forward, their implications for American Christianity became especially pronounced in the nineteenth century.[99] As Calvinist understandings of theology were challenged so also understandings of the

---

98. For further reflection on the development of this model from the church fathers to the present, see Green, *Empty Cross*.

99. For more on these developments, see chapter 3.

atonement underwent great nuance and transformation. A leading voice in that change was the theologian Horace Bushnell (1802–1876).

Bushnell, one of the preeminent liberal theologians of the nineteenth century, was a Congregationalist minister whose greatest theological contribution came in his discussions on the atonement in his treatise *The Vicarious Sacrifice, Grounded in Principles of Universal Obligation*. He introduces his work by describing the debate as he sees it.

> There has been a litigation of the sacrifice going on for these eighteen hundred years, and especially for the last eight hundred; yet still it remains an open question with many, whether any such thing as vicarious sacrifice pertains to the work of salvation Christ has accomplished. On one side the fact is abjured as irrational and revolting. On the other it is affirmed as a principal fact of the Christian salvation; though I feel obliged to confess that it is too commonly maintained under definitions and forms of argument that make it revolting. And which of the two is the greater wrong and most to be deplored, that by which the fact itself is rejected, or that by which it is made fit to be rejected, I will not stay to discuss.[100]

Bushnell desired an alternative to a penal substitution model of the atonement. He admits that God was involved in the crucifixion of Jesus of Nazareth but nuances orthodox understandings of Jesus of Nazareth being both God and man and understands the Trinity less as a metaphysical understanding of God's essence and more in line with God's self-revelation to humanity.[101] His third way response is less an assent to orthodox belief and more a desire to find a compatible mystical and affective understanding of God's involvement with the cross. On one side of the debate was Charles Hodge (1797–1878), the great Presbyterian theologian, who argued for penal substitution. On the other was Nathaniel William Taylor (1786–1858), who argued for a moral governance understanding of the atonement. This

---

100. Bushnell, *Major Works*, loc. 16520.

101. Bushnell held a modal Trinity, or, as he preferred to say, an "instrumental" Trinity. He regarded the word "Trinity" as a term which designated the threefold aspect of God's historic self-revelation. He did not deny that, corresponding to this threefold revelation, there might be similar distinctions—aspects or principles—in God's being. Indeed, in his essay, "The Christian Trinity a Practical Truth," he spoke of God "eternally 'threeing' himself." Rather than arguing against the threefold essence of God's being, Bushnell argued that language is inherently limiting and that the infinitude of God, while he may be three, cannot be known. Since language will fail to capture God's essence, it cannot be useful to assert if God's being is triune or not. Therefore, we know God's threefold revelation but his inner mystery we will never know as God's essence is not open to our inspection. See Bushnell, "Christian Trinity," 161–88.

model teaches that Christ suffered for humanity so that God could bypass punishment for humanity while still maintaining divine justice. It holds that Christ's suffering was a real and meaningful substitute for the punishment humans deserve but Christ did not receive the exact punishment due humanity. Instead, God publicly demonstrated his displeasure with sin through the suffering of Jesus as a propitiation. Therefore, Christ's suffering and death served as a substitute for the punishment humanity might have received. On this basis, God is able to extend forgiveness while maintaining divine order, having demonstrated the seriousness of sin and simultaneously allowing his wrath to pass over humankind.

The moral government view disagrees with this premise and does not affirm that Christ endured the precise punishment that sin deserves or paid its sacrificial equivalent. Instead, Christ's suffering was a moral example. In contrast, penal substitution holds that Christ endured the exact punishment that sin deserved. The satisfaction model states that Christ made the satisfaction owed by humans to God through the merit of Christ's propitiatory sacrifice.

Bushnell, caught between polarizing factions, developed an alternative that centered around God's love (not offended honor, punishment or moral exemplar).[102] He writes:

> Thus, it is that every sort of love is found twining its feeling always into the feeling, and loss, and want, and woe, of whatever people, or person, or even enemy, it loves; thus, that God himself takes our sinning enmity upon his heart, painfully burdened by our broken state, and travailing, in all the deepest feeling of his nature, to recover us to himself. And this it is which the cross and vicarious sacrifice of Jesus signify to us, or outwardly express. Such a God in love, must be such a Saviour in suffering—he could not well be other or less. There is a Gethsemane hid in all love, and when the fit occasion comes, no matter how great and high the subject may be, its heavy groaning will be heard—even as it was in Christ. He was in an agony, exceeding sorrowful even unto death. By that sign it was that God's love broke into the world, and Christianity was born![103]

God's love is central to Bushnell's theory of the atonement. The atonement is not about God's desire for judgment or punishment. Instead, God is

---

102. While love is *implied* in the view mentioned earlier, punishment and sacrificial language remain primary. Bushnell sought to develop a model of the atonement that more *explicitly* presented God's loving posture.

103. Bushnell, *Major Works*, loc. 16639.

motivated out of love. But this love is not the more common understanding of God's love that blends God's mercy with God's justice and holiness. Instead, God's affection for his creation calls him to take our "sinning enmity" upon himself.[104] This is the vicarious substitution of God's atonement. As Bushnell writes earlier in his treatise:

> The whole Gospel is a texture, thus of vicarious conceptions, in which Christ is represented, in one way or another, as coming into our place, substituted in our stead, bearing our burdens, answering for us, and standing in a kind of suffering sponsorship for the race.[105]

Bushnell adamantly claims that this substitution is not literal as is required for a belief in expiation that is central to the satisfaction model of the atonement. Rather, he argues that such an understanding is repugnant to the modern ear. Arguing from modern experience and sensibility, he remarks:

> We are not to hold the Scripture terms of vicarious sacrifice, as importing a literal substitution of places, by which Christ becomes a sinner for sinners, or penally subject to our deserved penalties. That is a kind of substitution that offends every strongest sentiment of our nature. He cannot become guilty for us. Neither, as God is a just being, can he be . . . punishable in our place—all God's moral sentiments would be revolted by that. And if Christ should himself consent to such punishment, he would only ask to have all the most immovable convictions, both of God's moral nature and our own, confounded, or eternally put by.[106]

Circumventing any understanding of the atonement as punishment, Bushnell argues that its impetus is found in God's affections for his creation. "Love is a principle essentially vicarious in its own nature, identifying the subject with others, so as to suffer their adversities and pains, and taking on itself the burden of their evils."[107]

Clarke would agree with the vicarious love of the Bushnell's atonement theory. "The necessity of punishment," he writes, "certainly cannot be present to God as an obstacle to his willingness for reconciliation between himself and sinful man. Grace does not wait for punishment to be inflicted."[108]

---

104. Bushnell, *Major Works*, loc. 16639.
105. Bushnell, *Major Works*, loc. 16639.
106. Bushnell, *Major Works*, loc. 16566.
107. Bushnell, *Major Works*, loc. 16583.
108. Clarke, *Christian Theology*, 332.

Adding to Bushnell's adjective of Christ's sacrifice as "vicarious," Clarke elaborates that even though this sacrifice "has been called forensic, commercial, vicarious, substitutionary, penal, vice-penal, governmental, ethical, moral," a more helpful description is that it was "direct and vital."[109]

Clarke steers the conversation away from substitution utilizing, instead, the phrase "sin-bearer" to describe Christ's work on the cross. Christ's "sin-bearance" occurs in two ways:

> [He became a sin-bearer] first by way of endurance, as a hater of sin and lover of men.... In another way, God became a sin-bearer by way of endeavor. He is a Saviour. Holiness and love conspire to make him such, and a Saviour, while he bears the burden of endurance that has just been spoken of, has to bear besides a burden of endeavor. A sinful world throws upon God the burden of a Saviour's work.[110]

Christ first bears our sin through his pursuit of us and then bears our sin through his example to us. Bushnell, remains in agreement with Clarke but offers an addendum—Christ's sacrifice was never about punishment or expiation. It was about penance. It was simply a covering provided by the Passover lamb.[111] As such, it is wholly subjective as the one making the sacrifice is covered, hidden, by the blood of the sacrifice. To atone, he notes, is to

> remove transgression itself, or reconcile the transgressor. It fulfills, in a figure, the original physical sense of the word to cover.... It is such a working on the bad mind of sin as at-ones it, reconciles it to God, covers up and hides forever the wrong

---

109. Clarke, *Christian Theology*, 338.
110. Clarke, *Christian Theology*, 342.
111. Bushnell writes in another section of Vicarious Sacrifice: "The original of the word atone, or make atonement, in the Hebrew scripture, carries no such idea of expiation. It simply speaks of covering, not expiations, making cover for sin, and is sufficiently answered by anything which removes it, hides it from the sight, brings into a state of reconciliation, where the impeachment of it is gone. Accordingly, it is sometimes translated to reconcile or make reconciliation; sometimes to pardon; sometimes to purify, cleanse, purge.... Atonement then is a change wrought in us, a change by which we are reconciled to God. Propitiation is an objective conception, by which that change, taking place in us, is spoken of as occurring representatively in God. Just as guilty minds, thrown off from God, glass [sic] their feeling representatively in God, imagining that God is thrown off from them; or just as we say that the sun rises, instead of saying, what would be so very awkward to us, and yet is the real truth, that we ourselves rise to the sun. The necessity and uses of this objective language will be considered more at large, in the remaining chapter, and therefore need not be insisted on here, as in reference to the single word propitiation." See Bushnell, *Major Works*, loc. 22590.

of transgression, assures and justifies the transgressor. In one word, constantly applied to it in the atonements of the old ritual, it makes clean. The effect is wholly subjective, being a change wrought in all the principles of life and characters and dispositions of the soul.... The sprinkling of the far more sacred blood of Jesus, dying as the Lamb of God, in the volunteer obedience of his vicarious sacrifice, reconsecrates the law broken by our sin, dishonored and defiled by our defilement, and by its life-touch in our feeling and faith, purges our consciousness from dead works, to serve the living God.[112]

Out of the vicarious love of the atonement flows the ethical dimension of imitation to the world. Questions still remain for both Bushnell and Clarke: What is the purpose of Christ's death? Why was such a violent death required? Who is inflicting the violence and what is the purpose of that violence?

Bushnell and Clarke return to the love of God that always desires to be in relationship with his people. Their understanding of divine love is nuanced and deserves further exploration. While their understanding of God is one of supreme and immanent love, little, if anything, is ever mentioned about his holiness, justice, or anger at sin. Instead, Clarke argues that something entirely different is occurring on the cross—what he terms "love suffering":

> [Love's suffering] is a substitute for punishment that God is offering, and in which he will forever delight. His true heart is willing that the pain of sin-bearing should be borne by himself and by all whom he can win to join him; for he does not desire the death of the wicked, but that the wicked turn from his way and live.[113]

Clarke never addresses why the particularly violent death of Christ was required. Yet he is intentional to note that those who follow the example of Christ and "bear the sins" of others must be prepared to meet that same fate. When the powers are challenged by "love's suffering," it may entail the potential for death. The hope is that the example of such suffering will continue to call others to rise above violence, brokenness and injustice. This is the purpose of Christ's death. Sin is the sickness and the example of Christ on the cross is our cure. Christ's death fully reveals what God is like.[114]

112. Bushnell, *Major Works*, loc. 22564.
113. Clarke, *Christian Theology*, 344.
114. While Clarke and Bushnell will each write of the centrality of Christ's death, both depart from orthodox Christology in that they separate God from the person of

Bushnell agreed with Clarke on the centrality of love although he is more committed to a substitutionary atonement theory. Where Clarke wanted the cross to show us what suffering on behalf of love looks like, Bushnell believed something more mystical was occurring—hence the language of "vicarious" used to describe Christ's sacrifice. If there is no vicarious connection between Christ's sacrifice and our own lives, Bushnell believed, then an important impulse at the core of Christian belief would be missing.

> If God's love has no vicarious element, theirs of course will have as little; if he simply stands by law and retribution, if he never enters himself into human evils and sins, so as to be burdened by them, never identifies himself with souls under evil, to bear them—enemies and outcasts though they be—then it will be seen that they, as believers, are never in affliction for the sin of others, never burdened as intercessors for them; for there was in fact no such mind in Christ Jesus himself.[115]

With this vicarious suffering, however, Bushnell insisted that the substitutionary language of the Bible could not be taken literally. "Christ bore [our sins] on his feeling," he argues, and "became inserted into their bad lot by his sympathy as a friend, yielded up himself and his life, even, to an effort of restoring mercy; in a word that he bore our sins in just the same sense that he bore our sicknesses."[116] While Bushnell saw more transpiring on the cross than Jesus as mere moral exemplar (moral government) or a punishment/penalty (penal substitution), the centrality of love was paramount as God entered into the fallenness of humanity and in solidarity laid down his life so that humanity may know mercy.

In a similar fashion, Clarke argued that the "same sin cannot be both punished and forgiven."[117]

> Forgiveness is the withdrawal of such punishment, and the infliction of such punishment implies that forgiveness has not occurred. . . . The central element in the penalty of sin is the disapproval of God, and the heart of the penalty is taken out when withdrawn. But forgiveness implies the withdrawal of this element in penalty.[118]

Jesus. The cross becomes less an act of God on our behalf and more the act of a moral exemplar that reveals what God is like.

115. Bushnell, *Major Works*, loc. 16673.
116. Bushnell, *Major Works*, loc. 16624.
117. Clarke, *Christian Theology*, 330.
118. Clarke, *Christian Theology*, 330.

God forgives *or* punishes. If God punishes, then God's love is negated. If God forgives, then it is not in response to a punishment or judgement but to create a people shaped by forgiveness.[119] As David Wells comments:

> In Bushnell [and Clarke] the transition from the centrality of the holiness of God to his love was complete. His approach was to use human experience to fashion an understanding of how God is able to forgive. Human and divine forgiveness do not differ from one another; the way individuals forgive one another is the way God forgives them. In both cases there is propitiation. Human suffering, in other words, propitiates sin. Thus, the atonement is a declaration of a universal principle, namely, that suffering and forgiveness are the ways in which sin is erased in both human and divine relations.[120]

While Miller would agree with much of the theological perspective described by Wells, he would differ from Clarke and Bushnell by discerning a difference between punishment and sacrifice. Miller found expiation as accompanying the work of Christ all while not emphasizing God's wrath nor any understanding of the Father abusing the Son.

Miller was well aware of these conversations regarding the atonement. As was described in chapter 3, the atonement was central to the liberal controversy that swept over Ashland College in the early 1900s revealing that the Brethren of the late nineteenth and early twentieth century experienced the same theological struggles and debates as other Protestant groups. Miller's challenge, like Bushnell and Clarke, was finding a moderate position between the extremes. Unlike Bushnell and Clarke, Miller takes his cues not from modern sensibilities or experience but rather from the biblical data. Revealing a theological mind that keeps the whole life of Christ and the revelation of Scripture central, Miller quickly rejected any theology that pit incarnation against atonement. Liberal theologians prized the former over against the latter. Fundamentalists stressed the latter and often ignored the former. Miller notes:

119. Clarke writes later: "The men who are this 'in Christ' do truly constitute a New Humanity. Christ, the first perfect man, was the first in whom God's idea in creating mankind was fully realized. To come into spiritual fellowship and moral unity with him is to enter into that ideal humanity which fulfills God's design. Christ is thus the beginning of a new humanity in fellowship with God, and when he brings men to himself he brings them into this humanity. Every soul that is joined to him thereby enters it." See Clarke, *Christian Theology*, 359. Here Clarke's theory is blending with the moral governance theory of the atonement whereby Christ's death starts a new humanity that lives out the ways of the kingdom. The difference for Clarke's theology is that the moral governance theory reveals God's disgust and judgment of sin in the sacrifice of Christ.

120. Wells, "Debate over the Atonement," 367.

> It has been said that the central fact of Christianity is the Incarnation of our Lord and that the main object of the Incarnation is the Atonement. The facts stated in the simplest manner are: man is a sinner and as such is estranged from God; sin involves penalty because of guilt incurred; sin also enslaves, weakens, and at last destroys moral endeavor; sin ends in spiritual death. Now man cannot redeem himself. He can in no way secure release from the power of sin by his own effort. He can never deliver himself from the guilt and the penalty of his sin. Redemption must come from God. It must be a gift of grace. It must fully meet the demands of God's righteousness and justice as well as set the sinner free and secure his salvation. All this God does by the redemption he wrought in and through Jesus Christ.[121]

Such an emphasis on the redemptive work of Jesus is central to a Brethren Christology and subsequent understanding of the atonement. Yet, even though Miller never commented on penal substitutionary theologians, specifically, his writings reveal his disagreement. Like Bushnell and Clarke, he cannot agree with any transference of guilt so that Christ is punished in our place.

> In a simple and concise statement, we must say that guilt attaches to sin committed and to him who commits it.... There can be no transfer of guilt. Guilt is blameworthiness experienced by the individual who is conscious of wrong, wrong done by himself of any sort whatsoever. Penalty is the just retribution from such wrong done.[122]

Christ is never to blame. Nor does God ever make Christ to blame. God's justice is not retributive for Miller. Instead, Miller nuances the language used in atonement conversations identifying significant distinctions between the concepts of sin, guilt, and penalty. "To transfer, were that possible, the guilt and penalty of one to another who knew no sin and was utterly innocent and thus attempting to make him the object of God's wrath, not only violates these moral distinctions but it contradicts God's justice."[123] While humanity was guilty of sinning against God, there is no justice in the person of God to transfer humanity's guilt to a sinless being. Such a transference models neither God's justice nor his love.

---

121. Miller, *Christian Doctrine*, 35. While Miller mentions both incarnation and atonement, he does seem to subordinate incarnation to atonement in a way this is typical of penal substitutionary atonement.

122. Miller, *Christian Doctrine*, 38.

123. Miller, *Christian Doctrine*, 39.

Insisting that the New Testament never reads "that Christ died *instead* for us,"[124] Miller argues, contrary to liberal theologians that, "[Christ] did die in our behalf, for our interests, for our sake, for our sin. He died in our behalf and because of our sin. We were under the death penalty."[125] The last line is a direct challenge to the overly optimistic understandings of sin and humanity presented by liberal theologians as he tethers his atonement theology to more conservative paradigms regarding the totality of sin's effect and humanity's inability to save themselves. Sin is not a bad feeling or simply a condition. Sin is a distortion of God's will for humanity that has both individual and social expressions. This belief was evidenced in an article written in the July 27, 1910, *Brethren Evangelist* in which Miller elaborated on his doctrine of sin and asserted that Scripture teaches:

1. Sin as primarily involved in a personal relation.
2. Sin as disobedience to a Divine law or self-assertion against God.
3. Since the race is a unit sin is a unit and hence the universal consciousness of sin.
4. Sin involves guilt and consequent punishment. The solidarity of the race does not free the one sinning from personal responsibility.
5. God graciously and fully pardons sin upon his own necessary conditions.[126]

Miller, as if reinforcing his orthodoxy against accusations of liberalism, closed the article with strong words: "The one phase of human inability which we can assert with positive certainty is that man cannot save himself. Jesus is the only Savior. He is the Divine Savior."[127]

A point Miller found missing from many within theological liberalism was salvation from spiritual death. Liberalism envisioned a world perpetually renewed by the efforts of those faithful to the kingdom. Miller reappropriates a more conservative understanding of the atonement when he writes:

> His dying a bodily death, a kind of dying, saves us or delivers us from spiritual death, an altogether different sort of dying. Thus, in this particular, his death was symbolic of the death from which he saves us. It was not strictly and literally the same. If we hold this distinction in mind we may say with due propriety that

124. Miller, *Christian Doctrine*, 39.
125. Miller, *Christian Doctrine*, 39.
126. Miller, "Doctrinal," 7.
127. Miller, "Doctrinal," 7.

he died instead of us. There is not in this, however, the slightest hint that he was punished instead of us in his dying for us.[128]

Thus, Miller found Christ's "experience of the consequences of sin [as] entirely vicarious and representative."[129] It is here that Miller cites George Barker Stevens—even explicitly borrowing Steven's language from *Theology of the New Testament* (1902). Though Christ served as our substitute through his sufferings, Christ was not punished. He willingly suffered the consequences of sin so that we could experience freedom.[130] Therefore, God's wrath was not visited upon Jesus. Christ was not made the "guilty object of retributive justice."[131]

While Jesus voluntarily associated with us in his suffering and love triumphed, Christ's vicarious sacrifice simultaneously addressed the consequences of sin (ignored by both Bushnell and Clarke). Writing on the Apostle Paul's exposition on Christ being made sin on our behalf (cf. 2 Cor 5:21), Miller remarks:

> This is far from saying that Jesus was made a sinner or that he was regarded as such. He did experience the consequences of sin. He was treated as a sinner. He shared the lot of a sinner but in no personal sense but entirely and absolutely in a representative manner. Thus, in a representative manner he came into the shame and suffering of sin for us.[132]

Miller stood in full agreement with Bushnell, Clarke, and Stevens. Stevens asks in *The Christian Doctrine of Salvation* (1906), a work published to analyze the various models of the atonement:

> Is not punishment correlative to guilt or blameworthiness? Is not the principle of distributive justice "suum cuique" ["to each

---

128. Miller, *Christian Doctrine*, 39.

129. Miller, *Christian Doctrine*, 40.

130. Stevens, *Theology of the New Testament*, 411. Stevens writes: "The apostle is careful not to say that Christ was a sinner, or that personally he was regarded as such; he says that he 'was made sin for us' (2 Cor. v. 21); that is, he was, for the sake of others, and not for his own sake, treated as a sinner. His experience of the consequences of sin was entirely vicarious and representative. These considerations look toward the conclusion that with Paul substitution means, not the substitution of Christ's punishment for our punishment, but the substitution of his sufferings, which were not of the nature of punishment, for our punishment; in other words, the substitution of another method of revealing and vindicating the divine righteousness in place of the method of punishment. God in his grace adopts another course of procedure with sinful man than that of retributive justice and a course which more fully displays his glorious perfections."

131. Miller, *Christian Doctrine*, 40.

132. Miller, *Christian Doctrine*, 41.

his own"]? Is it conceivable that God should spend his punitive wrath upon his eternally holy Son? Can the sufferings to which a perfectly holy Being voluntarily submits properly be called penal? Can God in his wrath punish the supreme object of his love?[133]

Ironically, the very concept Stevens (along with Bushnell and Clarke) reject—expiation—in their desire to make divine love central is the very concept Miller employs to exemplify God's love. The voluntary offering of Christ on our behalf is central to his understanding of expiation. Expiation claims that a debt is owed and that humankind cannot pay. The debt is that humanity has sinned and broken God's law. What proponents of penal substitution and satisfaction models of the atonement claim is that we deserve death, Christ takes our place and therefore our punishment, and his blood covers us. Propitiation claims that Christ is killed to assuage the wrath of God. To such an explanation, liberal theologians like Bushnell cried foul even while confusing expiation with propitiation.

> What is expiation? It does not, I answer, simply signify the fact that God is propitiated, but it brings in the pagan, or Latin idea (for expiation is an evil given to buy the release of an evil—Latin word), that the sacrifice offered softens God, or assuages the anger of God, as being an evil, or pain, contributed to his offended feeling.[134]

Bushnell's concern, like other liberal theologians of the period, with which Miller fully agrees, is that if it is "a mere feeling in God which is to be placated by an expiatory sacrifice, then we have to ask, is God such a being that, having a good mortgage title to pain or suffering as against an offender, he will never let go the title till he gets the pain—if not from him, then from

---

133. Stevens, *Doctrine of Salvation*, 246. Stevens and Miller both agreed with Bushnell and Clarke that something is inherently wrong with the traditional presentation of both penal substitution and satisfaction models. Stevens writes later: "For reasons like these I cannot help feeling that there is something erroneous in the initial definitions on which the dogma of atonement in seventeenth-century Protestantism rests. When wrought out to its logical issue, it seems to me to be contrary to fact in logically excluding salvation altogether, contrary to experience in teaching that benevolence is no necessary part of goodness, contrary to reason in breaking up the unity of the moral nature of God, and contrary to morality in holding that God is so 'just' that he cannot forgive the guilty, but so unjust that he can punish the innocent. Logically, carried out, it makes God a strict accountant who is, indeed, strictly 'just,' but is also nothing more. This result does not seem to me to coincide with the Christian concept of God." See Stevens, *Doctrine of Salvation*, 250.

134. Bushnell, *Major Works*, loc. 22114. Bushnell is either confusing expiation with propitiation or he is attempting to reject expiation by tying it to propitiation.

some other?"¹³⁵ He further presses: "Does then God's right hand offer pains to his left, and so make expiation for the sins of the world? How many Gods have we?"¹³⁶

Miller challenges Bushnell (and Clarke) on this last point revealing a christological difference between theological liberals and Miller. While Bushnell claimed that Christ and God were one, he did not believe in oneness the same as Miller. Bushnell described Christ as a mediator even though Christ was not separate from God, even in his capacity as mediator: "Whatever we may say, or hold, or believe, concerning the vicarious sacrifice of Christ, we are to affirm in the same manner of God. The whole deity is in it, in it from eternity, and will to eternity be.... It is *God* who enters the world in Christ, shares our condition, and suffers and dies for us."¹³⁷ There are subtle differences in the Christology espoused by Bushnell and Miller. Miller is much more comfortable to allow language to indicate that Jesus can be known as both God and human. Bushnell, in contrast, predicted that the church of the future would recognize the futility of definite dogmatic solutions to the metaphysical problem of Christ's person. He instead found the divinity of Jesus in the ethical, not the metaphysical.

> God is a Spirit, not merely ontologically, but ethically, and of what quality his Spirit is the man Jesus declares. God is love, and what divine love means the ministry of Jesus in life and death shows. God is good in the specific sense of being gracious, generous, philanthropic, and the historic life of Jesus interprets for us the philanthropy of God. All we really know of God in spirit and in very truth we know through Jesus.¹³⁸

While Miller would agree with the ethical underpinnings of Bushnell's claims, he would also argue that the biblical data indicates that we need not have any concern in assigning both humanity and divinity to Christ. His conception of Christ involves two chief points: (1) the divinity of Christ is to be found in what he is and does for men as the Revealer of God and Savior from sin and (2) the nature of the indwelling of God in him is a mystery on which theological metaphysics throws no light.

Consequently, Miller did not find expiation as a punishing of God's mediator. Instead, expiation, for Miller, was God choosing to suffer on our behalf to meld the justice *and* love of God. As Miller notes:

---

135. Bushnell, *Major Works*, loc. 22180.

136. Bushnell, *Major Works*, loc. 22227.

137. Bushnell, *Major Works*, loc. 22227. For further discussion of Bushnell's understanding of Christ as mediator, see Dorrien, *Making of American Theology*, 168–69.

138. Bruce, *Apologetics*, 350.

We find that Jesus Christ is Himself an expiatory sacrifice voluntarily offered by him for sin, the merit of which must be appropriated by faith. At the same time, it is such a sacrifice in his blood as exhibits the righteousness of God, that is, God's attitude toward and his dealing with sin. The student must guard against any idea of propitiating God. God does not need to be appeased. He is not angry in any such sense. God reconciles man to himself but not because God has a personal feeling of anger.[139]

The sacrificial posture and death of Jesus made all the difference for Miller. He saw an unfair caricature being used by theological liberals regarding more conservative understandings of the atonement. While Miller appreciated their critique of the traditional understandings of penal substitution and satisfaction models, he was cautious to not couple their critique (and his own) with a dismissal of expiation. The following chart reveals the areas of agreement and disagreement between Miller and the other theologians mentioned:

Atonement Component	Bushnell	Clarke	Stevens	Miller
Christ's Humanity	X	X	X	X
Christ's Divinity	X	Possibly	X	X
Propitiation			X	
Expiation				X
Reject Classical PST	X	X	X	X

While Miller adhered to expiation through Christ's voluntary suffering, he affirmed the larger critique of both penal substitution and satisfaction models offered by the other theologians listed. The irony is that Bushnell and Clarke, while rejecting a traditional Christology to circumvent the repugnant aspects of these two models, ended up at the same conclusion as Miller regarding the sacrifice of Christ—God's "love suffering," to quote Clarke, is the essence of Christ's sacrifice on the cross.

Regarding the necessity of Christ's death, Miller bridges both the ethical concerns of evangelical liberalism and the substitutionary concerns of more fundamentalist groups:

> Certainly, enough has been said to describe as fully as language can this marvelous, mystical and spiritual, yet real and vital change that takes place in the life of every person born again. It is a real, though mystical change.... It is a great moral and

139. Miller, *Christian Doctrine*, 43–44.

> spiritual adjustment to the verities of the Christ-life. It is oft-times [sic] a change so radical as to be a revolution in life and thought. It is the entrance of the life of a man into personal union and fellowship with his Savior and Lord, the Master of the souls of men, Jesus Christ.

This "real" and "personal union," as Miller understood such terms, was lived out within a kingdom-minded community that Miller understood as the church. With his rejection of imputed guilt and his stress upon a life that now lives covered by the voluntarily shed blood of Jesus, new believers live out a new covenant in relationship with God through the Son and empowered by the Spirit together as the church. Miller, while not rejecting expiation, redefined agency, and forged a new path.

Though Miller held differences with the theologians presented, he would have agreed with Clarke's "three expressions of the moral nature of God":

- A. God so constituted the order of things that sin should be visited with punishment. This is nature.
- B. God specifically and urgently forbade men to sin, warning them of the inevitable punishment. This is law.
- C. When men had sinned, God sought to bring them out of sin into reconciliation with himself. This is grace in Christ.

While Miller borrowed much from theological liberalism, especially evangelical liberalism, in his critique of the penal substitutionary theory of the atonement, he did not dismiss an understanding of expiation when describing the work of Christ on the cross. Instead, he embodied a both/and approach to theology where theological liberals and fundamentalists maintained an either/or. Christ was *both* God *and* man in his expiatory sacrifice. The atonement models *both* love *and* justice. Such a both/and theology was central to how Miller understood the atonement of Christ—sacrifice for us *and* a call to live sacrificially in obedience.

Concluding Observations

Miller's view of the atonement serves as an example of his strong commitment to the Bible coupled with an openness to and necessity for the Holy Spirit, not reason alone, to illumine his theology. His openness to new light from Scripture is a retrieval of an earlier Brethren approach to the Bible that was all but lost in the maintenance of the "old order" of the nineteenth century. While Brethren of all centuries have publicly confessed Word and Spirit as necessary for the witness of the church, Miller modeled the posture of a Word and Spirit theologian. It is his distinct approach to the Bible that marked him as not just a Brethren theologian of note but an evangelical theologian of importance. Rather than the specifics of Miller's theology guiding the conversation around Brethren and American evangelicalism in chapter 6, it will be his Word and Spirit approach, founded on his Brethren faith and elucidated in chapter 5, that will serve as a theological method, epistemology, and distinct biblical hermeneutic, that will guide such engagement.

5

The Theological Epistemology, Biblical Hermeneutic and Pedagogy of J. Allen Miller

Opening Remarks & Overview of Methodology

This chapter will move beyond the particulars of Miller's theology into an examination of the epistemological and biblical hermeneutical underpinnings of his thought and pedagogy. There are two key terms in this chapter that must be defined before they are further employed. The first is "epistemology," which has among its tasks investigation into what differentiates justified belief from opinion.[1] For something to count as knowledge—that

---

1. As Joel Garver notes, "Epistemology is broader than discussions of justification, including the nature of knowledge, the structure of knowledge, different kinds of knowledge, internalism and externalism, intellectual virtues, truth, skepticism, politics of knowledge, and certain dimensions of cognitive science. There's also a distinction between justification as a process (the giving of reasons, justifying) and justification as a status (the state of having warrant, reliability, being justified)." See interview with Joel Garver, March 2019. Epistemology will assist this chapter's exploration of the frameworks with which Miller thought by examining the nature, sources, and structures of the Christian claims he made—how Miller distinguished justified belief from opinion.

we can *know* it—it must consist of some element of truth. Verifying that truth within theological epistemology can be inherently difficult but need not be abandoned. This is part of the quest of Christian, theological epistemology—how do Christians claim to know what they say they know about God, the Bible and God's will? For all the theologians mentioned in this chapter, Scripture is an essential tool for that process.

Since epistemology is informed by the sources of authority that serve as frameworks for how one discerns and interprets the world around them, the second term to be defined are hermeneutics that serve as a subset of our Christian, theological epistemology. While hermeneutics, broadly speaking, consists in the lenses through which read the world around us—literature, cultural moments—*biblical* hermeneutics is how we interpret and extrapolate meaning from Scripture and the Spirit. Miller's epistemology was anchored in the revelation of Jesus Christ to the world. His hermeneutic was one of Word and Spirit as discerned in community. Thus, Miller's approach is best termed "Word-Spirit Communal Revelationalism."

Naming early Miller's theological method is important for understanding Miller in his own era and to apply his approach to own. Unlike chapter 4 that explored his writings in detail, this chapter will move behind the specific content of his writings and begin to discern the larger meaning and frames of reference that informed his conclusions. This is important as an individual's or community's beliefs and justifications form frameworks for dialogue and pathways for the discernment of truth and application.

Plato famously explores the foundation for how we understand "knowledge" in his work *Meno*, a tale about Socrates's uneducated slave, named "Menon," who helps him deduce geometric truths. Plato uses the juxtaposition of wisdom (Socrates) and ignorance (Menon) to create the foundational process of knowledge. Plato writes:

> For true opinions, as long as they remain, are a fine thing and all they do is good, but they are not willing to remain long, and they escape from man's mind, so that they are not worth much until one ties them down by giving an account of the reason why. . . . After they are tied down, in the first place they become knowledge, and then they remain in place. (See Cooper, *Plato*, 90)

Plato's work is one of the earliest to distinguish the epistemic difference between true knowledge, or truth, and mere opinion. The former is buttressed by justified belief. Often referred to as BJT (belief, justification, truth), it is not without criticisms. One of those criticisms is pertinent for any exploration of theological epistemology. How do we know that we're operating with correct data in our justification of belief? Who determines said truth? Plato's discourse speaks to a modern anxiety. Fundamentalist and liberal theologians of Miller's period were attempting to answer these questions through rationality alone. As will be shown, Miller introduces the role of the Spirit and the revelatory authority of Scripture. Revelation and reason are not synonymous and the latter, for Miller, must submit to the former.

Miller's era witnessed cul-de-sacs in such pathways as both Fundamentalist and liberal voices continued to spin in the morass of anxiety about rationalism. Each camp attempted to found their faith either explicitly or implicitly on rationalism. Theologians like Miller offer a helpful, revelatory epistemology that informs their biblical hermeneutic and allows them to bypass the angst of the polarization that existed between Fundamentalist and liberal theologies. Revelation (in all forms and expressions) denotes God's method by which he reveals himself to his creation. With revelation, hermeneutics serves as an important subset of Christian theological epistemology as serious consideration must be given to the role and authority of revelation through Scripture.

Miller and the contemporaries with whom he will be brought into dialogue are not advocating hermeneutical strategies that deny revelation. Miller's hermeneutical approach, specifically, does not advocate a *revelational positivism* in which the fact of revelation is simply acknowledged and upheld as true apart from the confirmatory witness of the Spirit in concert with reason.[2] He is not articulating a *presuppositionalism* in which we begin with postulates that are unprovable but provide the key to explaining the whole of reality. Counter to numerous Fundamentalist and liberal theologians of his period, Miller does not propose a *foundationalism* that begins with *a priori* assumptions impressed on the mind. Nor is his posture an *evidentialism* that develops a robust apologetic of empirically demonstrable certainty.

Miller's thought cannot be characterized as *coherentism* as Miller does not attempt to justify his position by showing the cohesive unity of his beliefs. Often times, Miller's thought is a series of ideas brought into conversation that encourages his students to arrive at their own conclusions. Miller's hermeneutic and larger epistemology never claim a rationally demonstrable or apodictic certainty. Instead, it is an embodied certainty that is realized in a life of repentance and obedience. This is why Miller's approach is best understood as a "Word-Spirit Communal Revelationalism." This understanding captures the role of the individual (and their faculties of reason), Bible, Spirit, and the community (church and classroom) evident in his writings. This will be further developed over the course of this chapter.

In this pursuit, this chapter will employ a six-part strategy. First, it will examine his theology to discern the hermeneutics behind it. Second, it will compare and contrast Miller's epistemology and subsequent biblical hermeneutic with that of William Newton Clarke who, as evidenced in the prior

---

2. As noted in chapter 3, John Calvin himself, not one to be seen as indifferent to the revelation of Scripture, argued for the internal witness of the Spirit. See Calvin, *Institutes*, 1.7.4–5.

chapter, strongly influenced Miller's theology. Third, the epistemologies and hermeneutics of a few of Miller's contemporaries will assist in locating him among his peers. "Contemporary" here denotes theologians of similar denominations, during the same time period as Miller, who sought a middle ground in their biblical hermeneutics specifically. The theologians utilized for this task will be the Mennonite leader Daniel Kauffman (1865–1944), and the Swedish Pietist David Nyvall (1863–1946). Fourth, the comparison of Miller with each of the aforementioned theologians—Clarke, Kauffman, and Nyvall—will elucidate how Miller both appropriates and nuances parts of their respective theological outlooks. Sixth, and finally, a synthesis of the above steps will explicate Miller's distinctive epistemology and biblical hermeneutic. This is foundational for how Ashland Brethren approach Scripture and theology and forms their distinct contribution to American evangelicalism. Before we explore the epistemic approaches of the above theologians, it is essential to understand the epistemic components that are constitutive of his theology.

The Epistemic Foundation of Miller's Theology

Miller's writings examined in the last chapter reveal a personality shaped by the interplay of Radical Pietist emphases of Spirit, individuality, and openness alongside Anabaptist emphases of outward form, community and order.[3] Miller embodied this paradox allowing the fulcrum to be the revelation of the Living Word of Jesus manifested through the cooperation of Word and Spirit in the life of community. "The eternal purposes of God," he wrote, "are centered in Jesus Christ. It is Christ that has perfectly manifested the will of the Father. It is Christ who effected man's redemption by his atoning death. It is Christ who assists man to first see his infinite possibilities."[4]

In an article entitled "The Sure Foundation" in a December 1928 issue of the *Brethren Evangelist*, Miller stressed the centrality of Jesus Christ for Brethren theology (indeed biblical Christianity):

> Jesus Christ came into our world as God's son, incarnate in perfect man;
>
> Jesus Christ spoke for God to men; he revealed the will of God to Men;
>
> Jesus Christ commanded men to hear his message, believe it and obey it.

---

3. Stoffer, *Brethren Doctrines*, 165.
4. Allison, "Miller" 54.

> This message which he revealed personally and through chosen men is the New Testament; as such record it is God's revelation given through Inspiration.[5]

The "why" to Jesus' appearance among humanity is seen in the revelation of God's kingdom to humanity. If Jesus is the "why," then the church is the "how" and the kingdom is the "what"—"the kingdom [is] the greatest theme of the New Testament. Everything there looks forward to its realization. Christ's personal return will precipitate the final crisis which will usher in the age to come."[6]

The authoritative revelation of this kingdom vision of Christ occurs through the dual influence of Word (Scripture) and Spirit buttressed by the loving accountability of the church. Stressing the Word over against the Spirit leads to legalism—an accusation occasionally made against conservative Anabaptist groups especially. To stress Spirit over Word results in a hyper-mysticism in which the outward evidences of faith are lost—an accusation made of Radical Pietists. Word *and* Spirit produces the mystical reality of Christ's presence. This revelation allows the church not to fear cultural engagement within the larger marketplace of ideas but to embody a paradox of being "in the world but not of it" (cf. John 17:16; 1 John 2:15).

As the church lives in this paradox, Miller was adamant that it not be underprepared in dialoguing with the ideas of surrounding cultures. Furthermore, under no circumstances should the church be apologetic about its distinct witness and mission:

> We must hold a faith that is reasonable, intelligent and compelling. We ought never as ministers and teachers of the Word of God have to beg the question when asked for the grounds upon which our faith rests by replying evasively or charging our questioners with unbelief.... I plead for an informed and intelligent ministry. I covet a ministry for the Brethren Church that knows the grounds upon which faith can be rested—grounds that cannot be shaken by any discovery of history, science, or philosophy.[7]

Miller's confidence stemmed from his understanding of the spiritual authority of the New Testament as "our ultimate source of information and the final word of authority." While "one must of necessity hold some philosophic worldview... there must be consistency in one's thinking and one's

---

5. Miller, "Sure Foundation," 3.
6. Allison, "Miller," 57.
7. Miller, "Sure Foundation," 3.

conclusions ought not . . . be contrary to the Teachings of Christ and the New Testament Revelation."[8] Therefore, Miller challenged the Brethren Church

> to take the Gospel of Jesus Christ and interpret it anew to the men of our times in the terms of the life of our day. Here we have made mistakes in the past and are still making them. Such mistakes continued will be all but fatal to any marked degree of success in the days to come. Now it is not with the Gospel that we have to find fault. It is with our handling of the gospel that we must break. . . . What I am insisting upon now is that we should be less held by man's apprehension of the Gospel and his interpretation thereof than by the Gospel itself. We must take the Gospel as it comes from Jesus and give it to men as we find them today.[9]

Not buying into the false dichotomy of Fundamentalism which posited that righteous conviction was at odds with cultural engagement, he allowed the foundation of the New Testament to provide preachers of his day with a different understanding of dogmatic claims (which often connoted sectarianism). Commitment to the whole gospel, he argued,

> makes us dogmatic. It makes us doctrinal preachers. Mark the words and their order—*belief, conviction* then *character*. Also, these words in their order, *the truths of the Gospel, their unequivocal acceptation,* then *their fearless proclamation to men.* This means that character cannot be divorced from conviction and conviction grows out of one's beliefs. Therefore, it does make all the difference possible what a man believes.[10]

A commitment to both character and conviction united both belief and behavior. This life change, Christlike character, was indicative of the authority of the Bible. Discipleship was an essential bridge across the divide between revelation and reason. Miller believed in both the revelation of the Bible and a reasonable faith that must be evidenced in a Christlike character. This is why "both liberal scholars . . . and conservative scholars . . . appear in Miller's works."[11] He did not adhere to either a

---

8. Miller, *Christian Doctrine*, 280.

9. Miller, "Forward Look," 1.

10. Miller, "Does It Matter," 1. "Dogmatic" in Miller's estimation is not logical certainty about faith but, instead, is in line with his Pietist roots—a transformation of the entire person.

11. Stoffer, *Brethren Doctrines*, 227. This theological worldview is captured well in his exploration of salvation, with special emphasis on the atonement (as described in

liberal or Fundamentalist system. His theological commitments were the product of "a reason enlightened by the Word and the Spirit."[12]

Miller employs a spiritual hermeneutic in his reading of the Bible that finds the text infallible but not claiming it to be inerrant—finding the rational tool of inerrancy used by fundamentalists as missing the import of the Spirit for the text. The Bible is infallible when enlivened by the Spirit. Then, and only then, will the Bible not fail in fulfilling its divine purposes in humanity. The Bible is "authoritative in its religious teachings. It has been and ever must be the ultimate authority and source of appeal in matters pertaining to spiritual life and Divine institutions."[13] Yet "apart from every other consideration," Miller is sure to mention, "the holy Scriptures are supreme because of the work and life of Jesus Christ."[14] The primary source of authority comes from the revelation of Jesus Christ transmitted to us by Scripture and our experience of the Holy Spirit.

Miller argues that the only creed of the Bible is that "Jesus is the Christ the Son of the living God." He comments further that

> [no statement] could be more simple yet more comprehensive. This creed needs no revision. It never becomes obsolete. It comprehends every other statement of Scripture as to the plan of human redemption. The Messiah, the Christ of God—there is salvation in none other.[15]

This central revelation of Christ's identity is the ultimate standard by which Scripture must be interpreted if the Bible is to be the ultimate source of our authority. However, an experience of the Spirit within the text is critical for us to move beyond belief *about* the Bible to becoming a people *of* the Bible. The "supreme demand of the Holy Scriptures centers in Jesus and his will. Jesus is to be believed on."[16] His understanding of belief as *both* noun *and* verb reveals the influence of the Spirit to be the "[transformation of] the whole man; and the transformed man gives undivided allegiance to his Master."[17] Miller is adamant that being a people of the Bible is not merely a rational or intellectual task. It is a spiritually empowered reality whereby

---

the last chapter).

12. Stoffer, *Brethren Doctrines*, 227.
13. Miller, "Our Plea," 12.
14. Miller, "Our Plea," 12.
15. Miller, "Our Plea," 12.
16. Miller, "Our Plea," 12.
17. Miller, "Our Plea," 12.

"Christ faithfully preached brings every other teaching in the redemption scheme to assume its place."[18] A people of the Bible are invited by the Spirit to participate in the "redemptive scheme" of Christ.

In this redemptive invitation, it is vital that the authority of the text not just be seen as propositional and approached solely on a rational foundation. While this methodology is important in our study of the Bible, the text must be received relationally as revelation. With this reception of the Bible, rather than a defense of the text, Miller's posture was devotional and trusting. Writing declaratively in his lecture notes, he challenged his students that "THE CHRISTIAN SCHOLAR MUST SATISFY HIMSELF THAT THE GOSPELS, THE ACTS AND THE EPISTLES ARE AUTHENTIC AND TRUSTWORTHY DOCUMENTS."[19] A relationship of trust must mark our approach to the Bible. "The Bible," he writes, "claims to be God-inspired. This claim was supported by (1) its own direct testimony to the fact of inspiration, (2) its historic truthfulness, (3) miracles, (4) prophecy, (5) the moral sublimity of its teaching, (6) its exalted precepts and promises, (7) its harmony and unity of purpose, (8) its self-evident truths, (9) its influence in the lives of its readers, and (10) the witness of the Spirit, in the hearts of believers."[20] Biblical authority rested on internal, revelatory truths held in tension with the loving accountability of community, individual interpretation alongside communal discernment, and reason in submission to revelation.

With such an attitude, Miller could confidently maintain a conservative understanding of the Bible as inspired revelation and remain open to the tools of higher criticism—recognizing that the source of truth for higher critics still remained external to Scripture:

> The *Bible* I say, is to be studied. Much of our so-called study is only about the Bible. Take Biblical Introduction, and Archaeology, and Chronology, and Geography, —all very good and very necessary in their place; or take textual and critical work and go as far as "Higher Critics"—and this too has a legitimate place but my contention is that these are mere externals, things well enough to know *about* the Bible, but are not really study of the Word itself. The Word is too often altogether submerged. These things are mere machinery. What the soul wants and needs is

18. Miller, "Our Plea," 12.
19. Miller, *Christian Doctrine*, 108.
20. Miller, *Christian Doctrine*, 134. It is significant that Miller does not employ inerrancy. With the illumination of the Spirit, the Bible could be trusted—a relational rather than rational apologetic for Scripture. His biblical approach also includes the witness of the church.

the living water from the depths of the well; the sweet bread of life from the golden grain.[21]

With the Bible as the "sweet bread of life," Miller could enter the debates regarding the verbal and plenary inspiration of the Bible (of which he denies the former) not as a mere higher critic, to be written off by conservatives, but as one who submitted his life to the authority of God's word. Addressing plenary inspiration, he notes that "it was the Holy Spirit's work so to direct the apostles in the employment of their talents in speaking or writing."[22] Continuing, he notes that all parts of the Bible are equally inspired. "The individuality of the authors as seen in their writings is, instead of being proof against, the strongest evidence in favor of, the Plenary inspiration of the Bible."[23]

Even though Miller never mentions inerrancy in his writings, he provides a necessary corrective to this understanding of the Bible. His writings never contain anxiety about how we know the Bible is authoritative. Instead, his teaching is a *broad* fideism—not the narrow, sectarian fideism that separates faith claims from dialogue and intellectual examination. For Miller, our theological knowledge must be based on faith which entails a conversation between both revelation and reason as each assisted the other in offering greater clarity of theological claims. He writes:

> If objection be urged against Revelation, as being unscientific, then I shall simply reply, that, as all instruction of the youth of the Race is based upon principles, morally, logically, and metaphorically sound, so the higher instruction of the Race given by God through Revelation, can in every particular rest upon the same premises.[24]

Miller remained quite comfortable with the tension between revelation and reason, finding it to be a source of creativity rather than a threat to Scripture. He remained critical of revelation understood *a priori*, as if the Bible needs no context and its readers need no training. Likewise, he critiqued reason comprehended *a posteriori* as if revelatory experience of the Bible is not essential to apprehending its meaning. Miller understood a complementary and cooperative relationship between revelation and reason.

> Apart from Revelation, Reason is the ultimatum of man's capacity, and Conscience of his power. But neither reason nor

21. Miller, "Bible Study," 4.
22. Miller, *Christian Doctrine*, 128–29.
23. Miller, *Christian Doctrine*, 129.
24. Miller, *Christian Doctrine*, 117.

> conscience can solve the great problems of human life. Reason itself is by far too narrow in its range to be an unerring guide through life. Reason illumined, and Conscience quickened by a Divine Revelation will be adequate.[25]

With this partnership between reason and revelation, Miller was able to hold an authoritative understanding of Scripture that was not found in the perfection of reason (read liberalism) or in a quasi-rational proof of the veracity of the Bible (read fundamentalism). Instead, he centered the authority of Scripture in the person of Jesus—a christocentric hermeneutic.

> But one of the strongest evidences of the Inspiration and Authority of the Old Testament writings is found in the testimony of Jesus and the Apostles. Jesus Christ as a witness cannot be impeached. Possessed of the Spirit of God without measure; coming into the world to bear witness to the Truth; proving by His works that He was the Messiah; teaching as one having authority, we feel confident of the infallible truth of His testimony. And what is the testimony Jesus bears in the Scriptures? By a careful reading of the four records of the Gospel, we find Jesus everywhere speaking of the Scriptures as the Word of God. Jesus certainly regarded the Scriptures as clothed with divine authority, and infallibly safe when He thus used them.[26]

The centrality of Christ by experience of the indwelling Spirit allowed Miller to embody a distinct epistemology that granted him the ability to rise above the anxiety that marked others of his period. This calm posture emerged from a scholar whose devotional truth in Jesus found theological truth in the world around him and in the Bible he loved.

Miller's Theological Epistemology

Miller outlined four sources of theological knowledge in one of his earlier *Evangelist* articles. This article revealed his desire to remain faithful to the Bible, open and honest as a scholar, and practical and concise in describing the contribution of each of the four to what we can claim to know. The first was nature, the realm of general revelation, that includes "the existing universe of mind and matter; the sum and order of causes and resulting phenomena."[27] Miller finds that "nature embodies the totality of finite

---

25. Miller, *Christian Doctrine*, 117.
26. Miller, *Christian Doctrine*, 121.
27. Miller, "Sources," 2.

agencies and forces."[28] Unlike pantheism, however, that posits that God is manifested within creation (intrinsic to it), he regards God as being "independent from nature."[29] Yet nature does serve an important purpose to which the Bible speaks (cf. Ps 19) and that is the "*voice* of a Supreme Personal God, speaking to the intelligent conscious creature of His love in a language read by the weakest of the race."[30] General revelation is not complete revelation, but it opens our minds and hearts to realities beyond that made known by mere empiricism.

Second, there is the soul that represents humanity's "mental and spiritual activities . . . by the attributes of self-consciousness, reason, intuition, the higher emotions, and conscience."[31] Where liberals, like Schleiermacher, prized the role of religious affections/emotions, Miller sees the soul as including such experiences but not totally defined by them. The soul is the part of the human to which the Spirit speaks. It is the Spirit's cooperation with the soul that is central to the transformative nature of the Bible.[32]

Third is the study of history which serves as the "branch of human knowledge that embraces the past experiences of the race. . . . It is the record of these experiences transmitted to each succeeding generation."[33] Miller regards history as touching "every phase of the religious life . . . as no other science."[34] History is an essential bridge between general and specific revelation. It allows one to move from an impersonal causation in the cosmos to "the very central proposition, by way of example, of the Christian system, viz., the doctrine of the Being and Nature of the Personal Christ" that "is premised upon (a fact of history) the historicity of the Gospel accounts."[35]

One of the components of this very specific revelatory history is the fourth source of theological knowledge, the Bible. Miller finds both Old and New Testaments elemental to understanding the master, redemptive plan of God. The Old points to the New. The books of the New Testament, however, "comprise the authoritative record of the Holy Scripture. They are and always must be the Christian's ultimate source of appeal in all matters of faith and practice."[36]

28. Miller, "Sources," 2.
29. Miller, "Sources," 2.
30. Miller, "Sources," 2.
31. Miller, "Sources," 2.
32. Miller, "Sources," 2.
33. Miller, "Sources," 2.
34. Miller, "Sources," 2.
35. Miller, "Sources," 2.
36. Miller, "Sources," 2.

The mediating epistemic influence present in all the above sources of knowledge is the Holy Spirit, the experience of whom is central to Miller's theological approach. Writing on one's call to the ministry, he notes that

> the Holy Spirit does not supersede our faculties. We do not receive the call thro any audible voice, or physical impression, or even supernatural conviction. God's call certainly involves our searching out of His purpose concerning us.[37]

This appreciation and application of the Spirit is distinct and essential to understanding Miller's theology. His interlocutors of the late nineteenth and early twentieth centuries were marked by great anxiety—an anxiety prevalent among almost all-American Protestants. The urbanization of society, scientific progress, and the boom of the industrial age challenged agreed upon understandings of reality as understood biblically and societally. As a result, a schism was developing between Fundamentalist and liberal voices regarding the role of reason and its relationship with revelation. This polarization became a battle for the great idol of American society—certainty. Both sides employed classical foundationalism to buttress their claims to authority. Therefore, both embodied what Michael Langer calls a "Cartesian anxiety" as long held signifiers gave way to ambiguity and debate.[38] While Fundamentalists would champion the authority of the *inerrant* Bible, they failed to see how inerrancy was a *rational* defense of Scripture against the onslaught of *rationalism*. Meanwhile, as Protestant liberals assailed the ghettoization of theology into archaic propositions known as *The Fundamentals* (ca. 1910), they unknowingly established a solely rational foundationalism, known as "classical foundationalism," that postmodernism would begin to unravel in the latter half of the twentieth-century.[39] Classical foundationalism maintains that basic beliefs must be infallible if they are to justify non-basic beliefs. Furthermore, these basic beliefs are only received through deductive reasoning to justify one belief from another.[40] Laurence BonJour, an American philosopher, argues that the "classical formulation of foundationalism requires basic beliefs to be infallible, incorrigible, indubitable, and certain if they are to be adequately justified."[41]

Neither side championed the role of the Spirit. Fundamentalists founded the authority of the Bible on rational propositions. Liberals ensconced

---

37. Miller, "Call," 5.
38. Langer, "Idolatry of Certainty," 57–75.
39. See chapter 3 for further historical background on this polarization.
40. Lemos, *Theory of Knowledge*, 50–51.
41. BonJour, *Empirical Knowledge*, 27.

reason thereby reinterpreting the Spirit as the religious experience of the believer (or as the spirit of the age). Both denied the personality, the very personhood, of the Holy Spirit, whom Miller reminds his students "is distinct from the Father and the Son and . . . is Personal and Divine."[42] While Fundamentalists would have championed the personality of the Spirit, they would have placed limits on his activity. The elevation of reason is once more witnessed amid such limitations.

This climate of rational anxiety may explain why "Miller gives far more attention to the inspiration of and interpretive tools for Scripture than do preceding Brethren writers while he devotes far less attention to the Spirit's relationship to the proper understanding of the Word than his predecessors."[43] While Miller retained the classical Brethren emphases, he was in some respects a man of his time. The activity and influence of the Spirit is foundational for all aspects of his theology and what he does say about the relationship between the Word and the Spirit is consistent with past Brethren thought. Miller captures the epistemic influence of the Spirit which is central to Brethren thought. He holds that "until the darkened understanding of the mind has been illuminated by the Holy Spirit the individual is unfit to explain the word of God to others."[44] The Spirit and Scripture form a symbiotic relationship but ever the Biblicist, Miller argued that "the witness of the Holy Spirit and that of our own spirit dare not contravene the spoken word."[45] As Stoffer remarks, "When renewed by the indwelling Spirit and guided by the Word, reason and conscience become significant means by which to realize God's purposes for one's life."[46]

This renewal avoids a bounded set approach to theology whereby followers intellectually assent to the right points of doctrine and right belief maintains their membership in the group. "Bounded set" versus "centered set" is borrowed from Paul G. Hiebert. Hiebert differentiates group membership cross-culturally as bounded set and centered set. Bounded sets require uniformity before membership with the group is offered. Counter to bounded sets, centered sets maintain a compelling center that recognize a diversity of perspectives as pointing towards that center. Group membership is less an affirmation of statements of belief and more a commitment to the center. Hiebert's writing is helpful when exploring theological

---

42. Miller, *Christian Doctrine*, 10.
43. Stoffer, *Brethren Doctrines*, 213.
44. Miller, *Christian Doctrine*, 10.
45. Miller, *Christian Doctrine*, 10.
46. Stoffer, *Brethren Doctrines*, 214.

epistemologies. Fundamentalists of Miller's era were demanding a rigid, bounded set theological approach.

A respect for the diverse paths to the center perfectly describes Miller's faith as a tethering to the center that allows for a freedom of exploration. While doctrine and belief are important, they are never the heart of Miller's faith. The illumination of Jesus by the Spirit through the Bible remains central. Therefore, rather than just a scholastic assessment of Christian education, Miller advocates for a holistic assessment of the divine life where progress

> is measured by the strength and beauty of these noble, Christly characteristics in the individual: (1) love, (2) righteousness, (3) humility, (4) virtues and graces of the Christian life [beatitudes, devotion, justice, steadfast, zealous, unselfish, patient], and (5) the fruit of the Spirit—a life devoid of them certainly would indicate the absence of the Holy Spirit from it. If the Spirit of God is present in the life and dominates and controls it, the fruit of the Spirit's presence will appear. This is self-evident and necessary, for the Holy Spirit of God is neither fruitless nor inactive in the child of God.[47]

A life measured by the fruit of the Spirit fosters an epistemology that does not bracket out the Spirit (as others of Miller's day were prone to do). Nor does it allow for a hermeneutic without embodiment (which Western theology is still prone to do). Rather, Miller's appropriation of the Holy Spirit in his theology, a conviction he takes straight from the New Testament, shaped a theological epistemology that was similar to, and conversant with that of William Newton Clarke.

The Theological Epistemology of William Newton Clarke

Clarke's theology has been characterized as evangelical liberal and as postconservative evangelical.[48] Like other theologians of evangelical liberalism, Clarke's writings reveal several core commitments:

- An attempt to maintain fidelity to historical doctrinal and ecclesial traditions (as long as they coincide with modern thought).
- A desire to accommodate the Bible to scientific inquiry and reason

---

47. Miller, *Christian Doctrine*, 99–102.
48. See Sotak, *Wm. Newton Clarke*.

- A radical Christocentrism that attempted to moderate the miracles and resurrection of Jesus with scientific inquiry—central vision of Jesus as a great moral exemplar on behalf of God.
- A positive anthropology that called the church to greater concern for justice and societal renewal.

Clarke presented his epistemology in one passage:

> The Christian doctrine of God does not begin with proof, it begins with the announcement that is made by Christian faith in the pursuance of the Christian revelation. Faith does not set out to find an unknown God, or to assure itself that God exists: it has heard his voice, and begins in confidence in his reality. It assumes the existence of God as its first certainty, and then proceeds to learn about him all that can be learned. The Christian doctrine is reached by unfolding the conception of God that is assumed as true by the Christian revelation and experience. When the doctrine has been presented, and it is apparent what manner of God the Christian faith is assuming to exist, it will be time to inquire how far the doctrine thus obtained is commended as true by fitting in with other truth that we have reason for holding. Proof comes at the end, not at the beginning and bears the nature of confirmation, not of discovery. There may be other ways of approaching the knowledge of God, but the Christian way is the way of recognition rather than of demonstration.[49]

Clarke's method is experiential as he argues from an experience of God to supportive proofs that confirm what is recognized as Christian truth. Finding transcendental and traditional arguments as rationalizing Christian experience, Clarke argues that such opinions are not demonstrations or foundations of belief, but are valuable as confirmations of the God recognized in Christian experience.

Since theology is "preceded by religion," the subjectivity of knowing God in Christ is central to Clarke's method. Unlike Schleiermacher, however, Clarke believed religious experience was determined by Christian revelation, not the "God-consciousness" of a particular time. For Clarke, the Bible was more than a repository of doctrines for a static theology but, rather, a derivative product of revelation and religious experience—a servant and not a master. This nuanced presuppositionalism differs from later presuppositionalists whose apologetics is based in transcendental, rational proofs for the necessity of God. Clarke's presuppositionalism is based in his

---

49. Clarke, *Doctrine of God*, 56.

religious experience of the Bible. Clarke never specifies how to verify the veracity of one's religious experience. There exists no greater tradition or ecclesial body to which such matters are appealed. Therefore, while Miller's hermeneutic shares a similar impetus with Clarke's that necessitated an experience of the Holy Spirit, Miller will nuance his particular approach with an appeal to community.

In Clarke's spiritual autobiography, *Sixty Years with the Bible: A Record of Experience* (1909), he ascribes the transformative authority of the Bible to the "historical and spiritual figure of Jesus Christ" who "showed me the principle on which he taught us to live the true life of men: it showed me the Saviour, and the salvation."[50]

> In this twofold vision I had the key to the Christian theology; or, to use a better simile, I had the light which it was my privilege to hold up for illumination of the field. This light which I as theologian was to use I found in my Bible just as it lay in my hands, without reference to any theory as to how the divine Spirit influenced the men who wrote it. I could read the book and get my information.[51]

Yet Clarke is quick to note, information was not the end goal of Scripture. "I have learned that instead of being dictated by the Bible, a man's theology should be inspired in him by the Bible." Such inspiration occurred by "the Spirit that inspired the Bible." Theology, he notes, should be "a result of exegesis, but [only] as a second fruit, not a first. Between exegesis and theology there are intermediate processes, not only legitimate but Necessary."[52] Those "intermediate processes" included the experience and illumination of the Holy Spirit. Therefore, Clarke's hermeneutical approach can best be named "experiential presuppositionalism." Central to his theology was an individual's experience of the Spirit through the text.

It is only by the Holy Spirit that we "receive knowledge of Jesus."[53] Thus the Spirit allows the Bible to be "our guide to Jesus, to God, and to life divine."[54] With the encouragement and confidence of the Holy Spirit, Clarke sought to navigate the no man's land between conservative and liberal camps—between orthodoxy and innovation. At the end of his autobiography, he writes,

---

50. Clarke, *Sixty Years*, 199.
51. Clarke, *Sixty Years*, 196.
52. Clarke, *Sixty Years*, 197.
53. Clarke, *Sixty Years*, 253.
54. Clarke, *Sixty Years*, 254.

> The chief danger about the Bible at present is . . . that [on the one hand] it will be studied too much in the mere spirit of criticism, without regard to its religious value. . . . On the other, the timidity of Christian people on critical grounds will prevent them from holding that religious value in its true rank and place.[55]

Clarke's fear was that the victimization of the Bible by the great polarization occurring within American Protestant Christianity would erode the church's hermeneutic of "intelligent confidence" in its revelation into a cold hard rationalism. It is this type of "religious confidence in the Bible to which I have been led," he further writes, "and that to which the Christian people are entitled, and I wish they all might have it."[56]

Clarke as a Precursor to a Postconservative Approach to Revelation

With this religious confidence, when Clarke was asked to translate 2 Tim 3:16, he held that a probable translation was: "'Every inspired Scripture,' or writing, 'is profitable.'"[57] He goes on to affirm that there "is no authority in the Scriptures for applying the verse to the Bible as a whole" since it refers to the Old Testament. Nevertheless, all canonical Scripture gives evidence of the quality of inspiration, albeit unequally.[58] Thus, Clarke affirms a dynamic view of inspiration: the thoughts of the writings were inspired but the words used were left to the individual writers. Their sacred content conveys their authority, not by an infallible form of words influencing the intellect from without, but by the Holy Spirit's use of infallible Christian truth from within. The Holy Spirit is the infallible guide, not an infallible church or book: "The Holy Spirit is our teacher, and the Bible is his servant, to show us Christ."[59] This centrality of the experience of Christ as revelation and authority of Scripture is what brings some to consider Clarke as a precursor to postconservative evangelicalism which Roger Olson describes as follows:

> Postconservatives do not reject a propositional, factual, and informational aspect to divine revelation, but they wish to stress that revelation is given primarily for the purpose of redemption through personal encounter and relationship, and

---

55. Clarke, *Sixty Years*, 255.
56. Clarke, *Sixty Years*, 255.
57. Clarke, *Christian Theology*, 36.
58. Clarke, *Outline*, 44.
59. Clarke, *Outline*, 44.

that non-propositional aspects of revelation can be useful for theological endeavor.⁶⁰

Postconservative evangelicalism attempts to reanimate the *experience* of revelation. Classical foundationalism quickly disintegrates into a cold, rigid rationalism. As Kevin Vanhoozer articulates, the drama of doctrine is lost as the story of Scripture is replaced by rational constructs to buttress the authority of the Bible (i.e., inerrancy).⁶¹ In this vein, Vanhoozer accuses both liberal and fundamentalist theologies of "de-dramatizing" revelation and thereby making it lifeless—the purpose of revelation is to be a *means of transformation* more than a *carrier of information*. As Vanhoozer remarks:

> To equate God's Word with the content it conveys is to work with an abbreviated Scripture principle that reduces revelation to the propositional residue of its locutions.... It fails to see that what Scripture is doing is witnessing to and hence mediating Christ, and it fails to do justice to the role of the Holy Spirit in making sure that this witness is effective.⁶²

Unlike Vanhoozer, Miller does not subjugate the Spirit to simply being a tool of interpretation for Scripture. Both Word and Spirit are necessary to capture the centrality of Christ that is evident in both his writings and those of Clarke.

Miller's Epistemological Posture regarding the Bible

Miller and Clarke saw experience and reason as both submitting to Christ. The difference between Miller and Clarke is subtle but profound. Clarke saw the proof of revelation as ultimately confirmatory instead of discovery. Miller, sounding almost Barthian, finds general revelation to be totally unlike the revelation in Christ as general revelation is unable to save. Clarke, revealing his liberalism, would have been far more open to natural theology.

Natural theology understands revelation as not exclusively being in Jesus Christ. While Clarke would have centered his faith on the example of Christ and appreciated his divinity, his confirmatory understanding of revelation would have been far more open to natural theology than Miller would have been comfortable. For Miller, as made known in the last chapter, if there is no salvation except through Jesus Christ, then there is also no revelation except through Christ. Unlike the confirmatory understanding

60. Olson, *Reformed and Always Reforming*, 54.
61. See Vanhoozer, *Drama of Doctrine*.
62. Vanhoozer, *Drama of Doctrine*, 68.

of Clarke, Miller would have understood the discovery that is central to the Bible—Jesus is God's self-revelation of salvation.

While Miller would have appreciated Clarke's experiential presuppositionalism, he would have been leery of the inherent danger of emotionalism or experientialism trumping a biblical Christology. Nuancing Clarke, Miller would have approached the Bible and recognized the role of experience in that endeavor. This experience, however, would have submitted to Christ, community, and his Brethren faith.[63] For each theologian, however, both reason and experience of the Spirit were foundational in discerning truth in Scripture.

Miller held a distinct epistemology that allowed him to maintain a theological epistemology that remained tethered to the Bible and open to the developments and innovations of the world around him. This commitment to a tethered theological exploration even shaped his hermeneutic of the Bible. In a letter to Louis Bauman regarding accusations against Ashland College of teaching heresy by allowing evolution to be taught in the classroom, Miller replied graciously to the staunch Fundamentalist:

> I am always very frank and open with my teaching both in the classroom and from the pulpit. I never try to force the acceptance of my teaching upon the students. Nor have I paid any attention thus far to rumors that I have heard that I am suspected of teaching heresy or infidelity. I dislike to be misrepresented but I am willing to let my work tell as to my loyalty to the Church and the Bible in all essentials. It would be a sure mark of error should we all agree upon every detail of Biblical interpretation.[64]

The last line succinctly captures Miller's theological commitment to an open and communal discernment regarding the text of the Bible. His hermeneutic allowed for a posture of openness, curiosity, exploration, and genuine playfulness in theology. While the Bible, itself, was seen as infallible, his interpretations were not. Experience was even allowed to shape his understanding of the Bible—a truth for which Miller was unapologetic. Rather than bracketing out our experience of the Spirit, Miller calls followers of Christ to lean in to such experiences while remaining tethered to the Bible.

---

63. Miller once again sounds Barthian. In Jesus Christ is God's self-revelation, God revealing Godself. In his article "The Subject of Divine Self-Revelation—No. 3," mentioned in chapter 4, Miller is adamant that while creation can testify to God as creator is does not reveal God. Only Christ reveals God. See Miller, "Subject of Divine Self-Revelation," 2.

64. Miller, "Miller to Bauman," 1.

Miller models an Anabaptist hermeneutic of obedience that is similar to what theologian Donald Bloesch called *fideistic revelationalism*—a posture with which Bloesch aligned. This hermeneutical approach stresses that the

> decision of faith is as important as the fact of revelation in giving us certainty of the truth of faith. The revelation is not simply assented to but is existentially embraced as the truth or power of salvation. Certainty of its truth becomes ours only in the act of decision and obedience by which the external truth becomes internalized in faith and life. This is not fideism in the narrow or reductionist sense because our faith has a sure anchor and basis in an objective revelation in history.[65]

For Bloesch, revelation is more than the epistemic extremes of fideism and empiricism. Fideism quickly leads to sectarianism as faith claims become subjective experiences that demand further faith as proof. Empiricism, or positivism, demands rational demonstrations of certainty which revelation cannot fully satisfy. Instead, Bloesch sees Christian revelation as an objective reality through the in-breaking of Christ—a historic event to which Christian theology is tethered and on which it is centered. Consequently, Christian faith can also not devolve into a cold, hard rationalism in which experience and perspective are bracketed out so as to preserve the perception of autonomous reason. With rationalism, faith becomes a series of proofs for God's existence and human experience is not seen as necessary to our acquisition of Christian revelation. Belief becomes the hallmark of true Christianity.

While Bloesch would never argue that correct belief is unimportant (or that experience is not essential) to Christian revelation, the pendulum of Protestant Christian epistemology too often lives at the extremes rather than a hermeneutic grounded in the Spirit's revelation received by faith. As Bloesch notes:

> It is the Spirit who converts and convicts, but he does so through human instrumentality. He does not need our aid, but he grants us the privilege of being covenant partners with him in making known the truth that alone can bring meaning to those who drift in aimlessness, and peace and joy to those crippled by depression and fear.[66]

---

65. Bloesch, *Theology of Word & Spirit*, 161.
66. Bloesch, *Theology of Word & Spirit*, 67.

The Word and Spirit that animate Bloesch's epistemology of fideistic revelationalism is very similar to that which animates Miller's understanding of Christian revelation. Miller offers an important corrective to Bloesch's *fideistic revelationalism*. In Bloesch's approach, the role of the church is, at best, implied. Bloesch does value the role of the church but does not explicitly give it a role in hermeneutics. Like most evangelicals who have any understanding of ecclesiology, Bloesch sees the church primarily as a missiological tool of the kingdom.

Miller, in line with his Anabaptist heritage, sees the church as *both* missiological instrument *and* hermeneutical context. It is only by understanding the church as both that its alternative witness is revealed in the world. The church holds a Word and Spirit epistemology and finds biblical authority only in the person of Jesus mediated through the Spirit's illumination of the text. This authority produces a telos to make Christ and his kingdom known by serving as eschatological first fruits of the kingdom. In Bloesch's approach, revelation is understood personally by default and communally by potential effect. In Miller's thought, revelation is seen as both personal and communal in relationship. The church exists as a sort of hermeneutical circle that regularly allows its members to bring their personal experiences of the Bible into conversation with each other and to be shaped and nuanced by that same community. Therefore, higher criticism was not a threat to Miller's theological method. Ultimate authority didn't come from some meaning behind the text (liberalism), under the text (fundamentalism), or over the text (transcendentalist presuppositionalism). The Bible was a living document because of the Spirit's activity in community. Rather than language of certainty or security to describe this language, Miller instead calls upon a relational vocabulary of assurance and confidence. If Bloesch does not fully capture Miller's hermeneutic, then how is his thought best understood? To answer that Miller must be brought into conversation with his contemporaries.

Miller's Hermeneutical Approach—Word-Spirit Communal Revelationalism

The relationship of Word and Spirit created for Miller an encounter with Christ.[67] His understanding of the authority of the Bible moved beyond rational proofs toward an experience of the risen Christ via the Spirit's

---

67. Brethren will often refer to the Holy Spirit as the "Inner Word" and Scripture as the "Outer Word." These two manifest the transformative presence of Jesus Christ, the "Living Word." See "How Brethren Understand God's Word."

illumination. This allowed him to embrace a centered set, faith over a dogmatic, bounded set approach espoused by fundamentalists. In this sense, Miller and Clarke are quite similar in their understanding of the revelation of the Bible. Yet Miller parts from Clarke regarding ecclesiology. For Miller, the Spirit's inspiration is confirmed by Scripture discerned in community. In contrast, Clarke has no developed ecclesiology and never clarifies how to properly discern the work of the Spirit. Two further contemporaries of Miller deserve attention to better elucidate Miller's hermeneutic. One was a Pietist contemporary while the other was Mennonite-Anabaptist.

First, Miller is similar to David Nyvall (1863–1946), who helped establish North Park College (a denominational school of the Evangelical Covenant Church which has a background in Swedish Pietism) and served as its president from 1912–1923. Both Miller and Nyvall were from Pietist backgrounds, were linguists with a love of the New Testament, had experience teaching at a seminary, and both held a deep appreciation for a liberal arts approach to education—this will be foundational to understanding Miller's application of a centered set epistemology in his pedagogy. Nyvall wrote on his rationale for such an approach in describing the ethos of North Park circa 1895:

> North Park College strives to attain the high mission of becoming a school home for knowledge thirsting youth from a thousand homes throughout the country. It aims with God's help to offer the clear unadulterated waters from the springs of knowledge to the thirsting ones. . . . We are trying to establish this education on a broad foundation. . . . Our opinion is that a preacher needs to be a [person] also educated in the liberal arts. He should not be educated into a separate caste and thus through his education destined to live in a world totally alien to the life interests of common people.[68]

Nyvall's Pietist roots shaped his theological epistemology. The Swedish Pietists that would form the Evangelical Covenant Church were a people intimately aware of their immigrant story. They had been, and in many cases were still being treated as, outsiders. Nyvall's vision is a pragmatic and Pietist vision to assist his church in the larger acculturation into American society. Contrary to Pietism's critics, Nyvall's vision is not otherworldly, highly subjective, nor overly emotional.[69] Both Nyvall and Miller embody a distinct

---

68. Nyvall, "North Park," 36–38.

69. Pietism is notoriously misconstrued as a quietistic, passive movement that maintains a sectarian posture of the heart. This speaks more to the Radical variant of the movement rather than Classical Pietism. Classical Pietism was, and is, quite

epistemology that serves as a corrective to the classical foundationalism of the Fundamentalism and liberalism of their period.

When an inerrant authority of the Bible was claimed, Nyvall objected that such a claim weakened the authority of the Bible. Insisting that the Bible was not inerrant nor claimed inerrancy, Nyvall, instead, reminded his listeners of the biblical understanding of inspiration over against the verbal inspiration championed by inerrantists. Regarding "inspiration," Nyvall provided a helpful summary of the historical development of the term:

> The difference may be best shown in that in its classical meaning the word refers to the person who is inspired, but in the Christian theological sense it refers especially to the result of the inspiration. And most of the misdirection in the teaching of the Bible's inspiration can be traced back to this starting point: a tendency to fasten chiefly upon the supernatural and divine in the Bible's origin and at the same time to deify or canonize the Bible writers, instead of fastening upon the Bible's divine content as a present-day fact.[70]

This is an important distinction between the *process* of inspiration and the *result* of inspiration. Fundamentalists and liberals alike underwrote their epistemologies with a rational process of inspiration. In that pursuit, Nyvall maintained, they both lacked a coherent understanding of the result of inspiration. They both fundamentally missed the greatest evidence for inspiration, the transformation of a human life by the Spirit. Fundamentalism produced disciples with *faith as cognition*. Liberalism produced disciples with *faith as experience*. In their anxiety regarding belief and the modern world, they both denied the spiritual authority of the Bible. Nyvall, however, asserts that "Scripture should be taken as a fact, exactly as we take other realities, and it's worth will be proven by its influence and fruit. . . . I do not need to know the whole history of an apple and understand its origin and development before I can enjoy its juice and flavor."[71] Like Miller, Nyvall recognizes the agency of the Spirit for biblical authority:

> No one has such access to and receptivity of disciplinary influence of the Scripture except by the indwelling Spirit. The Spirit who is active in the Scripture is also active in the believer. Here, therefore, it is not a question of only chiefly sharpening the

---

progressive in education, justice and missiology. A misunderstanding of Pietism is further reinforced by liberal theologians like Schleiermacher who exploited Pietism to buttress their defense of religion as merely religious experience and affection.

70. Nyvall, "Inspiration."
71. Nyvall, "Inspiration."

intelligence and gifts of understanding but of the sanctification of the whole being to become good soil for the living planting of the truth.[72]

Nyvall offers a distinct Pietist hermeneutic that Roger Olson calls "Pietist Perspectivalism."[73] Counter to the rationalistic epistemology of classical foundationalism, Pietist Perspectivalism is epistemology-as-posture towards the world. Such an epistemology argues that the acquisition of objective knowledge is not possible because no one starts from a neutral location. This "epistemology-as-posture" advocates conversional piety in which there is an ongoing transformation of the whole person by the power of the Spirit. Pietist Perspectivalism recognizes that our posture to the text begins with a personal encounter with the Spirit. It is not a rationally objective experience but is rather, in Nyvall's words, a "sanctification of the whole person." Miller would resonate with this but, like his differences with both Clarke and Bloesch, recognizes the role of individual, Spirit *and* church—in line with the Anabaptist stream of his heritage.

It is in his ecclesiology that Miller brings a "Pietist Perspectivalism" into conversation with the Anabaptist witness of the church that is central to the Brethren. Shirley Hershey Showalter writes regarding theologies of Anabaptist traditions that they, "are likely to be lurkers on the periphery rather than upholders of the dominant consensus."[74] The reason for such a location is the Anabaptists' concern for the life of the church rather than positions of power or influence.[75] Furthermore, it is a suspicion of hermeneutics too closely aligned with power, privilege and privacy.

Among Anabaptist theologians of Miller's period, a Mennonite contemporary was Daniel Kauffman (1865–1944).[76] Kauffman was born June 20, 1865, in Juniata, Pennsylvania. After making a failed attempt to enter politics in 1890, he experienced a crisis of faith precipitated by the death of both his wife and newborn daughter. Faced with the responsibility of raising

---

72. Nyvall, "Inspiration."

73. Gehrz, *Pietist Vision*, 105.

74. Showalter, *Minding the Church*, 255.

75. Miller had opportunities to teach at other colleges but turned them down out of a commitment to Ashland and, most importantly, to the Brethren. See interview with Dale Stoffer, June 2015.

76. For more on Kauffman, see Wetzel, "Fundamentalists," 104–28. Wetzel, specifically, addresses the common antagonistic reception that Kauffman receives from several Mennonite historians and theologians that he capitulated too far to either liberalism or Fundamentalism. Instead, Wetzel convincingly argues that the accusations from both ends of the spectrum of Kauffman's defection to the other side is indicative of a leader who modeled a "third way" amid the polarization.

a son alone, he was converted through the preaching of Mennonite leader J. S. Coffman (1848–1899). After this conversion, he joined the Mennonite Church and was ordained in 1892 and became a bishop four years later and supported the creation of the Mennonite General Conference, which he moderated in 1898.[77] Kauffman soon began his work as editor of the *Gospel Witness* (1905–1908) and of the *Gospel Herald* (1908–1943)—important Mennonite periodicals of the period. It was in his capacity as editor that Kauffman exercised great influence in the Mennonite Church during the first half of the twentieth century.[78]

Along with his editorial work, Kauffman was also a popular author for the Mennonite General Conference. A cursory glance at his works over a period of thirty years (roughly 1900–1930) demonstrates his opposition to any corrupting of traditional conceptions of orthodoxy. Furthermore, he resisted Darwinism, "erroneous views" of the atonement, and higher criticism.[79] In fact, Kauffman's views on science, Scripture, and Christology were very much in line with mainstream Protestant Fundamentalists.

In addition to holding many of the same positions as mainstream Fundamentalists, Kauffman evidenced his reliance on their works in his books either published or edited on biblical doctrines. In the preface to *Doctrines of the Bible* (1928), he listed R. A. Torrey (1856–1928), a contributor to *The Fundamentals*, and William Evans (1870–1950), author of the *Fundamentalist Great Doctrines of the Bible* (1912) as sources that he consulted in preparation for the project.[80] In fact, on all of the issues regarding Christology and the nature of Scripture, Kauffman was sympathetic to Fundamentalism. Despite his agreement with certain segments of Protestant Fundamentalism, however, Kauffman remained distant from the movement as a whole, believing Mennonites, in line with their Anabaptist faith, should remain distinct from these broader trends. In fact, just as Kauffman opposed modernists at Goshen College, a Mennonite liberal arts school in Goshen, Indiana, on the theological left, he also found himself at odds with Mennonite fundamentalists on the right. "We are," he said, referring to the Mennonite Church, "fundamentalists with a small 'f.'"[81]

More than simply distancing himself from the larger Fundamentalist movement, however, Kaufmann charted a third way displaying his

77. Erb, "Kauffman, Daniel," 3:156–57.
78. Erb, "Kauffman," 3:156–57.
79. For example, see Kauffman, *Doctrines of the Bible*, 42, 248–50. See also Kauffman, *Bible Doctrine*, 113–28.
80. Kauffman, *Doctrines of the Bible*, 8.
81. Quoted in Wenger, "Inerrancy Controversy," 112.

commitment to traditional Anabaptist-Mennonite doctrine and practice. Among the more notable ordinances that he defended were nonconformity to the world, nonresistance, the necessity of believers' baptism, and the devotional covering for women. Interestingly, Miller discusses all but the last in his writings on Brethren identity. Kauffman also opposed the taking of oaths, worldly fashion, and membership in secret societies.[82]

Kauffman demonstrated the importance of traditional Anabaptist teachings through his advocacy of the doctrine of nonconformity understanding the doctrine as the necessity of a transformed life and its consequent—"an entire separation from the world."[83] He became most emphatic about this doctrine in his later life. In 1941, reflecting on his fifty years of service in the church, he remained unambiguous about the need for separation from the world—a continued commitment to a central, Anabaptist distinctive.[84] Kauffman seems to have nuanced this commitment with Fundamentalist sectarianism.[85]

In Kauffman's 1930 work, *The Way of Salvation: Including Thoughts on What to Do After We Are Saved*, he explained his understanding of salvation and exhorted his readers concerning its ethical implications. Mere intellectual assent to correct doctrine without evidence of regeneration was unthinkable in this work. "If we have really been saved from sin," he declared, "we walk 'in newness of life.' This means that our former sins . . . must now be kept out of our lives."[86] It is here that he mirrors the thought of both Clarke and Miller. The newness of life was manifested in a commitment to ethics, to traditional Mennonite teachings, and to the necessity of a transformed life.[87] Through his opposition to modernism and his emphasis on correct doctrine, Kauffman led his church away from beliefs that were not part of its history. At the same time, his defense of Mennonite ordinances

---

82. Wetzel, "Fundamentalists," 119. "In addition to traditional ordinances," Wetzel notes, Kauffman "also defended other less well-known, though equally distinctive Mennonite practices. These included feet washing, the Christian salutation (holy kiss), anointing oil, self-denial, and opposition to life insurance, musical instruments, and birthday celebrations."

83. Wetzel, "Fundamentalists," 201.

84. Kauffman, *Fifty Years*, 74–75.

85. As Brenda Colijn notes, "Anabaptist theology requires that the church be distinct from the world, but not necessarily separate from it. The early Anabaptists certainly weren't separate from the world; the Amish are. Fundamentalists are separate from the world so that they won't be contaminated by it. Anabaptists are distinct from the world in order to be a living witness to it." See Colijn, interview by author, Ashland, OH, March 20, 2019.

86. Kauffman, *Way of Salvation*, 27–28.

87. Kauffman, *Way of Salvation*, 28.

and his unwillingness to join ranks with Fundamentalists in the Mennonite Church allowed him to simultaneously avoid any capitulation to Protestant Fundamentalism.[88] Kauffman's hermeneutical approach can best be coined "Mennonite Distinctivalism" as he saw the ordinances of the church, properly executed, as being the centering force necessary for Mennonites amid the polarization of the period.

Miller's convictions resonate with Kauffman's commitment to the life of the church. Miller is first and foremost a churchman and his overarching desire is to develop leaders for the Brethren. At the same time, Miller can be a provocateur to the Brethren, serving as a prophetic voice into the life of the denomination. Under his prophetic words, however, is a deep concern for the Brethren to know who they are and why they exist. Consistent with Anabaptist scholarship, Miller's approach reflects Shirley Hershey Showalter's observation that Anabaptist scholars

> write to serve and to know. They write to understand their deepest questions and in hopes that their communities will benefit. They write to unmask, to defamiliarize, and to challenge, even as they seek the "implicate order" or "hidden wholeness" underneath.[89]

This is at the heart of Miller's witness. While he argues for Brethren distinctives just as Kauffman contended for Mennonite ordinances, Miller remains open to new light and understanding by arguing for the complexity of the search for truth. Kauffman would not have held such an understanding. He appreciates the diversity of ways in which people approach truth, even Christian understandings of truth. Contrary to bounded set belief systems (like the fundamentalist insistence on creeds and statements of faith), Miller espoused a centered set seeking to affirm each believer's approach to Christ. In a lecture entitled "My Philosophy of Life," a series of conclusions he arrived at from his study of philosophy, he ascertained the following truths about the universe. The universe, he proposed, was

> rational, purposeful and meaningful. In other words, the world is end-realizing and value-conserving. We believe this with full knowledge of the problems of the evils and the failures the world presents. What I mean here is just this—this is the best possible world we can conceive for the purposes it subserves. It is my conviction that the findings of modern science, revolutionary as they may seem to be, especially the findings of Astronomy,

---

88. Wetzel, "Fundamentalists," 125.
89. Showalter, *Minding the Church*, 258.

Chemistry, Mathematics and Physics will confirm the view here stated.[90]

His centered set approach to education fostered an imagination that saw truth as multifaceted. Science, mathematics, and philosophy did not threaten Christian truth. While Jesus remained the central truth of his life, Miller desired "to find truth rather than to establish a theory."[91] It was this centering on the truth of Christ that allowed him to reject the anxiety of Fundamentalists who feared even a conversation regarding faith and the scientific developments of the period. Yet Miller remained sensitive to the limitations of both Fundamentalism and liberalism. In another lecture, entitled "The Philosophy of Life," Miller, in an almost playful tone, called both faith and science to an appreciation of mystery. This appreciation of wonder allowed for a posture of gratitude toward the pursuit of truth. "Let Science and faith in God go hand in hand in ferreting out God's way OF DOING THINGS—as in this respect, His way of Creating LIFE. How God did so is a question the Bible does not answer and the one with which Science delights to wrestle."[92] While remaining curious, Miller was also committed to the authority of the Bible and the church. This made him a trusted scholar and leader who simultaneously served as a prophetic voice to the Brethren Church. The Brethren were both his sounding board and anchor.

His obedient service in response was the development of leaders and scholars for its witness. His life and teaching assist the Brethren in better understanding their distinct epistemological witness. This is why, first and foremost, the gravitational force of his theology is Christology. It is Christology that holds everything together (in the spirit of Col 1:17). The mission of the church is the mission of Christ, and the Spirit connects the two through the revelation of Scripture discerned in community. It is the Spirit in our midst that serves as the standard for the mission of Christ.[93] This is a significant shift from theologians like Kauffman as Miller, perhaps unknowingly, was assisting the Brethren in retrieving their Radical Pietist heritage.

Many Reformation leaders, including Lutheran and Reformed, held a theological progression that differed very little from that of their Catholic counterparts:

Christology → Ecclesiology → Missiology

Miller proposed a new theological flow for the mission of Christ:

90. Miller, *Christian Doctrine*, xv.
91. Miller, *Christian Doctrine*, 205.
92. Miller, *Christian Doctrine*, 307.
93. Stoffer, *Brethren Doctrines*, 227.

Christology → Pneumatology → Ecclesiology → Missiology[94]

This import given to the role of the Spirit is an essential guard against the rationalism and scholasticism that was and is prevalent in many Reformation groups. Miller took what was implicit in many Reformation traditions, the role of the Spirit, and makes the Spirit's influence more explicit. The Spirit continually makes the work of Christ fresh and the pages of Scripture transformative for believers. The witness of the church is created by faithful, regenerate disciples who are continually being transformed by the influence of the Spirit.[95] With the inclusion of both the Spirit and reason, Miller's thought is both a recovery and redefinition of Brethren thought for later generations. His thought exposes an omission in several evangelical sources of authority—the person of the Holy Spirit. While experience became a dangerously, slippery slope in Protestant liberalism, Miller found the fear and removal of experience to be an overreaction by Fundamentalists. It is not simply *an* experience of Scripture that makes it transformative. It is the experience *of the Spirit* through the Bible—a truth held by both Clarke and Miller—that illumines the text to change our hearts. Miller's hermeneutical process consisted of (1) an encounter with Scripture and Spirit (occurring simultaneously in the individual's experience), followed by (2) spiritually empowered reason to interpret, that necessitates the (3) discernment of the greater community for verification or correction, and (4) creates a communal response that then produces a transformative, revelatory encounter with the Bible for both the individual and the community. This individual and corporate teaching on interpretive posture is the gift of Miller's legacy. Miller was committed to the narrative of Scripture (conservative) all while being engaged with the world's ideas in humility and service (progressive).

Miller's hermeneutical approach can best be described as a *Word-Spirit Communal Revelationalism*. At the heart of Miller's theology, and

---

94. Miller would clearly disagree with Hochmann regarding the constitution of the church, with Hochmann stressing the spiritual, invisible nature of the entity: they both would have high regard for the influence of the Holy Spirit. In many ways, Miller's elevation of the role of the Spirit is just another way that he helped Brethren rediscover the original Word and Spirit dialectic at the heart of the early Brethren.

95. This distinction of pneumatology will be very important in the next chapter as the relationship of Brethren and American evangelicalism is explored. Recent developments in evangelicalism have stressed that ecclesiology flows out of missiology. The missional church movement, as it is known, proposes an order as follows: Christology → Missiology → Ecclesiology. While this appears to be a corrective on paper, it too brackets out the Spirit and is not as christological as it appears. With the calling of his apostles, Christ modeled the formation of a people distinct from others who would go out and fulfill his mission. John's gospel proclaims the promise of the Holy Spirit in that task (see 24:15–31).

Brethren theology for that matter, is the revelation of Christ. This revelation is mediated to us by the creative dynamic of *both* Word *and* Spirit. Yet our hermeneutic remains incomplete without the epistemic influence of the church. It is the community of faith shaped by Word and Spirit that affirms or corrects our personal revelatory experiences. Miller takes what may be implicit in each of the above theologians and makes the influence of the Spirit more explicit.

Likewise, while Miller embodied the Pietist role of spiritual experience in agreement with orthodoxy detailed by Nyvall, he also understood and appreciated the importance of the witness of the church evidenced in Kauffman's writings. Miller appropriated, nuanced and offered helpful correctives to these other theological views all while remaining connected to the Word-Spirit community of his Brethren heritage.

Miller brought a Brethren plain reading of Scripture into dialogue with conservative and liberal voices of his day. Like Clarke, Nyvall and Kauffman, he was attempting to find a distinct way amid the schismatic voices of modernistic liberalism and Fundamentalism. The experience of the Spirit would have given him a greater affinity for the thought of both Nyvall and Clarke. But the role of the church, as evident in Kauffman's writings, would have been apparent in Miller's thought as well. Miller's gift to the Brethren was a hermeneutic marked by the involvement of the Spirit discerned in community—Word-Spirit Communal Revelationalism. The graphic below assists in locating Miller with his contemporaries and in capturing the role of Word with Spirit and individual in community—in his theology.

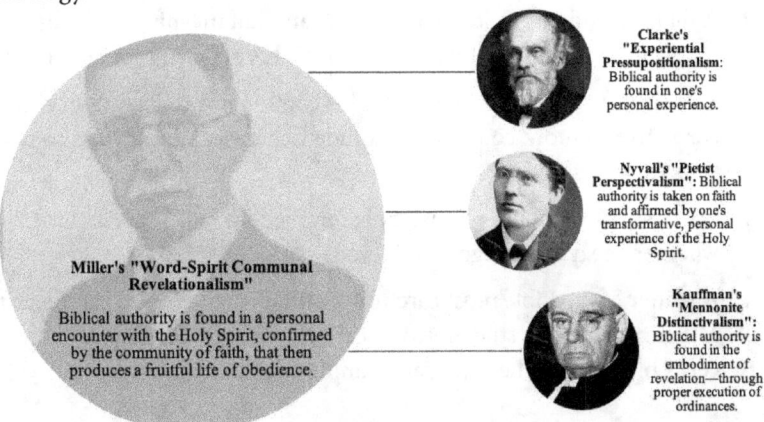

Applying this hermeneutic to the life of the community of faith, Miller, like Clarke and Nyvall especially, argued that one need not fear tools like higher criticism but that the true spirit of Bible study must include a thorough knowledge and an openness to truth often missed by higher critics of the Bible.[96] To maintain this interpretive posture, one must have the qualities of (1) a deep conviction of truth, (2) a thorough conviction that we must personally apply truth before applying it to others, (3) a childlike spirit, (4) a spirit of prayer, and (5) an ability to keep the end in view at all times (eschatology).[97] This interpretive posture does not abandon or relativize truth (as sometimes occurs in postmodern approaches to knowledge). Instead, Miller maintained a strong belief that every passage of the Bible has one true meaning, there is a unity of biblical truth, and the meaning of each passage is capable of being investigated.[98] "Do not think that the translator has done [the interpretation] for you," Miller warns. "It is not a translator's part to explain. He translates the words; *you must translate the ideas.*"[99]

Our interpretive task, according to Miller, is buttressed by common laws of interpretation. These laws reveal an interpretive approach that weds higher criticism of the Bible with a more Pietist approach to reading a part of Scripture in light of the whole. These laws assist us in discerning the meaning of a text:

6. The principles of interpretation are common to sacred and ordinary writings (words are signs of ideas). The Bible is sacred text but not immune to basic interpretive techniques.

7. One must study the historical antecedents (author, time of writing, etc.). Only by studying the world behind the text can one appropriately apply the text to the present. Rather than seeing this as a threat, Miller found it enhanced the application of the Bible to one's life.

8. A biblical student must learn the exact and full meaning of words and phrases used. It is here that Miller reveals his penchant for languages.

9. All texts must be read in context. This command would also serve as a corrective to more conservative/fundamentalist proof texting to buttress their positions.

10. The mode of thought must be examined to properly understand whether a text was allegory or literal.

11. A reader of the Bible must carefully distinguish the "sense" of the text. Miller instructs his students to discern the temporal and spiritual concerns of the text. The spiritual meaning of the text is not anathema to

---

96. Stoffer, *Brethren Doctrines*, 227.
97. Stoffer, *Brethren Doctrines*, 138–39.
98. Stoffer, *Brethren Doctrines*, 139.
99. Stoffer, *Brethren Doctrines*, 142.

the temporal concerns but it is a meaning that one cannot find utilizing tools of higher criticism alone. This is again a product of Miller's Pietist heritage.

12. All texts must be interpreted in harmony with the general teachings of the Scriptures. Again, Miller reveals his Pietist inheritance. The Pietist approach to the Bible was to read the part in the light of the whole.[100]

These "laws" are critical in our approach to the Bible since "interpreters have no right to explain as figurative that which is clearly literal because it may conflict with preconceived or denominational views."[101] When one used the Bible to merely justify a position, whether individual or denominational, such a theoretical approach to the Bible missed its ultimate import. The end goal of Bible study was a transformative encounter with Christ through the illumination of the Holy Spirit. Only in this manner could the true purpose of God in Christ be accomplished which "was the perfection of individual character, redemption from sin, [and] the recreation of man in the image and likeness of Jesus Christ."[102]

This transformative experience was Miller's hope for students at Ashland College. Miller's Word-Spirit Communal approach shaped him as a professor who modeled a pedagogy of discipleship in the classroom. Miller as professor was a teacher who saw his role not merely as carrier of information but also as a maker of disciples for the Brethren Church and for the kingdom. He would have seen the chief goal of Christian education to be the development of people into the character of Christ.

The Pedagogy of J. Allen Miller—a Liberal Arts Approach to Truth

With his approach of Word-Spirit Communal Revelationalism Miller was not threatened by examining Jesus' life as a moral exemplar for his own. He was especially drawn to the pedagogy of Jesus. He remarks in an *Evangelist* article that "Jesus was an incomparable teacher of men" and then lists three

---

100. Stoffer, *Brethren Doctrines*, 148. Miller's view of the Bible fits well with the Pietist theologian Philipp Jakob Spener's approach to the text. In his classic *Pia Desideria*, Spener writes: "It is not enough that we hear the Word with our outward ear, but we must let it penetrate to our heart, so that we may hear the Holy Spirit speak there, that is, with vibrant emotion and comfort feel the sealing of the Spirit and the power of the Word." See Spener, *Pia Desideria*, 117.

101. Miller, *Christian Doctrine*, 145.

102. Miller, *Christian Doctrine*, 215.

essentials of a great teacher as modeled by Christ.[103] They must hold (1) a thorough knowledge of the subject to be taught, (2) a keen and true insight into the mental and spiritual state of the learners or hearers, and (3) a striking aptness and wondrous skill in the art of illustration.[104] This pedagogy is not simply a transmission of information but also a sensitivity to both emotional and spiritual promptings.

Miller was impressed not only by the teachings of Jesus but also the manner of his teaching. One wonders if Miller felt that a truly Christ-like pedagogy might avoid the fault lines developing in American Christianity between belief and experience. He observes that "the [teaching of parables by Jesus] furnishes the most attractive and at the same time the most effective form of expressions to set forth moral and religious truth."[105] This style of teaching "arouses attention, it rebukes without giving offense, it warns because it interests, it reveals as well as conceals truth, it makes great truths easily remembered."[106] His reflections on the parables reveal a communicator intimately aware of the crisis and failure of theological dialogue of the period.

One of the first of many articles authored by Miller for the *Brethren Evangelist* came in an 1899 issue in which Miller outlined courses offered at the college. The listing reveals a surprisingly deep appreciation of the classics for a small denominational college course catalog. Courses offered during the 1899 fall term (right after the school was reopened in 1898 by both Miller and his wife, Clara Worst) were: "English—classes in Grammar, Composition and Literature will be taught; in Mathematic—Algebra, Advanced Arithmetic and Trigonometry; in Latin—Beginning Latin, Caesar and Cicero; in Greek—Beginning Greek and Xenophon; in Bible—Old Testament History and an elective in New Testament; also General History, U.S. History, Civics, Physics and German."[107] The reason for such a course of study is laid out in a subsequent issue of the denominational magazine:

> We are trying to make the College stand for the highest and best in life. We believe that the Christian cultured soul is the most highly cultured. We believe that the best life is the life of service. We believe that life's greatest compensation and chiefest joy is in living and doing for others. Who will help make the College

---

103. Miller, "Parables," 6.
104. Miller, "Parables," 6.
105. Miller, *Christian Doctrine*, 97.
106. Miller, *Christian Doctrine*, 97.
107. Miller, "College Notes," 14.

the power it can and ought to be? Who will help us in this most difficult and yet most important work of the church?[108]

Early on an emphasis on character becomes central to the educational vision of Miller. Education is not simply a cognitive exercise. There is in Miller a delight in learning. The liberal arts capture a deeper spiritual value for education. In many respects, the liberal arts *humanize* education as students learn "two things, to some extent at least, namely: that the best investment in this world is in character—cultured, empowered, Christianized manhood and womanhood; and secondly, that there is no way to accomplish so much along this line as thru the college."[109]

This call to character is not merely theoretical to Miller's vision. Character is the practical application of a Christ-centered life. This Christ-centered formation necessitates a liberal arts education. His argument in a 1903 special issue of the *Evangelist* is fourfold—education must be practical, it must be cultivated, a liberal education is the best for such cultivation, and such an education is not pie-in-the-sky.[110] It makes a difference to the one receiving it and to those impacted by such a person. In the end, a liberal education is best conducive to the development of the leaders that the church needs. He writes:

> Ashland College insists upon an education that is practical. We hold that the highest motive in the securing of an education is power *to live the best life and to help others to that life*. The words of our Master—"I came not to be ministered unto, but to minister"—are our motto.
>
> Ashland College believes in the worth and sacredness of life. It believes that the powers and capacities for growth implanted in the soul were meant to be developed, cultured, freed, to the highest possible degree.
>
> Ashland College believes that a liberal education will do all this and much more for every young lady and gentleman. All true education aims at character. This is worth many times more than all things else.
>
> And yet, the advantages which can be measured by worldly standards, are not to be despised. It is a well-known fact that if a man aims only at material success the discipline of a college

---

108. Miller, "College Notes," 14.
109. Miller, "College Notes," 14.
110. Miller, "Ashland College," 1.

> gives him four hundred times as many possibilities as his untrained brother enjoys.
>
> The heedless and indifferent young people live chiefly for themselves and for the day. Those who are seeking a college education are as a rule preparing themselves for service and a life of blessed usefulness in the world.[111]

Miller's passion for this vision was underscored by Ashland College serving as a vessel for leadership development within the Brethren Church. It existed as a "center of the strongest and most fruitful spiritual life and power. [Ashland] gives annually to the service of Christ the very best trained minds and most consecrated lives."[112]

This was accomplished because Ashland "gives opportunities in training and practical Christian work, the value of which is inestimable." He continues:

> The years of the College life of our young men and women are in many respects the most critical in their life—habits are formed, friendships are cultivated and the life-work is chosen, each and all for good or ill. Of what infinite importance therefore that they be given the proper direction in their study and the most healthful social and spiritual environments. Here the Christian College holds the most distinguished and characteristic preeminence.
>
> It is our ambition to give to the deserving and earnest student an opportunity to secure a higher education. In our own church and within our reach outside of the church are hundreds whom we are anxious to help to the higher and better things . . . to prepare [them] for lives of usefulness.
>
> We seek first of all to give direction and power to the life of the student. We hope always to educate for service. We hold that every power of the soul is divine and meant by the Creator to be given freedom and fullest possible development and culture.[113]

Christ-like character forms a "life of usefulness." Education is innately related to leadership and influence in the world. Christ-centered character is expressed in an irenic spirit for the common good. "If there is a single class of young people that the whole Church should make an object of thoughtful prayer," Miller writes passionately, "it is that class which will in the home

---

111. Miller, "Ashland College," 1.
112. Miller, "Ashland College," 1.
113. Miller, "Ashland College," 1.

churches become their leaders. All experience and students' records show that the young people who receive a College training become the leaders of Christian thought and activities at home."[114] Yet the impact of this education is not just for pastors and missionaries, though that is often a concern in his writings. Miller finds education to be imperative in all spheres of society. Regardless of occupation, Christian character is embodied in lives that have a useful, leadership-oriented, influential vision and impact. He writes in a later *Evangelist*:

> We must train a group of strong *men and women* for our leadership. Preachers? Yes. But also, teachers, doctors, engineers, businessmen, in short men and women in every walk and profession of life, for consecrated, effective, and worthy leaders in every local congregation. But first only sound, forceful, gospel preaching and teaching will lead in this direction. Therefore, we must educate.[115]

Yet Miller's focus on character and service do not diminish his commitment to a liberal arts education. Counter to sectarian Christian colleges, he writes that "[Ashland] College is not a proselyting institution; nevertheless, many learn to know our church and her teachings who could not otherwise be reached."[116] He maintains an appreciation for the role of crisis in education. True education is meant to challenge and stretch students, all while providing a security in that endeavor. Like a greenhouse, Ashland offered safety for a new life of ideas to take root. Therefore, Miller understood mentoring as essential to formation since a liberal arts college like Ashland realizes that "the years [spent at college] are the most impressionable of [youths'] lives. These college years are the crises years in which multitudes of instances and the influences surrounding young men and women then make or unmake them for Christ and the church."[117] An appreciation for crisis in both faith and intellectual development, an understanding of risk in the development of adolescents into adulthood, and an anchoring in a liberal arts education made Miller's vision for education distinct in the Brethren movement.

Even while traveling, Miller embodied this openness to learning and a childlike naiveté to the potential and opportunity around him. In a travel

---

114. Miller, "Prayer for the College," 3.

115. Miller, "Educate," 4, emphasis mine. Miller's writings are some of the first Brethren voices highlighting the necessity for both male *and* female leadership. This emphasis is consistent with the founding of Ashland College as a coeducational school.

116. Miller, "Duty," 9.

117. Miller, "Denominational College," 2.

diary he kept during a 1926 trip to the Middle East and Egypt he captures all three of the characteristics of his educational vision (character, service, openness).[118] Regarding travel, he notes:

1. That one must be open-minded. He must be willing to see the good even in unfamiliar. . . . He must see values even in systems or customs of folks where his own opinions or beliefs might be utterly antagonistic. And . . .

2. He must be fair toward others while remaining honest and true from himself. He must learn to discriminate, to be impartial, to be unprejudiced. All this is hard. Learning it one becomes more sympathetic, less superficially critical, less censorious and dictatorial in speech or conduct and earnest in his own beliefs and life to escape duplicity and hypocrisy.

Briefly my present reflections lead me to the following conclusions as fairly summing up the contributions of the travel experience of an earnest man:

1. One's own outlook upon life becomes much broader, more meaningful and consequently more directly definite and purposive.

2. The petty and trifling provincialisms of life, and the racial and political prejudices which he may have felt, must go into discard. My conviction is that spiritual and intellectual leadership must go to those prepared to assume it.

3. This . . . brings me to the inescapable conviction that the religious aspects of human life, or if you prefer the things of the Spirit—are primal, basic, essential. Here all men are kin; all are one. Christianity must assume the leadership. And it must be a Christianity that is regnant with truth and with a message. It must be a Christianity with Jesus Christ in His highest expression of character, in His supreme and unique place of Son of God and in His complicit and finished work as Redeemer of men and Revealer of God.

4. To me, as an American, I have seen the unparalleled, incomparable heritage which is mine in my Native Land—a heritage of home traditions, of personal freedom and opportunity, of political rights and the comforts of life, such as

---

118. Upon returning from this trip, which included the Holy Land, Miller made dozens of speaking engagements where he shared his travelogue with those that attended.

few other peoples if any possess and which none surpass. I thank God for this.[119]

Themes of character, service, and openness to new truth and evidence emerge in this snapshot of Miller's journey into Egypt, a land for which he held a large research passion. While standing in the Valley of the Kings he wrote, "From my student days Egypt has had a pull on my mind's strings. . . . But Ashland College and deep conviction of duty to my church cut all else off and away from me until at last I awoke to the stern reality that nothing else remained."[120] Miller's own character, service, and approach to truth had been shaped by a college and denomination centered in northeastern Ohio.

Ashland College was the lab in which Miller explored his educational experiment. His vision for education was laid out most clearly in a 1905 educational issue of the *Brethren Evangelist*, entitled "The Educational Ideal." It is included in its entirety below:

> The end to be aimed at in all education ought always to be character. Character at its best must be Christian. The most important years of life are the formative years of childhood and youth. These are the years of the school-life. Direction determines all the way of life and the end. The teacher largely determines direction. Acres, buildings, libraries, all material equipment are of vast importance. *But men are first*, men of character; men able to inspire, men who give out life, power as they instruct. Men are first and all else secondary. The teacher makes the College or University. . . . The teacher determines the ideal. I wish briefly to note four elements of a true educational ideal.
>
> True education stands for the perfection and culture of the whole man. Man's powers and capacities are all but infinite in their extent and variety. It cannot but be that the Creator meant these to be perfected.
>
> True education stands for the higher and better thing of life first. The mere training of the physical man can never be the highest ideal of the Gymnasium. No more can we stay at the development of the mental as the goal. The spiritual powers, the graces and virtues of the soul must be cultured. There are better things than the revel, the dollar, the throne.
>
> True education stands for the fullest and freest expression of life. Many are bound by the chains of ignorance or incapacity of indifference. Education sets all free, education in its highest

---

119. Miller, *Travel Journal*, 219–21.
120. Miller, *Travel Journal*, 104.

realization. Life's limitations are upon all but education vastly modifies all. Limitations are upon all but education vastly modifies all limitations.

True education stands for the life of service in the behalf of the less fortunate. Selfishness can never find a place in the best expression of one's life. It is a great blessing to anyone to be freed from the bondage of self. No motive can ever be quite so strong as that which found expression in the Man of Galilee. The cross is yet the way to the crown as well as to the salvation of multitudes of the unfortunate.[121]

The "truth" to Miller's educational vision was that through his leadership he was assisting the Brethren Church in articulating a progressive Brethren vision for both church and education. In quintessential Miller style, he did so by weaving together the two dominant streams in Brethren thought—Radical Pietism and Anabaptism—allowing him to converse with a wide spectrum of thinkers while never sacrificing core convictions he found rooted in Scripture.

Concluding Observations

Miller's theological epistemology and biblical hermeneutic is helpful in better understanding the theological method of the Ashland Brethren. The Word-Spirit Communal Revelationism that characterizes his hermeneutic allowed for a conservative-progressive dialectic that remains essential for this distinct branch of Brethren thought (and assists in better understanding the early Brethren). The phrase "conservative-progressive" does not denote a mere compromise of conservative and progressive principles—such a view of tolerance does not animate Miller's thought. Instead, *conservative* captures the source of theological authority and *progressive* captures the application of theological thought. This dialectic makes it possible for faithful engagement with society alongside an engagement of scientific and philosophical developments with Scripture. The Bible is revealed to be more conservative than liberal optimism and more progressive than Fundamentalist entrenchment. Such a posture allows for a conservative foundation for thought that is always open to what the early Brethren termed "new light" without abandoning central tenets of faith too hastily. This open, centered set epistemology and engagement with the ideas from surrounding cultures was (and is) an affront to the posture of Fundamentalists.

121. Miller, "Educational Ideal," 8.

Fundamentalism embodied a conservative-conservative approach. While a conservative source of authority was found in the Bible, the militant ghettoization of theology made for little to no engagement with developments of science.[122] Such a hyper-conservative approach to theology quickly brackets out the work of the Spirit. Some denominations in this category even claim that the work of the Spirit ceased with the close of the apostolic period.[123] Such an approach quickly makes faith highly rational and propositional as "new light" cannot be trusted. Thus, the liberal arts ethos of Miller's pedagogy was greeted with great suspicion by Fundamentalists like Louis Bauman and McClain.

Liberalism, especially modernistic liberalism, consisted of a progressive-progressive method. This attitude proposes great tolerance but can quickly become as militant as its Fundamentalist counterparts. Both hyper-conservative and hyper-progressive branches of American Christianity respond similarly as they are both founded on rationalism and on a subsequent anxiety about certainty. Where Fundamentalists bracketed out the Spirit in their defense of Scripture, liberals attempted to translate the work of the Spirit into religious experience or affections—to maintain a foundation of rationality over and against supernaturalism. Progressivism seems similar to Miller's approach in its openness to new evidences and its exploration of new ideas but, unlike his thought, lacks a center to which it must be tethered. In a spirit of tolerance and translation, liberalism fails to offer anything beyond a religious humanism that bypasses transcendence in the spirit of immanence—spirituality and religious consciousness become synonymous. Miller, while open to new ideas like his liberal colleagues, can never be accused of religious humanism.

Furthermore, Miller's "evangelical faith" was a departure from the rationalism and scholasticism that has often been a hallmark of more Reformed expressions of evangelicalism. This was due in large part to the

---

122. As mentioned earlier, the irony is not lost that Fundamentalists would stake the authority of the Bible on a rational defense known as inerrancy. While Fundamentalists demanded "the faith as once delivered to the saints," they had surpassed the transmission of faith present in the early and medieval churches and in the Reformers. The very rational worldview they adamantly opposed shaped their fundamental apologetic for the authority of the Bible.

123. "Cessationism" is the position that there is a permanent discontinuance of the supernatural displays of God through activity like miracles or healings. Some have taken the position that everything supernatural ended with the last written word of Scripture (the canon established) and with the passing of the twelve Apostles. There is a small percentage of Christians or denominations that hold to this today. Most admit that supernatural healings and miracles can sometimes occur and that God still answers prayer.

Anabaptist-Pietist heritage of his life that shaped him for a devotional approach to truth that, rather than necessitating a defense of the Bible as inerrant, maintained a relational approach to Scripture in which he could trust amid ambiguity—retaining confidence but not always rational certainty. He spoke often about life *with* God rather than a defense for God—even noting that "the life of communion with God is prayer."[124] This prayerful understanding of the Christian journey flowed out of his Word and Spirit theological epistemology into a witness that ultimately serves as his greatest gift to the Brethren and to American evangelicalism. Miller helped the Brethren retrieve a centered set epistemology against the bounded set of both fundamentalism and liberalism. While bounded sets are doctrinally specific and develop postures of protection and defense, centered set epistemologies, while still being concerned with doctrine, realize that doctrine alone does not change the human heart. Therefore, their epistemic posture is more curious and discerning. This was the liberal arts approach to truth that was central to Miller's faith. It will serve as a distinct voice Brethren can have via postconservative evangelicalism to the larger American evangelical landscape.s

The next chapter will examine the present-day applicability of Miller's Word-Spirit Communal Revelationism for both Brethren identity and for the Ashland Brethren relationship with American evangelicalism. It is the hope of this last chapter that a usable past from Miller will be discerned to better assist Brethren of today to engage society in a manner that is faithful to the Brethren way and the Bible, to discern a helpful Brethren approach to theological education, and to encourage a fruitful path forward with other Christian groups—especially other evangelicals.

---

124. Miller, *Christian Doctrine*, 97.

6

Word-Spirit Communal Revelationalism and Brethren Engagement with American Evangelicalism

THIS PROJECT HAS UNCOVERED the Word-Spirit dialectic of the Brethren that was formative at Schwarzenau, embodied in central practices like immersion baptism and carried to the new world via their trans-Atlantic pilgrimage. From there it marked their witness in the new republic of America, animated the disputes around identity throughout the nineteenth century, and suffered great distortion through a variety of splits at the end of that century. Finally, it distinguished leaders, like Miller, in their ability to rise above polarization and schism with a distinct posture and method, defined in the last chapter as Word-Spirit Communal Revelationalism. It is only proper, given Miller's pedagogical foci of character, life of usefulness, and a liberal arts approach to truth, to end this venture with a more practical and pastoral application of Miller's theological method to the relationship between the Brethren Church and American evangelicalism.

This chapter endeavors to provide a working definition of what is meant by the term "evangelical." It will use the research of David Bebbington, Roger Olson, and Molly Worthen to discern a working definition of "evangelical." Miller will be brought into conversation with the distortions of Bebbington's now-famous quadrilateral through the work of theologian David Fitch. His book *The End of Evangelicalism? Discerning a New Faithfulness for Mission: Towards an Evangelical Political Theology* (2011) offers a critique of distortions he finds within American evangelicalism.

This chapter will also explore another facet of evangelicalism. Since the Fundamentalist-Modernist controversy, evangelicalism has been plagued by an awkward relationship between reason and revelation. Many evangelicals, it will be shown, have created bounded set ideologies that continue to inhibit the work of the Holy Spirit—the one who can ease their rational anxiety. This chapter will utilize Miller's teaching on the marks of a Spirit-filled life to suggest a path of spiritual formation that employs the fruit of the Spirit (Gal 5:22–23).[1] Pertinent exegetical scholarship will be used to offer the reader a contextual understanding of the importance of these characteristics for the Christian journey. This path of spiritual formation will be applied to the bounded sets described to show how it assists in moving toward a centered set theological approach. The center, the heart of the Christian journey, is life with God.

Miller's theological epistemology of Word-Spirit Ecclesial Revelationalism serves as an essential hermeneutical framework to allow reason to submit to revelation and assuage the anxiety that exists for evangelicals regarding the Bible. At the conclusion of this chapter, and the project as a whole, it will be presented that Miller assists Brethren, and evangelicals by the influence of the Brethren, to embrace evidence of faith that are not mere intellectual assent but are manifest in an embodied theology that is inner and outer, individual and corporate, and shaped by Word and Spirit. Before such an understanding of certainty can be appreciated, it is helpful to understand the current evangelical landscape.

Defining Evangelicalism and Identifying Distortions

In 2010, Scot McKnight, professor of New Testament at Northern Seminary and author of the "Jesus Creed" blog, authored a post responding to an article in *Christianity Today* about the role of Al Mohler, president of Southern Baptist Theological Seminary, as a reformer in American Christianity and American evangelicalism especially.[2] McKnight saw the article, which was a

---

1. Miller, *Christian Doctrine*, 99–102. *Doctrine* Miller's lecture notes are especially important on this topic. A central focus of this chapter will be Miller's discussion of the marks of a spiritual life. His reflections were noted briefly in chapter 5.

2. See Worthen, "The Reformer," 18–25.

cover story for the magazine, as a sign of the shift occurring in evangelicalism at large. He lamented:

> Evangelicalism is changing. What used to be called "fundamentalist" is now occupied by the word "evangelical" and we have in the case of Mohler a genuine fundamentalist—and I'm using this word analytically and not derisively—who is reshaping evangelicalism because he's reshaping the [Southern Baptist Church]. A number of folks in this article call Mohler a fundamentalist. The term fits . . . a part of evangelicalism. . . . What we also are witnessing is the end of generous evangelicalism, what I often call Big Tent Evangelicalism that has been noted by a coalition of gospel-oriented people.[3]

The end of "generous evangelicalism," McKnight noted, comes with a cost. Those who found safety and community in the "Big Tent" of evangelicalism are increasingly finding themselves without a home.

> This new story of evangelicalism is sad for people like me who have always believed Evangelicalism was a Big Tent coalition of those committed to the basics of the gospel but more than willing to tolerate differences on all kinds of levels. Evangelicalism for many of us has been a generous evangelicalism. As I said above the numbers are on the side of the older Big Tent coalition, but there is a major, major problem: the old guard coalition is not composed of fighters. They've only known peace and cooperation. What is perhaps the secret here is that many of us became evangelicals to escape fundamentalism. For us, there's no turning back, which means we may find ourselves disenfranchised from evangelicalism.[4]

McKnight, now Anglican with strong Anabaptist sympathies, has sought a recovery, or possibly even a rediscovery, of evangelicalism as a "Big Tent coalition." He desires for the term "evangelical" to overcome bounded-set expressions that have long held evangelicalism hostage. The "Big Tent" McKnight desires, is a centered set approach to evangelical theology that allows for a plurality of views on nonessentials and centers on the person of Jesus Christ as understood by core, fundamental truths.

Such an approach to theology produces an environment of hospitality rather than one of defense. As will be show, a centered set theological approach is difficult in environments shaped solely by rationalism. The "new story" that McKnight is describing is one in which hyper-rational

3. McKnight, "Shifting," lines 1–3.
4. McKnight, "Shifting," lines 1–3.

evangelical scholarship has produced bounded set approaches to evangelical membership that distort the "old guard" mentality. This "new guard" desires greater clarity of evangelical identity and in their intellectual pursuit of that identity, often overlook the lived posture that was indicative of earlier evangelicals. These new evangelicals, shaped by a Baptist-Reformed paradigm, move away from a simple gospel-orientation to a rationalistic, bounded set anxiety regarding an evangelical understanding of the gospel.

Donald Dayton elucidates the distortion that McKnight has found and similarly finds two paradigms within evangelicalism. In an article entitled "The Search for Historical Evangelicalism," Dayton names the two paradigms of evangelical history: "One emphasizing its Puritan and Presbyterian roots, as in Protestant Orthodoxy and scholasticism, and the other emphasizing its Pietist and Pentecostal roots, as in the Wesleyan-Holiness movement."[5] Inspired by Dayton's assessment, both Christian Collins-Winn and Roger Olson have attempted to retrieve a Pietist evangelical witness in their book *Reclaiming Pietism: Retrieving an Evangelical Tradition* (2015).[6] In their survey of the history of Pietism, which they correctly identify as constitutive of evangelicalism, they categorize Dayton's two paradigms as the "Puritan-Presbyterian paradigm" and the "Pietist-Pentecostal paradigm."[7] The Puritan-Presbyterian strand has stressed theological accuracy and doctrinal purity. The Pietist-Pentecostal strand has emphasized religious experience alongside doctrinal purity by detailing the experiential nature of doctrine and calling for a greater sensitivity to the Holy Spirit and the role of transformational experience in theological pursuits.

---

5. Dayton, "Historical Evangelicalism," 12–33.

6. Collins-Winn and Olson provide a wonderful survey of Pietist history and its influence on American evangelicalism. For more, see Olson and Collins-Winn, *Reclaiming Pietism*. A glaring omission in the book, for students of Pietism, is Radical Pietism. There are themes from Radical Pietism that have often run amok in American evangelicalism. The omission of a visible ecclesiology is one of the most glaring inheritances. While the book can cherry-pick Pietist sketches that suit its larger purpose, the book is still important to balance the often Reformed-Puritan history of evangelicalism. There is a robust Pietist inheritance in American evangelicalism and Collins-Winn and Olson reveal it for their readers (while hiding the more radical expressions). Collins-Winn and his colleague at Bethel University, Chris Gehrz, have sought to strengthen scholarship on Pietism and American Christianity. An annual conference is held at Bethel University in St. Paul, Minnesota, on Pietism's intersection with American Christianity. Lectures from the first conference were published for broader distribution. See Christian T. Collins-Winn, Christopher Gehrz, G. William Carlson, and Eric Horst, eds. *The Pietist Impulse in Christianity*. Eugene, OR: Wipf & Stock Publishers, 2011. Gehrz has even edited a book on a Pietist vision for Christian higher education. See Gehrz, *Pietist Vision*. Gehrz and his pastor, Mark Pattie, later published a less academic work geared toward a wider audience to share a vision for a Pietist, public theology. See Gehrz and Pattie, *Pietist Option*.

7. Olson and Collins-Winn, *Reclaiming Pietism*, 113.

In alignment with McKnight's observations earlier regarding the Southern Baptist approach to evangelicalism, it is probably better to rearticulate Dayton's "Puritan-Presbyterian" paradigm as "Baptist-Reformed." Scholarship from Mohler and others is often quite rationalistic and the scholarship is shaped by a bounded set approach to theology. This paradigm has become quite dominant in evangelical scholarship. This one of the reasons that while Pietism is recognized as having an influence on evangelical identity, very little scholarship has been done on such its impact. There are many reasons for the supplanting of Pietist evangelicalism by this more Reformed evangelicalism. Reformed Christianity has a greater propensity for scholasticism that has fared better in Western societies. Theological precision has held greater appeal in societies shaped by the Enlightenment. The historic irony, however, is that many Reformed expressions of evangelicalism are more Calvinist than John Calvin (1509–1564) himself.[8]

With these two streams of evangelical identity, often perceived as an antagonism, at the heart of American evangelicalism, it is difficult to define. If one is to attempt to chart a new engagement with evangelicalism, however, it is imperative to have a working definition of what *it* is. When attempting to define *it*, Olson and Collins-Winn suggest that it depends on whom you ask. The most widely used definition is that of British historian David Bebbington. The "Bebbington Quadrilateral," as it is known, pulls four streams together in its working definition. Bebbington writes:

> There are four qualities that have been the special marks of Evangelical religion: *conversionism*, the belief that lives need to be changed; *activism*, the expression of the gospel in effort; *biblicism*, a particular regard for the Bible, and what may be called *crucicentrism*, a stress on the sacrifice of Christ on the cross. Together they form a quadrilateral of priorities that is the basis of Evangelicalism.[9]

The definition can be deceiving as many have argued that it simply defines biblical Christianity. If this is the case, they contend, it is not nuanced enough for the purpose of rigorous scholarship on evangelical identity.

While there is truth to such claims, there is still value in Bebbington's work as it can elucidate some of the more popular and problematic expressions of American evangelicalism. Conversionism is easily recognized as a "conversion experience." Biblicism can be reduced to Restorationist

---

8. As noted in chapter 3, John Calvin himself, not one to be seen as indifferent to the revelation of Scripture, argued for the internal witness of the Spirit. See Calvin, *Institutes*, 1.7.4–5.

9. Bebbington, *Evangelicalism in Modern Britain*, 3.

sentiments, as evidenced in a historic Brethren slogan from the nineteenth century, of "the Bible, the whole Bible, and nothing but the Bible."[10] Activism is understood as a concern for evangelism and missions. Crucicentrism is demonstrated in the centrality of the cross and the atonement in evangelical thought. Yet its truncated version is noted in revivalist hymns like "Nothing but the Blood" which link Christ's sacrifice on the cross to one's personal decision at the altar. Bebbington, being generous in his appraisal of the global movement, chose to describe its essence to these four overarching characteristics. His work will be discussed later in this chapter to further explore the distortions mentioned. What these distortions demonstrate is a pervasive anxiety evident in evangelical scholarship about itself and its engagement with society.

Molly Worthen suggests that some of this anxiety within evangelicalism stems from a crisis of authority that, in her view, stands at the center of the evangelical mind. Evangelical intellectual history "is peppered with compromises, sleights of hand, and defensive maneuvers, a combination of pragmatism and idealism that has made evangelicalism one of the most dynamic and powerful phenomena in Christian history, as well as a minefield for independent thought."[11] Her central contention is that evangelicals are stuck in a permanent and insoluble predicament as they are caught between the claims of rival authorities, both within and without.

Faith, experience, and reason all compete for supremacy in the evangelical mind. Worthen argues that modern evangelicalism wants to hold fast to the faith and also earn the respect of the secular academy because it was born in an existential and epistemological crisis because of a perceived antagonism between revelation and reason. She characterizes evangelicals as

---

10. The Restoration Movement developed from several independent streams of revivalism of the nineteenth century that idealized early Christianity. Two groups, which independently developed similar approaches to the Christian faith, were particularly important. The first, led by Barton W. Stone (1772–1844), began at Cane Ridge, Kentucky, and identified simply as "Christians." The second began in western Pennsylvania and Virginia (now West Virginia) and was led by Thomas Campbell (1763–1854) and his son, Alexander Campbell (1788–1866). They eventually named their respective movement the "Disciples of Christ." Both groups sought to restore the whole Christian church on the pattern set forth in the New Testament and both believed that creeds kept Christianity divided. Phrases like "no creed but the Bible" and "the Bible, the whole Bible, and nothing but the Bible" marked these Restoration Movement groups. Among other things, they were united in the belief that Jesus Christ was the Son of God, that Christians should celebrate the Lord's Supper on the first day of each week, and that baptism of adult believers by immersion in water was a necessary condition for salvation. For more on the Restoration Movement, see Foster and Dunnavant, *Encyclopedia of the Stone-Campbell Movement*.

11. Worthen, *Apostles of Reason*, 2.

the children of both Pietism and the Enlightenment. Therefore, evangelicals are the offspring of estranged parents who "behave like orphans."[12]

While there is much to appreciate in Worthen's assessment and her focused critique of the apparent estrangement between Pietism and the Enlightenment, her assessment is ironically blind to the very wing of evangelicalism that stresses the "Christian worldview" that stands at the center of her critique, namely, the Reformed wing. Her criticism of the Reformed inheritance within American evangelicalism utilizes language that is innate to Reformed theology's assessment of Pietism. An exploration of the Pietist wing of American evangelicalism would strengthen her project as it could speak into the three anxieties she finds as central to evangelical identity. Rather than core beliefs (i.e., Bebbington) she proposes that what unites evangelicals are three dilemmas:

1. How to reconcile faith and reason—differentiating knowledge attained by faith, a hallmark of Pietism, from that attained by reason, a hallmark of the Enlightenment.

2. The nature of true salvation—what does it mean to have an authentic relationship with Jesus?

3. How is private faith reconciled with the secular, public square?[13]

These three questions frustrate evangelicalism as the movement wrestles with how it matters to the world all while trying to make sense of its own identity.

Worthen is correct to note central anxieties in evangelical identity in America and Olson would trace those anxieties to the reality that no one owns the label "evangelical." "Neither the NAE (National Association of Evangelicals) nor the Gospel Coalition nor any organization *owns* the label 'evangelical,'" he observes.[14] He then recommends an important difference between "movement evangelicalism" and "ethos evangelicalism."[15] *Movement evangelicalism* has a tendency of being hijacked by societal ideologies and antagonisms. For proof of this, one only needs to witness American evangelicalism's identification with a white, male Republican voting base.[16] When evangelicalism becomes a movement, Olson notes, it is often rejected by subsequent generations and by those perceived to be in the minority view

12. Worthen, *Apostles of Reason*, 6.
13. Worthen, *Apostles of Reason*, 5.
14. Olson, "Is Evangelicalism White?," lines 5–7.
15. Olson, "Evangelicalism Again," lines 10–12.
16. Olson, "Evangelicalism Again," line 13.

on politics, government, and social issues. *Ethos evangelicalism* is more in line with Bebbington's quadrilateral. It is tethered to a few core theological commitments that afford a diversity of expression. It is this *ethos* expression that McKnight longed for in his article for *Christianity Today*. Olson identifies five areas of concern within evangelicalism that must be addressed to transition from a *movement* to *ethos* expression.

1. Anti-intellectual perspective—evangelicals have been suspicious of higher education outside their respective institutions thus ghettoizing their thought from larger engagement with society.

2. Hero-worship—in the absence of central doctrinal commitments, evangelicals have tended to gravitate toward personalities, thus defining themselves by mega-churches and their respective pastors.

3. Tendency to eschew organized efforts at social reconstruction—this exposes a deeper issue for many evangelicals with liberation theology. Evangelicals have developed unhelpful dichotomies between evangelism and social justice thus revealing a significant way in which the movement (not ethos) has been shaped by the Enlightenment.

4. Christ-against-culture approach—borrowed from H. Richard Niebuhr's postures of Christianity toward culture, evangelicals have adopted this stance that remains suspicious of the arts.[17]

5. Spiritual elitism toward mainline—evangelicals consistently present themselves as the rightful heirs of the Reformation, claiming that only they hold both doctrine and piety together.[18]

From the Puritan-Presbyterian (or Baptist-Reformed) paradigm these concerns are forged out of the insistence of evangelical scholarship on doctrinal precision. From the Pietist-Pentecostal paradigm these core issues are founded on a belief that intellectual assent must be coupled with a warm-hearted piety. Thus, the core of American evangelicalism is often a movement, using this description in Olson's sense, that refuses to understand the central paradox of its own existence—Reformed *and* Pietist. In its pursuit

---

17. H. Richard Niebuhr's classic book, *Christ and Culture*, has influenced or at least informed the discussion, notably among Western evangelicals, since it was published in 1951. Niebuhr proposed five models, which he labelled as (1) Christ against culture; (2) Christ of culture; (3) Christ above culture; (4) Christ and culture in paradox; and (5) Christ the transformer of culture. The Christ *against* culture approach was the approach Niebuhr argued groups like the Mennonites held toward culture. Those of this posture have well defined lines of demarcation between the church and the surrounding culture. See Niebuhr, *Christ and Culture*.

18. Olson, "Dark Side," lines 6–8.

to quell rational anxiety, the dominant evangelical paradigm retrieved has been the Reformed, and often more conservative, stream of evangelicalism.

In response, Olson calls for a postconservative evangelical theology that is by and large a derivation of the Pietist side of American evangelicalism.[19] Postconservatives view evangelicalism as a centered rather than a bounded set. "The question [then]," Olson notes, "is not who is 'in' and who is 'out' but who is nearer the center and who is moving away from it."[20] Authentic evangelicalism, he argues, "is defined by its center which is Jesus Christ and the gospel."[21] Here, however, Olson is quick to note that the center includes the four Bebbington commitments plus one that he finds important. From Bebbington come commitments to biblicism, conversionism, crucicentrism, and activism in missions and social transformation. Olson argues that a deferential respect for historic Christian orthodoxy is essential to tether theological reflection to a community that transcends the present unless theology be held hostage to the imperialism of the present.[22]

As Olson further observes, postconservative evangelical theology approaches theological reflection and the Bible with six pre-understandings. First, it finds the goal of theological education to be transformation, inner to outer. While cognitive study of theology is part of theological education, it must never be the ultimate goal. Second, theological reflection is best understood as a journey or pilgrimage over against propositional understandings of truth. If our core truth is Jesus Christ, then our pursuit in theology must be relational and nimble like that required of a pilgrimage—there is a plan of study but there is an openness to mystery and new light along the way. Third, postconservatives have a great discomfort with modernity and find that many evangelicals do not often realize the subtle ways their theological pursuits have been shaped by and founded upon modernistic assumptions.

Fourth, the centered set, as mentioned earlier, animates postconservative evangelical theology. If evangelicals profess biblical Christianity, then Jesus, revealed by both the Bible and the Spirit must remain the only center of their faith. Doctrine must be conversant with fresh ways of experiencing him in the life of the church. Fifth, doctrine is as much an experiential

---

19. This is not to say that conservative evangelical theology is not influenced by Pietism; many conservative evangelical theologians are pietistic in their personal lives of devotion. Nor is it to say that postconservative evangelical theologians lack any interest in Protestant orthodoxy; many of them express strong appreciation for the contributions of orthodox theologians of the past. Unfortunately, there is often a split between doctrine and devotion on the conservative side.

20. Olson, *Reformed and Always Reforming*, loc. 925.

21. Olson, *Reformed and Always Reforming*, loc. 925.

22. Olson, *Reformed and Always Reforming*, loc. 925.

pursuit as it is cognitive/propositional inquiry. Doctrine that does not influence the lived experience of a people devolves into ideology. Doctrine that is embodied by core practices reveals an experiential truth that continues to transform the life of the faith community by the power of the Spirit. Sixth, and final, there is a respect for the broad tradition of Christianity, often identified as the "Great Tradition" of the Christian faith. The confessions of both the Apostles' Creed and the Nicene Creed serve as helpful parameters to tether the faith community. Such a standard connects the church to a spiritual community that transcends the modern era.[23]

Postconservative evangelicalism aptly reflects Miller's theological method. Furthermore, Miller embodies all of the characteristics of postconservative evangelicalism. His writings reveal a pedagogy geared toward transformation. Over against the rational foundationalism of both Fundamentalist and liberal theologians he is steadfast in his belief in the authority of the Holy Spirit. His centered set approach is noted by his radical insistence on the centrality of Jesus for theology. While his writings are systematic, they never favor doctrinal precision at the expense of a lived theology. Finally, Miller is quite deferential to the Great Tradition of the church and often uses it to better hone and nuance the distinctives of the Brethren Church.

It should come as no surprise, then, that Miller offers helpful correctives to the modernistic distortions of Bebbington's criteria. According to theologian David Fitch, Bebbington's criteria have suffered modernistic reduction and have become hollow signifiers within American evangelicalism. In regard to evangelicalism's high view of Scripture, over against the German historical-critical attacks on the reliability of Scripture that caused Fundamentalist anxiety, many conservative Protestants asserted various doctrines of the *inerrancy* of Scripture. This view gave an opportunity for Fundamentalists to champion biblical authority against a perceived liberal assault.

The evangelical emphasis on personal conversion was distorted by the revivalist inheritance of evangelicalism and became a "decision for Christ" made often as a response to an altar call. This was firmly welded to a commitment to the substitutionary atoning work of Christ on the cross during the Fundamentalist-Modernist controversy. Any semblance of social salvation was rebuffed and the centrality of the horrific death of Christ was magnified to eschew any notion of salvation apart from the salvific work of Christ. Thus, Fitch collapses conversionism and crucicentrism into the "decision for Christ" that still animates large portions of popular

---

23. Olson, *Reformed and Always Reforming*, loc. 925.

evangelicalism.[24] Ironically, Fitch does not address activism. As mentioned earlier, many evangelical approach evangelism and missions, and presently social action, from this core evangelical impulse. If evangelicals have concern regarding their engagement with society, then perhaps this is an area for further reflection by Fitch and others. For the purposes of this chapter, Fitch's articulated truncations will remain as they capture the reductionistic approach that evangelical scholarship imposes on itself as it seeks to make sense of its own identity. Therefore, the following chart illustrates Fitch's understanding of modernistic distortions to Bebbington's characteristics. A truncated, hyper-private witness emerges focused on a specific understanding of biblical authority and "getting saved."

Bebbington Criteria	Modernistic Distortion
Biblicism—Bible as Authoritative	Biblical Inerrancy
Conversionism/Crucicentrism[25]	Personal Decision for Christ

For Fitch, the damage of these modernistic reductions has made American evangelicalism a shell of historic evangelicalism:

> In the process, [evangelicals] gave up the true core of [their] Christian politics—the person and work of Jesus Christ—and set [themselves] up for a fall by in essence becoming a form of "religious ideology." [They] in essence emptied [their] social politic of its core in Jesus Christ for a politics buttressed by the temporary structures of modernity.[26]

Miller's thought can provide a healthy corrective to this distorted politic in current evangelicalism. His theology stresses the importance of the church—a church which serves as a hermeneutical community that is

---

24. It is important to note that Fitch is disagreeing with popular expressions of evangelicalism. While there are robust networks of evangelical scholarship, the evangelical expression that seems to animate many evangelical churches seems embedded in revivalistic methodologies. If evangelical churches are to become more theologically reflective, then it is imperative that works like Fitch's assist with the translation needed from the academy to the pew. Fitch's role in such reflection would be aided by articulating the role of activism in evangelical theology which would prove quite helpful in addressing his perceived evangelical anxiety regarding engagement with society. His interlocutor seems to be revivalist evangelicalism though he never mentions that by name.

25. Miller offers helpful nuance and correction regarding evangelical approaches to the atonement. For further study on Miller's understanding of the atonement, see chapter 4.

26. Fitch, *End of Evangelicalism?*, loc. 16. Fitch would identify the Bebbington characteristics as the hallmarks of this evangelical expression.

always exegeting both Scripture and culture together. The church is "a body of believers in Christ who have been called out of the world, who have been born again of the Holy Spirit and are, therefore, alive in Christ, and who, under the authority of Christ, are accomplishing the will of God on earth and among men."[27]

Fitch's ideas align with Miller's and begs his readers to embrace the

> need [for] a politic that embodies the integrity of [evangelical] existence "in Christ" incarnationally for God's mission in the world. [Evangelicals] need a restoring of the ontological core of [their] political existence in the life of the triune God that carries its own integrity. This is the path towards [their] political life in the world becoming evangelical again. . . . For if this is what takes shape among . . . evangelicals, [they] will not only hold onto the heritage of orthodoxy that [they] claim, [they] will also be shaped politically into Christ and what God is doing for his mission in the world.[28]

Fitch contends that while Bebbington's criteria are useful in their broad characterization, they run the risk of being shaped by modernity because they fail to communicate, either explicitly or implicitly, an ecclesiological witness. Therefore, while Bebbington's quadrilateral succinctly, yet broadly, communicates global, evangelical commitments, the distortions communicate baggage from the Fundamentalist-Modernist controversy of the early twentieth century. Miller's Word-Spirit Communal Revelationalism offers an important correction to these distortions:

Bebbington Criteria	Modernistic Distortion	Miller's Corrective
Biblicism	Inerrancy	Christocentric Hermeneutic
Conversionism/ Crucicentrism	Decision for Christ	Conversionary Discipleship

By recognizing Christ as the authority of the Bible, Miller is able to champion a christocentric hermeneutic. Also, his writings challenge the deeply held practice of the "decision for Christ" by articulating a conversionary discipleship model of salvation. Each of these correctives flows out of his reverence for and devotional trust in the Bible.

---

27. Miller, *Christian Doctrine*, 103.
28. Fitch, *End of Evangelicalism*, loc. 129.

Biblical Inerrancy to Christocentric Hermeneutic

Biblicism among certain American evangelical groups has become synonymous with inerrancy. While Miller never mentions inerrancy, he does provide a necessary corrective to such an understanding of the Bible. While his writings are not primarily concerned with epistemology (how we know the Bible is authoritative) they do provide an epistemic approach that Craig Keener has identified as a "Spirit epistemology." Such a theological epistemology does not aim to merely "inherit the right worldview [but seeks to discern the right] frame of mind given by the Spirit."[29] Miller's theological writings reveal a hermeneutic that takes both the humanity and divinity of Christ seriously and thus finds the Bible to be both a human *and* divine vessel of the revelation of Jesus Christ. It is a hermeneutic of trust in rather than suspicion of Scripture. It is founded on both an objective, historic reality—the birth, life, and death of Jesus—and also a fideism—trust in the authority of Scripture that claims that only the Spirit can empower us to accept. Therefore, the gospel is both a narration of God's activity and an inspired interpretation by the Spirit who, as Craig Keener maintains, confirms by faith what is founded on historical evidence,

> which is consistent with the mind of the Spirit, [as] an epistemic commitment. Evidence may be sufficient to invite belief, but rarely would thinkers today claim that evidence compels belief; belief involves a decision. Even when it often produces unconscious recognition of the truth, this recognition does not compel adherence that acts as if the recognized reality is true. Christian scholars sometimes guard their moral life but surrender their intellectual life to the world's skepticism. If Christ is Lord of our lives, however, his realm must include our intellect.[30]

Similarly, Steven Sherman argues that a healthy, theological epistemology must be one that is able to transcend the largely "text-only basis for theological knowledge [of much of evangelicalism]."[31] Such an epistemology must contain "symbol, metaphor, mystery, embodiment, and story [as] powerful ways into the truth of the knowledge of God."[32] Allowing these epistemic influences permits us to embrace faith and humility and move away from facts alone and overconfidence—products of empiricism.

---

29. Keener, *Spirit Hermeneutics*, 176.
30. Keener, *Spirit Hermeneutics*, 162–63.
31. Sherman, *Theological Epistemology*, 252.
32. Sherman, *Theological Epistemology*, 252.

Therefore, Sherman argues, "we must move beyond an exclusively textual referent with respect to the knowledge of God."[33]

Likewise, sociologist Christian Smith calls for evangelicals to reject biblicism, not to be confused with Bebbington's language, that posits that the Bible can be understood by a literal reading. By "biblicism" Smith means a "particular theory about and style of using the Bible that is defined by a constellation of related assumptions and beliefs about the Bible's nature, purpose, and function."[34] That constellation is represented by ten assumptions or beliefs:

1. *Divine Writing:* The Bible, down to the details of its words, consists of and is identical with God's very own words written inerrantly in human language.

2. *Total Representation:* The Bible represents the totality of God's communication to and will for humanity, both in containing all that God has to say to humans and in being the exclusive mode of God's true communication.

3. *Complete Coverage:* The divine will about all of the issues relevant to Christian belief and life are contained in the Bible.

4. *Democratic Perspicuity:* Any reasonably intelligent person can read the Bible in his or her own language and correctly understand the plain meaning of the text.

5. *Commonsense Hermeneutics:* The best way to understand biblical texts is by reading them in their explicit, plain, most obvious, literal sense, as the author intended them at face value, which may or may not involve considering their literary, cultural, and historical contexts.

6. *"Solo Scriptura":* The significance of any given biblical text can be understood without reliance on creeds, confessions, historical church traditions, or other forms of larger theological hermeneutical frameworks, such that theological formulations can be built up directly out of the Bible from scratch.

7. *Internal Harmony:* All related passages of the Bible on any given subject fit together almost like puzzle pieces into single, unified, internally consistent bodies of instruction about right and wrong beliefs and behaviors.

---

33. Sherman, *Theological Epistemology*, 252.
34. Smith, *Bible Made Impossible*, loc. 205.

8. *Universal Applicability:* What the biblical authors taught God's people at any point in history remains universally valid for all Christians at every other time, unless explicitly revoked by subsequent scriptural teaching.

9. *Inductive Method:* All matters of Christian belief and practice can be learned by sitting down with the Bible and piecing together through careful study the clear "biblical" truths that it teaches.

10. *Handbook Model:* The Bible teaches doctrine and morals with every affirmation that it makes, so that together those affirmations comprise something like a handbook or textbook for Christian belief and living, a compendium of divine and therefore inerrant teachings on a full array of subjects—including science, economics, health, politics, and romance.[35]

In response to Smith's "constellation," Miller would have affirmed the divine inspiration of the biblical writers but would not have bypassed the role of interpretation by the Spirit from their time to that of modern audiences. His writings never make the argument that the Bible is the total representation of God's communication as this would significantly undermine the importance and centrality of the revelation of Jesus Christ. With confidence in this fundamental revelation, his liberal arts approach to truth, that was evidenced by a penchant for philosophy, allowed him to grapple with theological issues from many angles instead of appealing to Scripture alone for all answers.

While Miller would agree with Smith's assessment regarding "democratic perspicuity," he would have held that the central revelation of the Bible, the person of Jesus, is accessible to all. Furthermore, the role of community is essential in maintaining the fidelity to Scripture. Later in his book, Smith remarks that a christocentric hermeneutic is how the church best responds to biblicism. Miller would have affirmed this response and invited the community into the discernment and application of such a hermeneutic. Miller would have appreciated Smith's concerns over a "commonsense hermeneutic." Miller invested his life into the development of pastors and teachers of Scripture at both Ashland College and Seminary. While the biblical application can, and should, be done by every member of the church, not just the clergy, it is also important not to avoid the complexity of Scripture or stifle those voices that could serve as guides—especially those who have pursued theological education. Additionally, believers must include the voice of the Holy Spirit discerned in community.

35. Smith, *Bible Made Impossible*, loc. 205.

Smith's comments on "solo Scriptura" and "internal harmony" would have made Miller perk up. Miller's writings would challenge Smith's claims regarding the need for creeds and confessions from two fronts. The first would be the absence of community from Smith's assessment. The community gathered around the Word and empowered by the Spirit produces not a static creed of intellectual assent but a robust, dynamic and living interpretation of Scripture for the ongoing edification of the community of faith. Regarding the harmony of the Bible, Smith reveals a highly rational challenge to such a formation. Brethren, influenced by their Pietist witness, would have interpreted the various parts of the Bible in light of the whole narrative of Scripture. While Miller would agree with Smith's later christocentric hermeneutic, his Brethren heritage would challenge the consistency of Smith's refutation of an *internal harmony* to the Bible. If no such harmony exists, as Smith seems to allude, then how does a christocentric hermeneutic manifest a coherent, overarching interpretation of Scripture? Smith's conspicuous absence of the role of community neuters the application of the very hermeneutic that he argues best responds to the biblicism he finds in evangelical churches. It is this absence of community that makes Smith's rebuttal to biblicism rather anemic.

Regarding the "universal applicability" of the Bible, Miller would have argued that this can occur but does not happen by bypassing the role of communal interpretation. Interpretation is the method by which the Spirit is invited into biblical reflection. Consequently, it is this same Spirit that fosters the environment necessary for the words of Scripture to pierce our hearts as the Spirit makes the Bible authoritative. Like the two strands of DNA's double-helix, Word *and* Spirit make the revelation of Jesus Christ universally relevant. It is the revelation that is universally applicable.

Related to the applicability of Scripture, Miller would not have negated an "inductive method" to the Bible but would have cautioned against principles of interpretation becoming a creed for the believer. In one's experience of Christ, certain values and principles may be discerned from the reading of Scripture. Those principles should be discussed in community to discern the context for such a "word" from the Lord. The issue for Miller would not have been an inductive methodology, in and of itself, but the propensity to apply principles discerned for the individual onto the community minus a process of communal discernment. Such application can quickly devolve into legalism which was antithetical to Miller's theology. This is why Miller would have not been as threatened by the use of the Bible as a handbook (of sorts). Scripture offers us the clearest revelation of Christ. Brethren, of all generations, have approached the Gospels, especially, as a handbook for living like Christ. Smith seems to be reacting to a more Reformed understanding of biblical engagement that seeks to find principles within the Bible to shape a perceived "worldview."

Miller, in alignment with his Brethren heritage, would have contended that the Bible does not necessarily shape a worldview but invites us to reflect on the mind of Christ discerned in community by the power of the Spirit. "Worldview" theologies seek to deduce rational truth claims that are then applied in the workplace, relationships, etc. Miller and the Brethren would argue that the central revelation of Christ shapes individuals in community for an alternative witness to the world collectively. Where *worldview* perspectives can quickly become individualistic, Miller and the Brethren would argue that the end goal of spiritual formation is not individual believers having greater faith expression in their respective spheres of influence, but, rather, a community that testifies to a reality greater than itself. This alternative witness is at the heart of Brethren ecclesiology.

While Miller would agree with much of Smith's critique, the bogeyman in Smith's theological closet is a hyper-Reformed expression of evangelicalism that is not the same evangelical witness that animates the Brethren or Miller. Miller's Anabaptist-Pietist faith would nuance Smith's thought all while calling Brethren to the same christocentric hermeneutic that Smith recommends. This hermeneutic would have allowed Miller to both agree and nuance the tension inherent in Smith's constellation between reason and revelation. Where modernity, and its use of foundationalism, has created a false dichotomy through these two sources of theological knowledge. Miller's Word-Spirit Communal Revelationalism is quite comfortable with the tension between revelation and reason finding it to be, as mentioned in the last chapter, a source of creativity rather than a source of division and harm. It is a theological framework that is both rational and spiritual—so long as the inherent tension submits and finds its resolution in the revelation of Jesus Christ. Similarly, Smith proposes:

> The purpose, center, and interpretive key to scripture is Jesus. . . . Truly believing that Jesus Christ is the real purpose, center, and interpretive key to scripture causes one to read the Bible in a way that is very different than believing the Bible to be an instruction manual containing universally applicable divine oracles concerning every possible subject it seems to address.[36]

Miller held the same standard of authority for the Bible. His understanding of Scripture was not found in the perfection of reason (Protestant liberalism) nor in a quasi-rational proof of the veracity of the Bible

---

36. Smith, *Bible Made Impossible*, loc. 1989.

(Fundamentalism). Instead, Miller centered the authority of Scripture in the person of Jesus—a christocentric hermeneutic.

> But one of the strongest evidences of the Inspiration and authority of the Old Testament writings is found in the testimony of Jesus and the Apostles. Jesus Christ as a witness cannot be impeached. Possessed of the Spirit of God without measure; coming into the world to bear witness to the Truth; proving by His works that He was the Messiah; teaching as one having authority, we feel confident of the infallible truth of His testimony. And what is the testimony Jesus bears in the Scriptures? By a careful reading of the four records of the Gospel, we find Jesus everywhere speaking of the Scriptures as the Word of God. Jesus certainly regarded the Scriptures as clothed with divine authority, and infallibly safe when He thus used them.[37]

Miller's Word-Spirit Communal Revelationalism allowed the Bible to be a living, transformative record of God's acts and an ongoing inspired standard for the life of the faith community. Jesus is both the authority of Scripture and testimony to the authority of Scripture. By shifting from an inerrant approach to Scripture to one that captures the centrality of Jesus as its source of authority, Miller's hermeneutical approach can show that a process of ongoing conversion through discipleship is a better model of salvation than the punctiliar "decision for Christ." Salvation is a continual process of being transformed into the likeness of Christ.

Decision for Christ to Conversionary Discipleship

A central aspect of evangelical religion in America has been the "decision for Christ." The *decision* has become the embodiment of the evangelical importance of conversion. Many modern theologians, even many evangelicals, have provided critiques of this core practice within evangelicalism. It is as a piece of evangelicalism's inheritance from the revivalist services of the nineteenth and twentieth centuries. The signature ritual of these services was some form of an "altar call," where one decided to put their faith in Christ. Upon making a "decision," the individual was called into the "Spirit-filled life"—a subsequent decision to live daily in dependence upon the Holy Spirit.[38]

Fitch cites the philosopher Slavoj Žižek and his work within semiotics—the study of language and symbols—to reveal how this "decision for

---

37. Miller, *Christian Doctrine*, 121.

38. This is a product of the Keswick influence on revivalism. For more on this, see chapter 3.

Christ" has become what Žižek identifies as a "master-signifier—a conceptual object around which people give their allegiance thereby enabling a political group to form."[39] While the efficacy of an altar call can be debated, the point is that a contextual expression became calcified and the central theological motif dropped out leaving a hollow signifier that no longer accomplishes what many evangelicals would like it to achieve.

The desire is for life transformation. Yet the danger of "hollow signifiers" is evidenced by sacramentalism (or the centrality of a specific mode of an ordinance minus the necessary theological framework to inform it). The mode ends up replacing the meaning. Modes are practices and expressions that serve to connect people back to the larger framework of their identity. When these expressions are disconnected from their meaning, they become calcified and hollow. While these specific expressions and practices shape behavior, they do not provide the transformation that only the meaning of such practices can supply. Modes are often time specific. Yet once they become calcified, they fail to create the life transformation desired and inadvertently position people for nostalgia or legalism.

The "decision" is an expression of such a hollow signifier. The initial mode was tied to a deeper meaning of one committing their life to Christ. It was a practice that viscerally acknowledged one's decision to follow Jesus. What has occurred in many evangelical churches and camps is that a fear of "going to hell" has supplanted this attitude of commitment. At one time, there was an acknowledged of life in Christ as one went forward to give their life to Christ. Now there is only an understanding of *eternal* life that has little impact on the present—rather than assuaging doubts of eternity present to the individual in the moment. Furthermore, these converts are shaped for self-preservation rather than the witness that Christ calls the church to have in the world. The central gospel command to follow Christ, even to death, is lost by an altar call message of saving oneself from the calamity of the world.[40]

The environment that produced the "decision" was one with which Miller was conversant. He heard the revivalistic-fundamentalist reduction of salvation to a *decision* and also heard the ethical demands of liberal

39. Fitch, *End of Evangelicalism?*, loc. 26. Fitch also argues that biblical inerrancy and the idea of a Christian nation also serve as master-signifiers for American evangelicalism. For more on Žižek's thought on "master-signifiers." See Žižek, *Sublime Object of Ideology*.

40. It is important to note that some altar call messages are more about being called to commit or recommit oneself to Christ. It's important to note that often times these appeals have an emotional appeal of needing to "find Jesus" once again. The emotional rhetoric is more about self-preservation and anxiety rather than a call to be on mission with Christ in the world.

theologians stressing the life of Jesus over against any substitutionary understanding of the atonement. Unlike both camps (fundamentalist and liberal), Miller stressed that while a new birth is necessary, it is but the beginning. In a section of his writings on salvation entitled "The Divine Ideal Set before the Christian," he writes:

> The saving work of grace conceived of as beginning in the new life in Christ Jesus is not regarded as fully accomplished in these initial acts. These are indispensable and primary conditions to salvation. We come now to consider salvation in its relation to the individual himself and that as it pertains to his whole being and through his whole life. We find that the New Testament holds before the believer an ideal of life and character, of behavior and accomplishment, to be attained in Jesus Christ. This attainment is a gradual and prolonged process. The ideal is exemplified in Jesus Christ himself and is enforced again and again by practically every New Testament writer.[41]

Writing later in the same section, he likens growth in Christ to the development of a human. "Newborn babes," he remarks, "grow into full-grown men. Men are not born full-grown. The beginning of the new life in Christ Jesus is a birth. The birth must not be confounded with the process of the development of the whole after life."[42]

The key to this process is a lifelong practice of repentance that makes salvation ever fresh. It serves as the connectivity needed between salvation in three tenses—past, present, and future. Miller writes of the inner and outer dimensions of repentance:

> [It] is a change of mind and as such it is an inward work of grace wrought upon the soul. But in its outward expression it requires fruit worthy of its profession. Repentance is itself a mighty revolution in the life, a change so great and so marvelous that it is well-nigh a miracle, and as such it manifests itself in the fruit of the Christian life. True repentance always makes all possible restitution for its past errors. . . . No one can truly repent and then allow any evil of his old and former life to continue if it is within his power to end them. . . . What a supreme teaching is this that enjoins so radical a change in a man's life as to make him all over into a new man when the process is completed. But such is the end of the process which repentance begins in a man's soul. It is the first step in salvation and salvation when it is

---

41. Miller, *Christian Doctrine*, 85.
42. Miller, *Christian Doctrine*, 87.

complete brings a soul into communion with God and crowns him by that very fact with eternal life.[43]

For Miller, repentance was the first step in salvation, counter to salvation and repentance being collapsed into one another as in the altar calls of revivalism. As Miller understood repentance and conversion over the course of a believer's life, it could be characterized as conversionary discipleship. Brenda Colijn, Brethren elder and theologian, captures this in an article entitled "Salvation: Past, Present, Future." Salvation, she notes, is "both an event and a process: it is an accomplished fact, a continuing walk, and a future hope."[44]

As such, salvation is a lifelong process that is intimately tied to a life of obedience, discipleship and repentance. In her assessment, evangelicals' (especially fundamentalists') fear of salvation by works has led them to omit the ethical implications of salvation in the New Testament which teaches that orthodoxy must produce orthopraxy. Therefore, believers

> must cooperate with God in carrying on the salvation process that He has begun in their lives. As they obey Him, He transforms their will and actions to more closely resemble His. The parallel between obedience and salvation indicates that the two are inseparable.[45]

The writings of both Colijn and Miller are exemplars of the Brethren witness that the fruit of obedience and discipleship is evidenced in a new, transformed life in the believer.

Similarly, they are also resolute in their defense of essential role that the church plays in salvation. "The context of salvation in the New Testament," Colijn writes, "is corporate; Christians are not called to be individual believers, but to be members of the Body of Christ."[46] The church is essential to the ongoing work of salvation in the believer. Counter to the individualistic (and often private) model of most evangelicals, conversionary discipleship requires the church. Conversion is simply the beginning of a lifelong process of discipleship.

Discipleship has remained a central Brethren emphasis and is woven throughout Miller's writings and his hermeneutic. A Word-Spirit Communal Revelationalism finds the revelation we receive as believers points us to a community shaped by the Word and the Spirit. "The church," Colijn

43. Miller, "Steps," 7.
44. Colijn, "Salvation," 4.
45. Colijn, "Salvation," 4.
46. Colijn, "Salvation," 4.

agrees, "must provide the context and the motivation for discipleship. This means a strong commitment to education, support for small groups and other means of spiritual growth, training in leadership, opportunities for ministry, and mutual accountability."[47]

Miller would have agreed with Fitch's assessment that American evangelicalism must address its reductionistic understanding of salvation and its anemic (often non-existent) understanding of ecclesiology. "Such a re-articulation of the gospel," Fitch writes, "results in a new communal disposition towards the world." Discipleship becomes the shaping of desires, vision, and character into Christ and his mission for the world which demands practices of spiritual formation in the situations of everyday life. Rather than being individualistic, often legalistic behaviors, these "disciplines . . . become a part of our everyday life together. They breed a new politic of fullness."[48]

Discipleship is the ongoing rhythm of these patterns of spiritual formation that sustain our salvation—the lifelong communal journey of becoming like Christ. Conversionary discipleship challenges the way many systematic theologies have divided salvation into theological silos and calls evangelicals to recapture a larger, more robust and biblical understanding of salvation in three tenses that avoids the separating of justification, sanctification, and glorification. As Colijn affirms:

> The past tense of salvation assures us that we have peace with God and that God is able to complete the work he has begun in us. The present tense urges us to grow in our faith as we participate in the redeemed community. The future tense encourages us to anticipate the day when God's work in us will be complete and we will receive our inheritance.[49]

Miller's understanding of salvation, which challenges the revivalist and Fundamentalist "decision for Christ" model, is a conversionary discipleship model that ties faith to obedience and conversion to discipleship. In the life of the church, faith and obedience are

> so vitally linked that they become in many instances all but synonymous. In the Old Testament . . . God constantly [calls] to His people, saying, "Obey my voice." . . . The finest Old Testament summary of the true religious life is given by Micah in 6:8. To do justly, to love mercy, and to walk humbly with God. True obedience cannot be better described than in these marvelous words.

---

47. Colijn, "Salvation," 6.
48. Fitch, *End of Evangelicalism?*, loc. 152.
49. Colijn, "Salvation," 6.

> In the New Testament obedience to the Lord is the test of true discipleship. Our personal relation to the Master is determined by this test. According to Acts 5:32 obedience is the condition upon which the Holy Spirit is given.... Obedience purifies the soul. So, the greatest of the blessings of the Christian life come to us through obedience, namely, the Holy Spirit and purity of soul.[50]

Miller speaks prophetically into a central anathema for many evangelicals—salvation including both faith *and* obedience. The hermeneutical approach of Miller, Word-Spirit Communal Revelationalism, is a theological epistemology that is dialectical. The revelation of God is for individual *and* communal purposes. Therefore, the Bible, contra-inerrancy, is received both spiritually *and* rationally and salvation entails both faith *and* obedience. It shapes a community of faith to receive the revealed *and* mystical character of God. Being comfortable with both divine initiative *and* human responsibility, it produces a centered-set epistemology that is at odds with the bounded set theologies of both Miller's day and the bounded set evangelical theological systems of the present.

Bounded Set Evangelicalism

Much of evangelicalism has long been underwritten by foundationalist epistemologies that seek to accommodate faith to reason. In a sense, it has blended the epistemic approaches of both Fundamentalism and liberalism, each of which accommodated to rationality in its own way. Fundamentalism was the most ironic posture in its development of a rational defense of Scripture. Liberalism established an epistemic response that located theological reflection in the affections (Schleiermacher) or in one's experience of the Bible (Clarke).[51]

While some evangelical scholarship has started to apply the adjective "postmodern" to itself, it generally remains quite modern. Actually, it is hyper-modern as it continues to accommodate itself to rationality instead of recognizing that reason is not as objective as once thought or that, in theology, reason must submit to revelation. Indeed, rationality must be sanctified

---

50. Miller, "Steps," 7.

51. The blind spot of Fundamentalism toward rationality has already been discussed. Liberalism failed to recognize that even accommodating its views to Christian theology was allowing revelation to shape its epistemology. The engagement with Christian claims was an appreciation for the role of revelation.

by the revelation of Jesus Christ.[52] Yet this accommodation to reason still informs epistemic approaches marked by rational anxiety. Rather than a trust of the interior witness of the Spirit in community, evangelicals react in various bounded set approaches to culture.

Donald Bloesch details several theologies that have been used by American Christians of the twentieth century in their engagement with larger culture. They are helpful to note because they have all been recapitulated, in some form or fashion, by modern evangelicals. The first, Bloesch notes, is a theology of restoration. Attempts are made to retrieve tradition as an anchor amid the storm of modernity. This marks the Anglo-Catholic-evangelical responses to modernity. The Eucharistic elements, ordinances, and liturgy become prominent in an attempt to ground Christian practice. Rather than a constructive interaction with reason, the symbols take on a life of their own. A sacramental positivism develops around the elements.

A second approach is a theology of accommodation that marked the project of Protestant liberalism. Bloesch identifies this with the "Christ-of-culture" approach outlined by H. Richard Niebuhr in *Christ and Culture*. Theological understanding is less a divide between natural and supernatural and, instead, is understood as a greater awareness and higher self-consciousness. This is evident in evangelicalism's "moralistic therapeutic deism" as described in *Soul Searching: The Religious and Spiritual Lives of American Teenagers* (2005) by sociologists Christian Smith and Melinda Lundquist Denton.[53] In this approach, revelation is predicated on reason.

---

52. For more on this topic of evangelicalism and hypermodernity, see https://albertmohler.com/2014/04/28/nearing-the-end-a-conversation-with-theologian-stanley-hauerwas/. In this podcast, Al Mohler, president of Southern Baptist Theological Seminary in Louisville, Kentucky, interviews Stanley Hauerwas. The conversation, entitled "Nearing the End: A Conversation with Theologian Stanley Hauerwas," is ironic given the two personalities and also prophetic in its critique of evangelicalism's engagement with modernity. Hauerwas argues that evangelicalism will die of exhaustion.

> I think evangelicalism is destined to die of its own success and it will go the way of mainstream Protestantism because . . . it depends far too much on charismatic pastors, and charisma will only take you so far. Evangelicalism is constantly under the burden of re-inventing the wheel and you just get tired. For example, I'm a big advocate of Morning Prayer. I love Morning Prayer. We do the same thing every morning. We don't have to make it up. We know we're going to say these prayers. We know we're going to join in reading of the psalm. We're going to have these Scripture readings. I mean, there's much to be said for Christianity as repetition and I think evangelicalism doesn't have enough repetition in a way that will form Christians to survive in a world that constantly tempts us to always think we have to do something new.

53. See Smith and Denton, *Soul Searching*. The authors' study found that many

A third relationship of theology to culture is found in a theology of correlation—or what was identified as a "Christ-above-culture" by Niebuhr. Whereas a theology of accommodation finds the gap between revelation and reason to be unbridgeable, a theology of correlation. Instead, this view argues that reason finds its fulfillment in revelation. Such a view is often found in conversations regarding justice and politics. Rather than eschatology serving as a corrective to political systems, these political systems become charged with eschatological rhetoric and hope. The Moral Majority of the 1980s and the Christian Left of the 2000s (in response) reveal a close alignment of Christianity with politics. While not all people and parties in these camps are guilty of a theology of correlation, the extremes of each of the movements reveal an eschatological confusion shaped more by political aspirations that the biblical data. In this posture, reason and revelation become synonymous.

Lastly, a theology of confrontation marks the response of early twentieth-century Fundamentalism. It is Niebuhr's "Christ-against-culture" posture. It entails a sharp divide between church and culture, often marked by a militant posture. Fundamentalism, for example, separated the Bible from constructive engagement with scientific and technological developments of the period. With this stance, reason is treated suspiciously and revelation is bracketed away from rationality.

Bloesch calls for a centered set, confessional theology that is "both conservative and radical (in the sense of going to the roots, *ad fontes*). Its adherents will respect and try to learn from the creeds and confessions in their own traditions, but instead of remaining with them, will aspire to go

---

young people believe in several moral statutes not exclusive to any of the major world religions. It is not a new religion or theology as such, but identified as a set of commonly held spiritual beliefs. It is this combination of beliefs that they label "Moralistic Therapeutic Deism":

1. A god exists who created and ordered the world and watches over human life on earth.
2. God wants people to be good, nice, and fair to each other, as taught in the Bible and by most world religions.
3. The central goal of life is to be happy and to feel good about oneself.
4. God does not need to be particularly involved in one's life except when God is needed to resolve a problem.
5. Good people go to heaven when they die.

These points of belief were compiled from interviews with approximately three thousand teenagers. It's important to note that the teens surveyed in 2005 are now young adults who are continuing to shape the engagement of faith and culture.

through them to a fresh articulation of the faith for our day."[54] Therefore, the relationship of theology to Scripture, and of reason to revelation, is one of servant rather than master. The approach of confessional theology is aligned with Scripture and attempts to deepen its understanding of and application to the modern world.

The four approaches have served as new articulations of foundationalism among evangelicals. Foundationalism is merely the acknowledgement of certain beliefs that anchor all others as these beliefs are seen as more basic, or foundational. Both Fundamentalism and liberal theologians of Miller's era sought to create rational foundations for their respective views—Fundamentalism with inerrancy and liberalism with faith as mere religious affection, experience or ethics in its quest to best accommodate reason.

This foundationalist quest among modern evangelicals shows striking parallels to that of science and philosophy. When many evangelicals were forced to admit that the biblical texts contained contradictions, a common move was to argue that only the original autographs were inerrant. This claim, Olson notes, "is incorrigible (since all of these are lost) but the incorrigibility comes at the cost of needing to ground theology on something inaccessible to contemporary theologians; the lost autographs are inerrant but useless."[55] Regardless of the location of the "original manuscripts," the attempt to found biblical authority in such a manner distracts from the central claims the Bible makes of itself and how it claims to find authority and justification. It is here that the late theologian, Lesslie Newbigin is helpful as he argued against foundationalism in religion, and particularly in Christianity, because it posits a criterion of truth alien to the gospel; in foundationalism, evidence and logic become the bases for belief in the gospel. For Christianity, however, "the truth surely is not that we come to know God by reasoning from our unredeemed experience but that what God has done for us in Christ gives us the eyes through which we can begin to truly understand our experience of the world."[56] In their quest for objectivity and certainty, foundationalist evangelicals have actually accomplished the opposite. As Richard Lints remarks:

> In banishing all mediators between the Bible and ourselves, we have let the Scriptures be ensnared in a web of subjectivism. Having rejected the aid of the community of interpreters throughout the history of Christendom, we have not succeeded in returning

---

54. Bloesch, *Theology of Word & Spirit*, loc. 3180.
55. Olson, *Reformed and Always Reforming*, loc. 2247–52.
56. Newbigin, "The Gospel and Public Life," 239.

to the primitive gospel; we have simply managed to plunge ourselves back to the biases of our own individual situations.[57]

For Miller's faith a Word-Spirit Communal Revelationalism manifests itself in a personal, transforming relationship with Jesus Christ and is expressed communally in shared stories (testimonies), hymns, witness, and worship. It spills over into a pedagogy that allows for the epistemic influence of the Spirit that animates his centered-set theological approach that remains curious while tethered to the revelation of Christ. In a similar vein, the late theologian Stanley Grenz (1950–2005) advocated a move from a "creed-based" to a "spirituality-based" identification of authentic evangelicalism, thus making the experience of conversion and its outworking in evangelical piety the defining center of the boundaryless broad evangelical "tent."[58] Like Miller, Grenz did not discard or discount doctrine as unimportant but gave it secondary status. "To be truly evangelical, right doctrine, as important as it is, is not enough. The truth of the Christian faith must become personally experienced truth" for authentic evangelical faith to exist.[59]

In *Beyond Foundationalism* (2001) Grenz and John Franke outlined theological sources and motifs for faith in a postmodern context. The sources are the streams that converge to shape a Christian, revelatory epistemology and witness in the world. These influences inform what a Christian can claim to know and how they are able to speak with confidence on the revelation of God. Grenz and Franke identified three such sources. First is Scripture which serves as the "norming norm" for the other two sources. It receives a primacy in Christian, revelatory epistemology. Yet Scripture must come into conversation with tradition, the second source, which is deemed a "hermeneutical trajectory." Tradition for Grenz and Franke is the community of faith that transcends, and includes, the present. It helps us to not allow the biases of the present to hijack and subvert the biblical witness.

These two, however, are never received in a vacuum as culture, the third source, serves as the "embedded context" for theological reflection. Language, even what we say about God, demands a context. The witness of the church, likewise, necessitates context. Culture brings questions and possibilities to which the church responds. It is always the milieu in which the church bears witness. At any moment in time, Grenz and Franke contend, Scripture, tradition and culture remain the three central sources of

---

57. Lints, *Fabric of Theology*, 93.
58. Grenz, *Revisioning Evangelical Theology*, 32.
59. Grenz, *Revisioning Evangelical Theology*, 57.

theology.[60] Their vision of these three sources lived out serves as helpful definition for Miller's Word-Spirit Communal Revelationalism:

> If theology is both the reflection of church practices and the articulation of the church's mosaic of beliefs for the sake of hearing the Spirit's voice, then ultimately all theology is "local." That is, it is the reflection and articulation of a particular moment of their ongoing existence in the world.[61]

Miller's hermeneutical approach, however, was much more explicit about the Spirit than Grenz and Franke's approach seems to be. While the Spirit is evident in their work, it does not serve as one of the three sources of theology. This could be that the Spirit is the meta-source that mediates the revelation of Jesus Christ through the three sources mentioned or the Spirit serves as the translation of the three sources into practice. This is not clear in their work but Miller would have located the work of the Spirit in both the mediation of revelation *and* the empowering, transformative influence to apply these sources to the witness of the church. This raises a question, if theology is inherently local, then what characterizes theological reflection beyond the local expression? Put another way, how are various local expressions understood to be held in common?

Grenz and Franke recommend three motifs—that each of these local expressions operates with a "similar pattern, shape, or 'style.'"[62] These motifs of theology are the Trinity, community and eschatology. The Trinity, the first motif, reveals that theological reflection identifies and centers on one God who is triune. This God exists in community. Therefore, community, the second motif, serves as the integrative motif as the revelation of Scripture is discerned and applied in the life of the church. Lastly, just as tradition served as a source for theological reflection, eschatology, the third motif, serves as a north star and orients the witness of the church in the world. Each source has a parallel motif. Scripture reveals the Triune life of God, tradition is the transcendent life of community, eschatology shapes the culture of the church and determines moments of relevance and moments of departure from the surrounding cultures.[63]

Sources and motifs could be misconstrued by some as a new foundationalism. Even Bloesch notes that a theology of Word and Spirit could be so confused "because it presupposes an indefeasible criterion outside ourselves

---

60. See Grenz and Franke, *Beyond Foundationalism*.
61. Grenz and Franke, *Beyond Foundationalism*, 166.
62. Grenz and Franke, *Beyond Foundationalism*, 166.
63. Grenz and Franke, *Beyond Foundationalism*, 166.

that becomes the infallible standard for faith and practice."[64] Yet this criterion or authority does not consist in *a priori* assumptions or universal principles or transcendental ideals.

> Foundationalism tries to anchor one's thought in basic premises that are beyond all possible doubt (indubitable) and beyond any need of correction (incorrigible). In a theology of Word and Spirit we receive or hear the concrete speech of God, which makes an indelible impression on the human soul but can never be fully assimilated by the human mind. To know the full import of what is revealed, we must act in obedience to what we presently ascertain to be the will of God.[65]

These sources and motifs of theology are received as part of the revelatory act of the Spirit in Miller's Word-Spirit Communal Revelationalism. This revelation and its subsequent authority are not simply what the Bible says but what God says *in the* Bible. Yet authority needs a witness and the church is such a witness, empowered by the Spirit. Hence the hermeneutic of Miller can never simply be a fideistic act of an individual. The church responds to the historic account of the gospel and, by an epistemic faith commitment, assimilates the central confession of the church through the ages that Jesus of Nazareth was/is simultaneously God the Son. This same Spirit that moves the church from general to specific revelation, from objectivity to faith, also serves to provide necessary wisdom to the community of faith regarding any and all issues that faith community may encounter. Even those issues not explicitly addressed in Scripture still have access to the wisdom of the Spirit. The Word and Spirit, in harmony, focus the church on central revelation of Christ which anchors the church amid dialogue with the ideas of surrounding cultures. The antagonisms of Fundamentalism and liberalism find their resolution in Christ as pictured below:

---

64. Bloesch, *Theology of Word & Spirit*, loc. 171.
65. Bloesch, *Theology of Word & Spirit*, loc. 178.

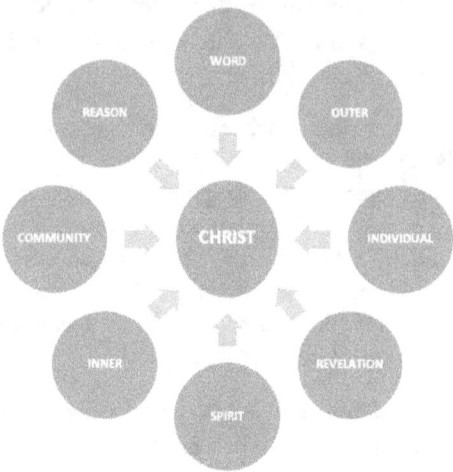

Christ as center allows for each generation to encounter a robust, biblical faith because the knowledge of God is rooted in the paradoxical unity of Word and Spirit. As Bloesch comments, "Against rationalism we do not appeal to the Bible in and of itself but to the Bible illumined by the Spirit. Against mysticism and spiritualism, we insist that the Spirit acts in conjunction with the revealed Word of God."[66] The central revelation of biblical faith exists on an objective to subjective trajectory. It is anchored in the historical life, death and resurrection of Jesus of Nazareth which then, by the power of the Spirit and our decision in faith to receive his supernatural claims as true, becomes the experientially received Lord and Savior of our life and the world. Contrary to dogmatism or mysticism, evangelical faith is a revelational-contextual posture. It is a transcendent revelation that is contextualized in our specific community and in each human heart.

The indicators of such a faith can never simply be cognition or propositions. These assess information transmitted but do not lead to life transformation. The struggle that many evangelicals have with the centered set faith of Miller's Word Spirit Communal Revelationalism is that it seems too subjective and difficult to measure. Those same evangelicals, in their quest for objectivity, have often enslaved the biblical text to their own, often subconscious, biases as they isolate the text from tradition and community and bracket out the Spirit. Scripture suggests how to assess this theological epistemology in a well-known passage of the New Testament. It is only fitting that to embrace the theological method of Miller this chapter must now turn to exegesis, pastoral pedagogy and practical application.

---

66. Bloesch, *Spirituality Old & New*, 85.

Fruit of the Spirit as Evidence of Spiritual Formation

A Word-Spirit Communal Revelationalism names the hermeneutical approach of both Miller and the Ashland Brethren. Word and Spirit operate in unison to testify to the central revelation of Jesus Christ (revelationalism) who is discerned in and for community. It connects the community to the Word and Spirit as they testify to the center who is Jesus Christ. A loving obedience is formed as Word and Spirit invite us deeper into Christlikeness and life with God. It captures the sources and motifs detailed by both Grenz and Franke.

A concern with such a centered-set approach is how to assess the growth of discipleship. How is growth in Christlikeness known? Subsequently, how is it measured? While Bible memorization and being a "good person" are not to be looked down upon, a Word-Spirit Communal Revelationalism produces transformation and is not simply intellectual assent. Transformation produces holistic life change. Much like the church detailed in Galatians, a propensity to follow the Mosaic law (bounded set) must continually be supplanted by the role of the Spirit (centered set). In alignment with Paul's admonishments in this New Testament text, Miller's Word-Spirit Communal Revelationalism is a biblical posture to evidences of faith that desires the transformation of a believer from the inside-out.

This is why Galatians is a helpful spot to begin a discussion on the spiritual formational application of Miller's hermeneutical approach. The Apostle Paul's correspondence details two factions emerging in the church. Some in the community, known as "Judaizers," appealed to both the death of Christ and the law for their justification. The other group were Gentile converts who were being swayed by the teaching of the Judaizers. Galatians often gets presented as Paul's clarion call to a gospel of justification by faith. Yet the biblical scholar F. F. Bruce saw another important theme developing in this letter:

> The Letter to the Galatians can be thought of as so completely devoted to the theme of justification by faith that its teaching on the Holy Spirit may be overlooked. In fact, its teaching on the Holy Spirit is so interwoven with its teaching on justification by faith that the one cannot be understood without the other, any more than in real life the justifying grace of God can be experienced apart from the Spirit.[67]

The Judaizers claimed that the Galatian converts needed to adopt the whole law to be completely redeemed before God because, in so doing, they

---

67. Bruce, "The Spirit in the Letter to the Galatians," 36.

would express their trust in the entirety of God's revelation and provide themselves with an adequate moral guide (the law). Therefore, they claimed that new converts must assume the yoke of the law. In doing so, these Gentile converts would acquire a social identity: Jewish proselytes who were part of Judaism, a religion recognized by Roman law.[68]

The Judaizers argued that Paul was teaching an abbreviated gospel (Jesus without Moses) in order to gain the Galatians' initial hearing; but had he stayed longer in Galatia, he would have revealed the need for the law of Moses to them. Therefore, they ought now to accept the law to finish Paul's work in their midst. Furthermore, they insisted that "life in the Spirit" was profoundly inadequate by itself. It would lead to immorality and would never counter the forces of the flesh in their lives. If they would adopt the law, then all would be solved: no immorality, no problem with the flesh, and full acceptance with God.

The letter to the Galatians reveals that these Gentile converts were responding favorably to this theology. Yet Paul contends that the flesh has actually been put to death already and that the means of moral guidance has already been given: God's Spirit. For Paul, just as Jesus was the fulfillment of the law, so the Spirit is the replacement (and fulfillment) of the law as God's instrument for such guidance. This is the historical context of Paul's application of the idea of freedom from the battle with the flesh. McKnight provides the bridge between the time of Galatia and our own:

> It does no good to talk about the Spirit's sufficiency as moral guide if we are not all agreed that the Spirit of God is the chief leader of our lives. We must agree here. Unless the two parties [Judaizers and Gentile converts] can stop and remember the sufficiency of the Spirit, there will be no progress. This is the hardest step for all those seeking to find peace and for those called in as arbitrators. Why? Because in that admission comes an intuition that one is going to get steamrolled into an answer that will roll over one's egocentrism or cherished viewpoint.[69]

It is in this context that the Apostle Paul outlines the fruit of the Spirit as "love, joy, peace, forbearance, kindness, goodness, faithfulness, gentleness and self-control" (5:22–23a NIV). Then, to punctuate his point, he reminds the Galatians that "[against] such things there is no law" (v. 23b NIV). These verses follow the list of fleshly vices that would have caused anxiety to the legally minded Judaizers. In a word, both parties, Judaizers and Gentile converts, were attempting to find foundation for their faith outside the Spirit

---

68. McKnight, *Galatians*, loc. 5309.
69. McKnight, *Galatians*, loc. 5410.

in the bounded set of the law. The Spirit, they believed, was too ethereal to combat matters of the flesh. The discipline of the law was deemed necessary.

It is fascinating in this dialogue that Paul uses the language of fruit to describe life in the Spirit. To rebuff the anxiety of the two parties to whom he is speaking, one might expect to find a list of disciplines. Instead, Paul lists characteristics that mark a life in the Spirit. Characteristics that flow out of a centered set life with God. As Richard Hays so rightly puts it, "The metaphor of 'fruit' suggests that the sanctified conduct Paul expects of the Galatians is not so much the product of moral striving as that of allowing the mysterious power of God's Spirit to work in and through them. Where God's Spirit is at work, Paul contends, the result will be peace and holiness, not moral anarchy."[70] Christopher Wright, inspired by the great evangelical theologian John Stott's interest in the fruit of the Spirit, has researched the spiritual formation implications of Paul's response. In his book *Cultivating the Fruit of the Spirit: Growing in Christlikeness*, Wright notes:

> Why does a tree bear fruit? Not because there is some law of nature that says it must. But simply because of the life within it, rising up from the soil and water that feed its roots and flowing in the sap through every branch and twig. A tree does not bear fruit by keeping the laws of nature . . . but simply because it is a living tree, being and doing what a tree is and does when it is alive.[71]

Wright recommends that if there exists a struggle to love other Christians (as was occurring in Galatia), there are two things one should do: "first, go to the source of love, God himself, and ask for his divine love to fill you; and second, look at the model of love, the cross of Christ, and follow his example."[72]

A life shaped by the Spirit will inevitably embody Gal 5:24 by "crucifying [the] flesh." The pathway produced by the Spirit is a formational journey that is quite similar to the Anabaptist concept of *Gelassenheit*, or yieldedness. The believer first submits their life to God, then to the community, and finally to suffering entailed as one is obedient to Christ. With such yieldedness, the believer experiences the tangible, visceral by-product of transformation, namely, the fruit of the Spirit.[73] As the late New Testament scholar, James Dunn noted:

70. Hays, *Moral Vision*, loc. 1148.
71. Wright, *Cultivating the Fruit*, loc. 188.
72. Wright, *Cultivating the Fruit*, loc. 330.
73. The fruit of the Spirit is not the only location for a list of spiritual characteristics that serve as evidences of faith. See also Matt 5:1–12; Rom 5:3–5; 2 Cor 6:3–10; Phil 4:4–9; 2 Pet 1:5–7; and Jas 3:17–18. Galatians 5:22–23 is simply used as an illustration

> For Paul the Spirit is the power of God which transforms believers into the image of their Lord degree by degree (2 Cor. 3.18). The Spirit is the power which, again as the prophets had hoped, enables the obedience which fulfills the law (Rom. 8.23) and bears the fruit of a transformed character (Gal. 5.22–23). The Spirit is the power which in the end will complete the lifelong process of salvation by changing our bodies of humiliation to conform them to Christ's body of glory.[74]

Such conforming occurs in community. New Testament scholar, Richard Hays provides a simple hermeneutical assessment for a communal, centered set life shaped by the fruit of the Spirit. He labels it "a fruits test" that asks, "Does the community manifest the fruit of the Spirit (Gal. 5:22–23)?"[75]

A centered set application of Miller's Word-Spirit Communal Revelationalism would utilize the fruit of the Spirit as a pathway for spiritual formation as it serves as an indicator of spiritual growth and discipleship. Miller himself, in his travel journal, used a threefold description regarding such indicators—what he identified as "things of the Spirit." In an entry from his tour of Egypt in 1926, Miller explored an "inescapable conviction that the religious aspects of human life, or if you prefer the things of the Spirit—are primal, basic, essential."[76]

Miller employs the use of triads often to emphasize an important point in a lecture or to highlight an important argument in a paper. The literary device drills down the point as Miller details life in the Spirit as "primal, basic, [and] essential"—a Word-Spirit Communal Revelationalism centers the community of faith on the relational, revelatory necessity of Jesus Christ who produces life change, evidenced by the qualities like the fruit of the Spirit, as we encounter him by through the Word and the Spirit.

Therefore, the fruit of the Spirit provides a helpful gauge on spiritual development within Miller's Word-Spirit Communal Revelationalism. In this centered set theological approach, it is important to assess the fruitfulness of an individual's life rather than simply their doctrinal precision/correctness. The latter is not unimportant but it is incomplete in our pursuit for evidences of faith. Fruit proceeds from transformation and is more determinative of a believer's walk with Christ than propositions. It is important to note that the

---

of the New Testament's call to evaluate believers on the fruit of their lives and ministry. When disagreements arise in the church regarding biblical interpretation, it is wise to heed the call of the New Testament to evaluate fruit as evidence of the Spirit's involvement and influence.

74. Dunn, *Jesus, Paul, and the Gospels*, 109.

75. Hays, *Moral Vision*, loc. 5863.

76. Miller, *Travel Journal*, 219–21.

life of the Spirit that marked Miller's hermeneutic produces frustration for those who desire rational certainty and/or demand doctrinal precision, yet it serves as a centered set theological approach to life with God that respects the role of the Spirit at the heart of a Christian, theological epistemology.

The Certainty Offered by a Word-Spirit Communal Revelationalism

The battle for certainty continues to wreak havoc within American Christianity in general and evangelicalism in particular. Though titles like "Fundamentalist" have come and gone, the postures of Fundamentalism and liberalism still remain. In this sense, the epistemic posture of Miller is fresh for each generation. Miller's Word-Spirit Communal Revelationalism is a hermeneutic that submits reason to revelation—not bifurcating reason from revelation. Revelation employs reason but can never be encompassed by reason alone as it also requires the Spirit. This Word-Spirit center of both Miller's faith and that of the Brethren is a helpful corrective to the underpinnings of rationalism and scholasticism that still exist at the center of many evangelical expressions. While doctrine is not unessential for Miller, it must never be separated from devotion. This is why the center for Miller was the revelation of Jesus Christ made known by the dual mediators of Word and Spirit.

Natural questions arise as to how Miller and the Brethren understand theological certainty and what a centered set looks like ecclesiologically? The Anabaptist and Pietist grounds of certainty, formative for the Brethren, are the quality of one's experience *and* the external marks of holiness. In many ways, this is quite similar to the theology of *habitus practicus* detailed by the Pietist theologian, Philipp Jakob Spener. Everything must be aligned to the praxis of faith and life. According to Spener, "theology is not merely a science but exists in affections of the heart and in the exercise. . . . [It] alone is learned in the light of the Holy Spirit."[77] Therefore, experience is not denied in Brethren theology but is brought into conversation with the community, the Bible and the Spirit—the agents of holiness in the life of a believer. The task of theology is ongoing and dynamic and not static and punctiliar. It is best characterized by the metaphor of pilgrimage. Christian theology is "pilgrim theology."[78]

---

77. Spener, *Pia Desideria*, 70–71. For more on Spener's relevance for the life of the Brethren, see chapter 1.

78. For further reflection on theology as a disciplined illustrated by the metaphor of pilgrimage, see Bauman, *Pilgrim Theology*.

Regarding what a centered set ecclesiology looks like one can explore the two ecclesiologies detailed by Michael Budde in his book *The Two Churches: Catholicism and Capitalism in the World System* (2012).[79] In this book, written for a Catholic audience, Budde differentiates between "tight" and "loose" ecclesiologies. *Tight ecclesiologies*, which could also be classified as centered set, are demanding for their adherents. They have mutual support and initiative and involve participatory decision making. *Loose ecclesiologies* generally involve a one-way transmission of religious resources from a minority leadership to a more passive membership. These ecclesiologies tend to focus on the outer to the exclusion of the inner life of the community. Budde's research, focusing on the shaping of America's Catholics by capitalism, found that the tighter the ecclesiology, the more resistant its people are to the global capitalist market order.[80] Tight, centered-set, ecclesiologies value participation and formation. Loose, often bounded-set, ecclesiologies may appear to minimize anxiety but they fail to invite participation which perpetuates identity confusion and continued anxiety. Furthermore, absent a defined center, something (or someone) else ends up forming adherents.

A tight, centered-set ecclesiology, in contrast, invites participation and works out anxiety and identity confusion in community. While the fuzziness of the edges of the centered-set may indicate ambiguity, the center is clear. Such a tight and centered ecclesiology is necessary for a Word-Spirit Communal Revelationalism as it calls each believer to take their seat at the table and to be a part of the discernment process around Scripture. It invites accountability and calls for obedience but all out of love for the center to which the body is tethered. Loose ecclesiologies wander into ideology as they fail to empower a corporate identification with and reflection upon the center. Tight ecclesiologies allow for the revelation of the Word and Spirit to bind us together by the power of the Spirit into a community of prayerful discernment and consensus.

Budde's research shows that centered sets appear ambiguous at first. The bounded set offers the appearance of structure and direction. However, without the dynamism between the center and its members at the heart of its ecclesiology, there exists little transformation of the faithful. For Budde's research, loose ecclesiologies did not foster greater participation (and subsequent transformation). Therefore, the dominant, societal ideology of capitalism was more transformative for these adherents. In contrast, tight ecclesiologies have a dynamic center that animates the life of its members.

---

79. Though written for a Catholic audience, Budde's insights are applicable to Christians in general.

80. For more information, see Budde, *Two Churches*.

These ecclesiologies are also protective of the center and recognize that theological reflection demands involvement marked by nuance and communal discernment—therefore there is greater contribution from the life of the community. Word-Spirit Communal Revelationalism necessitates a tight ecclesiology marked by the fruit of the Spirit.

Concluding Remarks

This chapter has explored the application of Miller's Word-Spirit Communal Revelationalism for Brethren engagement with American evangelicalism. It discerned that a postconservative, centered set evangelicalism was most congruent with Miller's theological method and then utilized such a methodology to speak into the modernistic distortions of Bebbington's quadrilateral. By differentiating between bounded and centered set theological approaches, it then offered a spiritual formational pathway utilizing the fruit of the Spirit to develop a centered set ecclesiology in line with Miller's continued call to recognize and respect the work of the Holy Spirit.

It then detailed the implications of such an ecclesiology for how it shapes Scripture reading and creates tight over against loose ecclesiologies. Consequently, it revealed that certainty for Miller and the Brethren is not rational but is experiential and communal in response to the revelation of Christ through Word and Spirit. Therefore, evidence of faith is marked by a life of obedience, holiness and fruitfulness. Miller noted that the divine life

> is measured by the strength and beauty . . . the fruit of the Spirit—a life devoid of them certainly would indicate the absence of the Holy Spirit from it. If the Spirit of God is present in the life and dominates and controls it, the fruit of the Spirit's presence will appear. This is self-evident and necessary, for the Holy Spirit of God is neither fruitless nor inactive in the child of God.[81]

The fruit of the Spirit captures a relationship between the rational and the spiritual. Like a Venn-diagram, Miller's Word-Spirit Communal Revelationalism invites us to live in the overlap. Similarly, every day of his life, Stott prayed, "Holy Spirit . . . fill me with yourself and cause your fruit to ripen in my life: love, joy, peace, patience, kindness, goodness, faithfulness, gentleness, and self-control."[82] Miller and Stott caught something of the ordinary beauty of dialectical living. The fruit of the Spirit shaped them personally for life communally. They were giants of biblical study who did not give up

---

81. Miller, *Christian Doctrine*, 99–102.
82. Wright, *Cultivating the Fruit*, loc. 62.

on the Jesus of faith. They pored over the Word and allowed their lives to be marinated in the Spirit. They refused to allow reason and revelation to be separated and the lives of their readers are better because of it. In agreement, and similar in his devotion to both Word and Spirit, Bloesch claimed:

> We are closest to God when we acknowledge our despair and need rather than boast of our capacity to understand and believe, but we cannot know our real despair and need until our inward eyes are first opened to the glorious grace and incomparable love that we see in the death and resurrection of Jesus Christ. It is not only faith that is a gift from God but the very condition to receive faith. We must never forget that the hope of the church rests not on its own strategies and wisdom but on the living God alone, who speaks and acts wherever his Word is faithfully proclaimed and wherever the prayers of his children are offered up in faith and repentance.[83]

All of these men (Bloesch, Stott, Miller, and a host of others throughout the pages of this project) were advocates of a Word and Spirit theology and acknowledged the relational certainty they had by the power of the Spirit. This promised Spirit illuminates the pages of Scripture, transforms the believer, and intercedes on our behalf (Rom 8:26).

Likewise, this same Spirit inspired a band of followers to immerse themselves in the Eder River of Schwarzenau, Germany, in a pact of radical obedience to Christ in 1708. He continues to speak to each subsequent generation of Brethren (and American evangelicalism through them). The gospel remains fresh because the central revelation is timeless by the power of this same Spirit. This is the overarching witness of the Brethren—a radical Christocentrism. Brethren have wandered into numerous bounded sets but their Christ centered theology has allowed the community of faith, by the power of the Spirit, to bring necessary corrective to the fellowship. This is an original aspect of the ethos that is Brethren. Therefore, as Miller would remind us, "[Whether] conservative or liberal, the best way [for us] to seek to do the right thing is by remaining loyal to our original deposit of faith."

---

83. Bloesch, *Word and Spirit*, loc. 3226.

Concluding Remarks

AFTER EXPLORING THE THEOLOGICAL pilgrimage, witness, epistemology, and biblical hermeneutics that marked Miller's life, several immediate points of application come into view. I first started writing this book due to my ongoing desire for Brethren to better understand their heritage. Second, I wanted to assist the Ashland Brethren to appreciate their unique position within the larger Brethren family. Miller proved to be the exemplar necessary to accomplish this task. Third, I became convinced that the Word *and* Spirit approach of the Brethren is especially helpful as we navigate the many streams of American evangelicalism and offer our distinct theological nuance to conversations that arise in that partnership—specifically regarding biblical authority and theological education.

In this project, I have defined my understanding of "Brethren," particularly, the Ashland branch of which I am a part, and how I understand the term "evangelical," namely, a postconservative evangelicalism that embodies Bebbington's fourfold characteristics, broadly defined, and locates the development of those characteristics in the life of a faith community. The evidences of this evangelical faith lie in the fruit produced by the believing community and not merely in the community's doctrinal correctness or intellectual assent. While the latter are important, they are not where the New Testament's own emphasis falls as it instructs believers to assess the quality of their faith. This accent upon lived fruit explains why Brethren theology has so often been based upon history and narrative. Biographical vignettes and historical development best capture the Brethren witness more so than a systematic theology. While Miller's thought is systematic, he always remains open to the influence of the Spirit and the larger narrative of the Bible.

Mentors and guides are essential with a theological approach like that of the Brethren. The need for such guides is hard-wired into a Word-Spirit Communal Revelationalism. While the Spirit continues to speak through the text of Scripture to us individually, revealed meaning must be further discerned together in community to determine its veracity. This communal revelational bent will continue to be essential as Brethren engage biblical texts and societal concerns that are likely to produce disagreement within the fellowship. As Brethren are invited by the Spirit to speak concerning disputed texts and moments, we must not merely assess the quality of anyone's faith by doctrinal agreement alone. Instead, Brethren must submit to the community's reading of a text or its approach to a societal issue. While disagreements persist, there is a recognition that the Spirit is seeking to create a people for himself and our submission is constitutive of that endeavor. Submission to the community in its reading of both the Word and the Spirit calls us back again to the essentials of the biblical revelation. As Donald Bloesch reminds us:

> The biblical text is entirely truthful when it is seen in relation to its divine center, God's self-revelation in Jesus Christ. When separated from this center, the text is not perceived in its proper context.... The truth of the Bible is available to us only when we strive to see the text in relation to the New Testament Gospel.[1]

Miller's evidences of faith, as outlined in his discussion on salvation in *Christian Doctrine*, are helpful to Brethren as they navigate disagreements and simultaneously examine one another for continuing evidences of faith. Miller notes that "progress in the divine life is measured by the strength and beauty of . . . noble, Christly characteristics in the individual."[2]

The first of these is love, which Miller calls the "most Christ-like character" as "love of the brethren in the Lord is the badge of true discipleship."[3] Second is righteousness which manifests itself as a loving obedience to Christ. "Righteousness," he remarks, "is a matter of heart and motive, of life and conduct. It is therefore of the inner Spirit. It is character in the likeness of God."[4]

Righteousness and love produce the third Christly characteristic, humility, which "is the spirit of teachableness and submission" that "is the

---

1. Bloesch, *Holy Scripture*, 37–38.
2. Miller, *Christian Doctrine*, 99.
3. Miller, *Christian Doctrine*, 99.
4. Miller, *Christian Doctrine*, 100.

opposite of pride and self-assertion."[5] This humble posture further begets attributes that Miller identifies as "virtues [or] graces of the Christian Life."[6] He first references the Beatitudes (Matt 5:1–12) and then provides a list of further virtues. Along with these truths of the Beatitudes, a Christian is devout, just, sincere, upright, steadfast, zealous, unselfish, and patient.[7] Miller remarks that

> it is just in the degree to which these virtues and graces are cultivated that the beauty and power and worth of the Christian life appear. It is just as the characteristics of the life of Jesus are reproduced in his disciples that they really enter upon their *heritage in him*.[8]

It is at this point that Miller turns to the fruit of the Spirit (Gal 5:22–23)—love, joy, peace, patience, kindness, goodness, faithfulness, gentleness, self-control. Concluding his entire section on salvation with these specific characteristics, Miller declares that

> a life devoid of them certainly would indicate the absence of the Holy Spirit from it. If the Spirit of God is present in the life and dominates and controls it, the fruit of the Spirit's presence will appear.[9]

The call of Miller to the Ashland Brethren and to American evangelicalism is for us to rise above the polarization of our current cultural and political landscape, and to search for the fruit of the Spirit among us. It is only by appreciating the fruit of a believer's life that we can disagree well without calling a person's entire theological journey into question.

Out of Miller's call to examine a life by its fruit, there are a few recommendations that I offer to the Brethren as they seek to apply the principles of his life to their own. First, we must better communicate the essentials of our faith. For too long the essentials have been our distinct ordinances. I fear these may become the "hollow signifiers" to which Žižek alludes if we do not connect them back to the foundational beliefs of our tradition.

Second, we must first learn to disagree, and then embrace conflict in a healthy manner. Brethren are both averse to conflict and struggle to nuance theological arguments. While the Bible is indispensable to our faith, we must respect the numerous interpretations of this seminal text and

---

5. Miller, *Christian Doctrine*, 100.
6. Miller, *Christian Doctrine*, 101.
7. Miller, *Christian Doctrine*, 101.
8. Miller, *Christian Doctrine*, italics mine.
9. Miller, *Christian Doctrine*, 102.

bring them into dialogue. We can trust the Spirit to align our various biblical interpretations and foster unity, even if not uniformity. Miller did not avoid conflict but trusted the Spirit to find a point of mediation. The Spirit produces fruit on which our conversations should be founded. Fruitfulness reminds us that the Spirit always works through broken vessels and it also nuances our conversation. Discipleship is not mere intellectual agreement. It is a mind and body expression. The fruit of the Spirit, mentioned explicitly in chapter 6, calls us to embody our faithfulness even when we disagree.

Third, we need to cease to apologize for being Brethren. This apologetic stance takes two main forms. We either dismiss "Brethren" in our pursuit of simply being "biblical" or we express ill-ease with our distinctive practices (i.e., footwashing). In response to the first, Miller's Word-Spirit approach reminds us that it is both/and. We are biblical *and* we have a distinct hermeneutical approach to the Bible that informs our interpretation. To the latter, these practices tie us back to a distinct heritage and story. Miller's life remained rooted in his Brethren faith but also conversant with the many ideas that sustain a liberal arts college.

Lastly, Brethren need to engage the life of the mind. While our devotional approach to the Bible focuses us on practical theology and obedience, we can sometimes fail to reflect on the theological frameworks that shape our reading of the Bible, our corporate worship, and our engagement with society. We tend to tell our story through shared practices and behaviors as if these expressions were not founded on a specific way of thinking theologically. Brethren would be prudent to heed Miller's example and allow the mind to be shaped by a Word-Spirit Communal Revelationalism. We do not hold a sectarian faith but, rather, one that can engage the ideas of society while sustaining its connection to the vine of Jesus Christ.

As Brethren look ahead and seek to be faithful to the call of God, it is the hope of this work that leaders like J. Allen Miller can serve as indispensable guides for us. Miller holds a unique place in our heritage and he deserves further study beyond this project. May his witness and example challenge us to "love God with all of our heart, and with all of our soul, and with all of our mind" (Matt 22:35–40 NIV). Similarly, just as the Apostle Paul urged the church in Corinth, may Miller call the Brethren to "follow [his] example, as [he] [followed] the example of Christ" (1 Cor 11:1 NIV).

Bibliography

Ahlstrom, Sydney E. *A Religious History of the American People*. 2nd ed. New Haven: Yale University Press, 2004.
Allison, Richard. "J. Allen Miller, 1866–1935." *Ashland Theological Journal* 15 (January 1983) 51–57.
Arndt, Johann. *True Christianity*. Translated by Peter Erb. New York: Paulist, 1979.
Arnold, Bill T., and David B. Weisberg. "A Centennial Review of Friedrich Delitzsch's 'Babel und Bibel' Lectures." *Journal of Biblical Literature* 121 (2002) 441–57.
Arnold, Gottfried. *Die Erste Liebe Der Gemeinen Jesu Christi, Das ist, Wahre Abbildung Der Ersten Christen*. Frankfurt: Gottlieb Friedeburgs Buch-handlung, 1696.
Bach, Jeff. "The Life and Influence of Alexander Mack Jr.: Introduction." *Brethren Life & Thought* 58 (Spring 2013) 1–7.
Baker, Mark David, ed. *Proclaiming the Scandal of the Cross*. Grand Rapids: Baker, 2006.
Bame, Charles A. "J. Allen Miller as a Bible Teacher." *Brethren Evangelist* 57 (April 27, 1935) 5.
Bauman, Louis S. "Literalization, versus, Spiritualization." *Brethren Evangelist* 24 (June 4, 1902) 5.
———. "What First Interested Me in Missions." *Brethren Evangelist* 30 (August 26, 1908) 10.
Beachler, William H. "In Memoriam—Dr. J. Allen Miller." *Brethren Evangelist* 57 (August 27, 1935) 8.
Bebbington, David. *Evangelicalism in Modern Britain: A History from the 1730s to the 1980s*. London: Routledge, 1989.
Bender, Harold S., and C. Henry Smith, eds. *Mennonite Encyclopedia: A Comprehensive Reference Work on the Anabaptist-Mennonite Movement*. 4 vols. Scottdale, PA: Mennonite Publishing House, 1955.
Benedict, Fred W. "The Life and Work of Elder Peter Nead." *Brethren Life & Thought* 19 (Winter 1974) 63–79.
Bloesch, Donald. *Christian Foundations*. 6 vols. Downers Grove: InterVarsity, 1995.
———. *A Theology of Word & Spirit: Authority & Method in Theology*. Christian Foundations 1. Downers Grove: InterVarsity, 2005. Kindle.

BonJour, Laurence. *The Structure of Empirical Knowledge.* Cambridge, MA: Harvard University Press, 1985.

Bowman, Carl F. *Brethren Society: The Cultural Transformation of a "Peculiar People."* Center Books in Anabaptist Studies. Baltimore: Johns Hopkins University Press, 1995.

Brecht, Martin, ed. *Geschichte des Pietismus.* 4 vols. Göttingen: Vandenhoeck & Ruprecht, 1993.

Brethren Encyclopedia Project. *Brethren Spirituality: How Brethren Conceive of and Practice the Spiritual Life.* Philadelphia: Brethren Encyclopedia, 2015.

Brown, Dale W. *Another Way of Believing: A Brethren Theology.* Elgin, IL: Brethren, 2005.

———. *Understanding Pietism.* Grand Rapids: Eerdmans, 1978.

Bruce, Alexander Balmain. *Apologetics; or, Christianity Defensively Stated.* New York: Scribner, 1892.

Bunner, Christian, ed. *Lieder des Pietismus aus dem 17. and 18. Jahrhundert.* Leipzig: Evangelische Verlagsanstalt, 2003.

Burkholder, Jared S., and David C. Cramer, eds. *The Activist Impulse: Essays on the Intersection of Evangelicalism and Anabaptism.* Eugene, OR: Pickwick, 2012.

Bushnell, Horace. "The Christian Trinity a Practical Truth." *Christian Examiner and Religious Miscellany* 60 (January, March, May 1856) 161–88.

———. *Major Works of Horace Bushnell.* Midas Classics. London: Midas Classics, 2016. Kindle.

Caldwell, Robert W., III. *Theologies of the American Revivalists: From Whitefield to Finney.* Downers Grove: InterVarsity, 2017.

Calvin, John. *Institutes of the Christian Religion.* 2 vols. Translated by Ford Lewis Battles. Edited by John T. McNeill. Philadelphia: Westminster, 1960.

Carlson, William G., et al., eds. *The Pietist Impulse in Christianity.* Cambridge: Clarke, 2012.

Cassel, J. C. "The Old Religion and the New (II)." *Brethren Evangelist* 36 (February 1914) 3.

———. "A Sermon." *Brethren Evangelist* 23 (July 18, 1901) 4.

———. "A Twentieth Century Forecast." *Brethren Evangelist* 23 (January 3, 1901) 6.

Cauthen, Kenneth. *The Impact of American Religious Liberalism.* 2nd ed. Washington, DC: University Press of America, 1983.

Clarke, William Newton. *The Christian Doctrine of God.* Edinburgh: T. & T. Clark, 1909.

———. *An Outline of Christian Theology.* Edinburgh, T. & T. Clark, 1904.

———. *Sixty Years with the Bible: A Record of Experience.* New York: Scribner, 1909.

Colijn, Brenda B. "Incalculable Grace: A Covenantal-Relational Understanding of Atonement." Paper presented at the annual meeting for the Wesleyan Theological Society, Northwest Nazarene University, Nampa, Idaho, March 7–8, 2014.

———. "Incarnational Hermeneutics: The Brethren Approach to Scripture." *Brethren Life & Thought* 36 (Fall 1991) 251–54.

———. "New Birth into a Living Hope: The Brethren Understanding of Regeneration." *Brethren Life & Thought* 52 (Spring 2007) 101–20.

———. "Salvation: Past, Present, Future." *Brethren Evangelist* 102 (October 1990) 4–6.

———. "Word and Spirit in Brethren Spirituality." Paper presented at the fifth Brethren World Assembly at the Brethren Heritage Center, Brookville, Ohio, July 12, 2013.

Collins Winn, Christian T., et al., eds. *The Pietist Impulse in Christianity*. Eugene, OR: Wipf & Stock, 2011.
Cooper, John M., ed. *Plato, Five Dialogues: Euthyphro, Apology, Crito, Meno, Phaedo*. 2nd ed. Translated by G. M. A. Grube. Indianapolis: Hackett, 2002.
Darby, John Nelson. *Collected Writings*. 34 vols. 2nd ed. Edited by William Kelly. London, 1967.
Dayton, Donald. "The Search for Historical Evangelicalism." *Christian Scholar's Review* 23 (September 1993) 12–33.
Delitzsch, Friedrich. *Babel and Bible: Two Lectures*. New York: Putnam, 1903.
Dorrien, Gary. *The Making of American Theology*. 3 vols. Louisville: Westminster, 2001.
Durnbaugh, Donald F. *The Believers' Church: The History and Character of Radical Reformation*. Eugene, OR: Wipf & Stock, 2003.
———. "Brethren Beginnings: The Origins of the Church of the Brethren in Early Eighteenth-Century Europe." PhD diss., University of Pennsylvania, 1979.
———, ed. *The Brethren in Colonial America*. Elgin, IL: Brethren, 1967.
———. *European Origins of the Brethren: A Source Book on the Beginnings of the Church of the Brethren in the Early Eighteenth Century*. Elgin, IL: Brethren, 1958.
———. *Fruit of the Vine: A History of the Brethren, 1708–1995*. 2nd ed. Elgin, IL: Brethren, 1996.
———. *Meet the Brethren*. Elgin, IL: Brethren, 1984.
———. "Vindicator of Primitive Christianity: The Life and Diary of Peter Nead." *Brethren Life and Thought* 14 (Autumn 1969) 196.
Durnbaugh, Hedwig T. *The German Hymnody of the Brethren, 1720–1903*. Philadelphia: Brethren Encyclopedia, 1986.
Eberly, William R., ed. *The Complete Writings of Alexander Mack*. Philadelphia: Brethren Encyclopedia, 1991.
Ensign, C. David. "Radical German Pietism (c. 1675–c. 1760)." PhD diss., Princeton University, 1963.
Erb, Peter C. *Pietists, Protestants, and Mysticism: The Use of Late Medieval Spiritual Texts in the Work of Gottfried Arnold (1666–1714)*. Lanham, MD: Scarecrow, 1989.
———. *Pietists: Selected Writings (Classics of Western Spirituality)*. Mahwah, NJ: Paulist, 1983.
Erben, Patrick M. *A Harmony of the Spirits: Translation and the Language of Community in Early Pennsylvania*. Chapel Hill: University of North Carolina Press, 2012.
Feinberg, Charles, and R. A. Torrey. *The Fundamentals: The Famous Sourcebook of Foundational Biblical Truths*. Grand Rapids: Kregel, 1990.
Felbinger, Jeremias. *Christliches Hand-Büchlein*. 3rd ed. Baltimore: Samuel Saur, 1799.
Finger, Thomas N. *A Contemporary Anabaptist Theology: Biblical, Historical, Constructive*. Downers Grove: InterVarsity, 2004.
Finney, Charles. *Lectures on Revivals of Religion*. New York: Leavitt, Lord, 1835.
Fitch, David. *The End of Evangelicalism? Discerning a New Faithfulness for Mission: Towards an Evangelical Political Theology*. Eugene, OR: Cascade, 2011. Kindle.
Flood, Derek. "Substitutionary Atonement and the Church Fathers." *Evangelical Quarterly* 82 (2010) 144.
Foster, Douglas Allen, and Anthony L. Dunnavant. *The Encyclopedia of the Stone Campbell Movement: Christian Church (Disciples of Christ), Christian Churches / Churches of Christ, Churches of Christ*. Grand Rapids: Eerdmans, 2004.

Frank, Douglas W. *Less than Conquerors: How Evangelicals Entered the Twentieth Century.* Grand Rapids: Eerdmans, 1986.

Funk, Benjamin. *Life and Labors of Elder John Kline, the Missionary Martyr.* Elgin, IL: Brethren, 1900.

Furry, W. D. "The Church and Education." *Brethren Evangelist* 33 (August 30, 1911) 3.

———. "The End of Creation." *Brethren Evangelist* 23 (August 15, 1901) 6.

———. "The Message of Higher Criticism." *Brethren Evangelist* 25 (May 20, 1903) 9.

———. "Our Father." *Brethren Evangelist* 25 (June 24, 1903) 3.

Gehrz, Chris, ed. *The Pietist Vision of Christian Higher Education: Forming Whole and Holy Persons.* Downers Grove: InterVarsity, 2014.

Gillin, J. L. "The Bases of the Christian Faith. (In Three Parts—Part II)." *Brethren Evangelist* 37 (October 13, 1915) 4.

———. "Here and There in Red Cross." *Brethren Evangelist* 43 (November 23, 1921) 14.

Gilman, D. C., et al., eds. *New International Encyclopedia.* New York: Dodd, Mead, 1905.

Green, Michael. *The Empty Cross of Jesus.* Eastbourne: Kingsway, 2004.

Grenz, Stanley J. *Theology for the Community of God.* Grand Rapids: Eerdmans, 1994.

Grenz, Stanley J., and John R. Franke. *Beyond Foundationalism: Shaping Theology in a Postmodern Context.* Louisville: Westminster, 2001.

Grenz, Stanley J., et al. *Pocket Dictionary of Theological Terms.* Downers Grove: InterVarsity, 1999.

Gross, Leonard, ed. *Golden Apples in Silver Bowls: The Rediscovery of Redeeming Love.* Translated by Elizabeth Bender. Lancaster: Lancaster Mennonite Historical Society, 2014.

Hatch, Nathan O. *The Democratization of American Christianity.* New Haven: Yale University Press, 1991.

———. "The Origins of Civil Millennialism in America: New England Clergymen, War with France, and the Revolution." *William and Mary Quarterly* 31. 3 (July 1974) 407–30.

Hays, Richard. *The Moral Vision of the New Testament: Community, Cross, New Creation; A Contemporary Introduction to New Testament Ethics.* New York: HarperOne, 2013. Kindle.

Heckman, Samuel, ed. *The Religious Poetry of Alexander Mack, Jr.* Elgin, IL: Brethren, 1912.

Hegel, G. W. F. *The Phenomenology of the Spirit.* Translated by A. V. Miller. Oxford: Oxford University Press, 1977.

Hiebert, Paul G. *Anthropological Reflections on Missiological Issues.* Grand Rapids: Baker, 1994.

Hillsdale College. "Theadelphic Society." College pamphlet, 1900.

Hiram College and Western Reserve Eclectic Institute: Fifty Years of History, 1850–1900. N.p.: n.p., 1900.

"History of North Central Ohio." Northeast Ohio Heritage Pursuits. https://www.heritagepursuit.com/Ashland/Ashland1909P750.htm.

Hodge, Charles. *Systematic Theology.* 3 vols. New York: Scribner, 1874.

Hoehnle, Peter, ed. *The Inspirationists, 1714–1932.* London: Pickering & Chatto, 2015.

Holland, Scott. "Sander Mack and the Poetics of Pietism." *Brethren Life & Thought* 58 (Spring 2013) 108.

Holsinger, Henry R. *History of the Tunkers and the Brethren Church.* Lathrop, CA: Pacific Coast, 1901.

———. "Introductory." *Progressive Christian* 1 (January 3, 1879) 2.
Horne, Harry L. "Dr. J. Allen Miller." Editorial. *Ashland Times Gazette*, March 28, 1935.
"How Brethren Understand God's Word." Denominational source. N.p: n.p., 1993.
Jacobs, Edwin E. "The Teaching of Evolution in Ashland College." *Brethren Evangelist* 55 (February 25, 1933) 6.
Johnstone, William, ed. *William Robertson Smith. Essays in Reassessment*. Sheffield: Sheffield Academic, 1995.
Kauffman, Daniel, ed. *Bible Doctrine: A Treatise on the Great Doctrines of the Bible Pertaining to God, Angels, Satan, the Church, and the Salvation, Duties and Destiny of Man*. Scottdale, PA: Mennonite Publishing House, 1914.
———. *Doctrines of the Bible: A Brief Discussion of the Teachings of God's Word*. Scottdale, PA: Mennonite Publishing House, 1928.
———. *Fifty Years in the Mennonite Church, 1890–1940*. Scottdale, PA: Mennonite Publishing House, 1941.
———. *The Way of Salvation: Including Thoughts on What to Do After We Are Saved*. Scottdale, PA: Mennonite Publishing House, 1930.
Keener, Craig. *Spirit Hermeneutics: Reading Scripture in Light of Pentecost*. Grand Rapids: Eerdmans, 2017.
Kettering-Lane, Denise D. "Evangelical from the Start? Brethren Origins and Evangelicalism." *Brethren Life & Thought* 61 (Summer 2016) 1–10.
Kraus, C. Norman, ed. *Evangelicalism and Anabaptism*. Eugene, OR: Wipf & Stock, 2001.
Kurian, George T., et al. *Encyclopedia of Christianity in the United States*. Lanham, MD: Rowman & Littlefield, 2016. Kindle.
Laërtius, Diogenes. *Lives of the Eminent Philosophers*. Edited by Pamela Mensch. Translated by James Miller. New York: Oxford University Press, 2018.
Langer, Michael. "The Idolatry of Certainty: Kierkegaard and Evangelical Covenant Faith in a Postmodern World." *Covenant Quarterly* 71 (February 2013) 57–75.
Langford, Michael J. *The Tradition of Liberal Theology*. Grand Rapids: Eerdmans, 2014.
Lemos, Noah Mercelino. *An Introduction to the Theory of Knowledge*. Cambridge: Cambridge University Press, 2007.
Liechty, Daniel. *Early Anabaptist Spirituality: Selected Writings (Classics of Western Spirituality)*. Mahwah, NJ: Paulist, 1994.
Lindberg, Carter, ed. *The Pietist Theologians*. Malden, MA: Blackwell, 2005.
Livingstone, David N. *Darwin's Forgotten Defenders: The Encounter between Evangelical Theology and Evolutionary Thought*. Vancouver: Regent College Publishing, 1984.
Longenecker, Stephen L. "Alexander Mack Jr.: Pennsylvania German and American." *Brethren Life & Thought* 58 (Spring 2013) 25–32.
———, ed. *The Dilemma of Anabaptist Piety: Strengthening or Straining the Bonds of Community?* Blue Hill, ME: Penobscot Bay Press, 1997.
———. *Shenandoah Religion: Outsiders and the Mainstream, 1716–1865*. Waco, TX: Baylor University Press, 2002.
Mack, Alexander. "A Letter concerning Feetwashing." In *Brethren in Colonial America*, edited by Donald F. Durnbaugh, 444–45. Elgin, IL: Brethren, 1967.
Marsden, George M. *Fundamentalism and American Culture*. Oxford: Oxford University Press, 2006.
McClain, A. J. "The Faith of Doctor Miller." *Ashland College Bulletin* 8 (May 1935).

McClendon, James. *Biography as Theology: How Life Stories Can Remake Today's Theology*. Eugene, OR: Wipf & Stock, 2002.

McKnight, Scot. *Galatians*. NIV Application Commentary. Grand Rapids: Zondervan, 2000.

———. "Shifting Evangelicalism." *Jesus Creed* (McKnight's *Patheos* blog), October 8, 2010. http://www.patheos.com/blogs/jesuscreed/2010/10/08/shifting-evangelicalism/.

Mead, Sidney. *The Lively Experiment: The Shaping of Christianity in America*. New York: Harper & Row, 1963.

Meier, Marcus. *Origins of the Schwarzenau Brethren*. Philadelphia: Brethren Encyclopedia, 2008.

Miller, Clara Worst, and E. Glenn Mason. *A Short History of Ashland College to 1953*. Ashland, OH: Ashland Brethren, 1953.

Miller, Donald E. "The Brethren Philosophy of Higher Education." *Brethren Life & Thought* 49 (Fall 2004) 173–87.

———. "Influence of Gottfried Arnold upon the Church of the Brethren." *Brethren Life & Thought* 5 (1960) 39–50.

Miller, J. Allen. "Ashland College." *Brethren Evangelist* 25 (February 25, 1903) 1.

———. "Ashland College." *Brethren Evangelist* 26 (January 6, 1904) 1.

———. "Bible Study and Its Relation to the Christian Life and the Work of the Church." *Brethren Evangelist* 24 (January 22, 1902) 4.

———. "The Brethren Church: Why?" *Brethren Evangelist* 35 (July 30, 1930) 1.

———. "The Call to the Ministry—No. 2." *Brethren Evangelist* 20 (April 27, 1898) 5.

———. *Christian Doctrine: Lectures and Sermons*. Ashland, OH: Ashland Brethren, 1946.

———. "College Notes." *Brethren Evangelist* 21 (August 23, 1899) 14.

———. "College Notes." *Brethren Evangelist* 21 (September 27, 1899) 14.

———. "The Divine Self Revelation—No. 1." *Brethren Evangelist* 18 (October 7, 1896) 4.

———. "The Divinity of the Lord Jesus." *Brethren Evangelist* 24 (May 28, 1902) 6.

———. "Doctrinal and Practical: Sin and Human Need (IV)." *Brethren Evangelist* 32 (July 27, 1910) 7.

———. "Does It Matter What a Man Believes?" *Brethren Evangelist* 40.44 (October 16, 1918) 1.

———. "The Duty of the Church toward Ashland College." *Brethren Evangelist* 27 (October 4, 1905) 9.

———. "An Educational Ideal." *Brethren Evangelist* 27 (October 11, 1905) 8.

———. "The Forward Look." *Brethren Evangelist* 39 (July 24, 1917) 1.

———. "How to Indoctrinate the Young Convert." *Brethren Evangelist* 18 (April 8, 1896) 4.

———. J. Allen Miller to Louis S. Bauman. March 3, 1908. Letter. Morgan Library Archives and Special Collections at Grace College, Winona Lake, IN.

———. "The Object of Divine Self Revelation—No. 2." *Brethren Evangelist* 18 (October 14, 1896) 3.

———. "The Origin and Spirit of the Brethren People." *Brethren Evangelist* 37 (August 18, 1915) 3.

———. "Our Plea." *Brethren Evangelist* 20 (August 3, 1898) 12.

———. "The Parables of Our Lord Jesus." *Brethren Evangelist* 23 (October 24, 1901) 6.

———. "The Place of the Denominational College." *Brethren Evangelist* 31 (June 16, 1909) 2.

———. "Prayer for the College." *Brethren Evangelist* 30 (April 29, 1908) 3.

———. "Sin and Human Needs (IV)." *Brethren Evangelist* 32 (July 27, 1910) 7.

———. "The Sources of Human Knowledge—No. 5." *Brethren Evangelist* 18 (November 18, 1896) 2.

———. "Steps in the Way of Salvation (V)." *Brethren Evangelist* 32 (August 10, 1910) 7.

———. "Steps in the Way of Salvation (VI)." *Brethren Evangelist* 32 (August 24, 1910) 7.

———. "Studies in Bible History." *Brethren Evangelist* 16 (April 11, 1894) 2.

———. "The Subject of Divine Self-Revelation—No. 3." *Brethren Evangelist* 18 (October 21, 1896) 2.

———. "The Sure Foundation." *Brethren Evangelist* 50 (December 28, 1928) 3.

———. "The Travel Journal of Dr. J. Allen Miller, Spring 1926." Ashland Theological Seminary Library, Ashland, OH.

———. "The Work of the Divine Self Revelation—No. 4." *Brethren Evangelist* 18 (October 28, 1896) 2.

———. "We Must Educate." *Brethren Evangelist* 49 (June 4, 1927) 4.

Moore, Brian H. *A Brethren Witness for the 21st Century: A Search for Identity and Cultural Relevance*. Hagerstown: n.p., 2008.

Nead, Peter. *Theological Writings on Various Subjects*. Dayton, OH: Ells, 1850. Kindle.

———. *The Wisdom and Power of God, as Displayed in Creation and Redemption*. Cincinnati: Morgan, 1866.

Niebuhr, H. Richard. *Christ and Culture*. New York: Harper & Row, 1951.

Noll, Mark. *America's God: From Jonathan Edwards to Abraham Lincoln*. Oxford: Oxford University Press, 2005. Kindle.

———. *A History of Christianity in the United States and Canada*. Grand Rapids: Eerdmans, 1992.

Nolt, Steven. *Foreigners in Their Own Land: Pennsylvania Germans in the Early Republic*. University Park: Pennsylvania State University Press, 2002.

Nyvall, David. "From North Park (1895)." *Covenant Quarterly* 13 (1953) 36–38.

———. "The Inspiration of the Bible." Lecture, Ministerial Meeting of the Covenant Ministerium, Princeton, Illinois, August 18, 1898.

Olson, Roger E. "The Dark Side of Evangelicalism." *My Evangelical Arminian Theological Musings* (Olson's blog at *Patheos*), February 12, 2019. https://www.patheos.com/blogs/rogereolson/2019/02/the-dark-side-of-evangelicalism/.

———. "Evangelicalism Again: Why Are They Not Using My Distinction Between 'Movement' and 'Ethos?'" *My Evangelical Arminian Theological Musings* (Olson's blog at *Patheos*), February 8, 2019. https://www.patheos.com/blogs/rogereolson/2019/02/evangelicalism-again-why-are-they-not-using-my-distinction-between-movement-and-ethos/.

———. "Is Evangelicalism White?" *My Evangelical Arminian Theological Musings* (Olson's blog at *Patheos*), January 29, 2019. https://www.patheos.com/blogs/rogereolson/2019/01/is-evangelicalism-white/.

———. "Pietism and Postmodernism: Points of Congeniality." *Christian Scholar's Review* 41 (2012) 367–80.

———. *Reformed and Always Reforming: The Postconservative Approach to Evangelical Theology*. Grand Rapids: Baker, 2007. Kindle.

Olson, Roger E., and Christian T. Collins Winn. *Reclaiming Pietism: Retrieving an Evangelical Tradition*. Grand Rapids: Eerdmans, 2015.

Pearce, Alan S. "Summary of Dr. Bauman's Life." *Brethren Missionary Herald* 13 (January 6, 1951) 3.

Porter, Frank C. "George Barker Stevens." *Biblical World*, 28 (September 1906) 162–75.
Quiet Observer [pseud.]. Untitled article. *Brethren Evangelist* 23 (January 3, 1901) 23.
Reid, Daniel G., et al., eds. *Concise Dictionary of Christianity in America*. Downers Grove: Wipf & Stock, 2002.
Rench, G. W. "As a Church Leader." *Brethren Evangelist* 57 (April 27, 1935) 5–6.
Renkewitz, Heinz. *Hochmann von Hochenau: 1670–1721*. Translated by William G. Willoughby. Philadelphia: Brethren Encyclopedia, 1993.
Rollins, Peter. *How (Not) to Speak of God*. Brewster, MA: Paraclete, 2006.
Ronk, George T. "The Present Issue. (I): Right of Perpetuity: Its Relation to Liberty of Interpretation." *Brethren Evangelist* 37 (August 11, 1915) 13.
Sandeen, Ernest R. *The Roots of Fundamentalism: British & American Millenarianism, 1800–1930*. Chicago: University of Chicago Press, 1970.
Sappington, Roger. *The Brethren in the New Nation*. Elgin, IL: Brethren, 1976.
Schneider, Han. "Alexander Mack's Notes about Immersion Baptism." *Brethren Life & Thought* 48 (Winter/Spring 2003) 18–28.
———. *German Radical Pietism (Pietist and Wesleyan Studies)*. Translated by Gerald MacDonald. Lanham, MD: Scarecrow, 2007.
Sharp, S. Z. *Educational History: Church of the Brethren*. Elgin, IL: Brethren, 1923.
Sherman, Steven B. *Revitalizing Theological Epistemology: Holistic Evangelical Approaches to the Knowledge of God*. Eugene, OR: Wipf & Stock, 2015.
Shiveley, Martin. "Some Brethren Church Leaders of Yesterday as I Knew Them: J. Allen Miller, H.M., D.D." *Brethren Evangelist* 57.32 (August 1935) 7.
Smith, Christian. *The Bible Made Impossible: Why Biblicism Is Not a Truly Evangelical Reading of Scripture*. Grand Rapids: Brazos, 2012. Kindle.
Smith, Christian, and Melinda Lundquist Denton. *Soul Searching: The Religious and Spiritual Lives of Teenagers*. New York: Oxford University Press, 2005.
Smith, John. "Elder Peter Nead." *Brethren Family Almanac*. Elgin, IL: Brethren, 1909.
Smith, Timothy L. *Revivalism and Social Reform: American Protestantism on the Eve of the Civil War*. Eugene, OR: Wipf & Stock, 2004.
Sotak, Max H. *Wm. Newton Clarke and Postconservative Evangelicalism*. N.p.: Sotakoff, 2017.
Spener, Philip Jacob. *Pia Desideria*. Translated by Theodore G. Tappert. Eugene, OR: Wipf & Stock, 2002 [1964].
Stein, K. James. *Philipp Jakob Spener: Pietist Patriarch*. Chicago: Covenant, 1986.
Stevens, George Barker. *The Christian Doctrine of Salvation*. New York: Scribner, 1917.
———. *Theology of the New Testament*. New York: Scribner, 1902.
Stoeffler, Ernest F. *The Rise of Evangelical Pietism*. Leiden: Brill, 1965.
Stoffer, Dale. "Alexander Mack Jr.: The Pilgrim of Love and Light." *Brethren Life & Thought* 58 (Spring 2013) 8–24.
———. *Background and Development of Brethren Doctrines, 1650–1987*. Philadelphia: Brethren Encyclopedia, 2018.
———. "The Brethren Church: Anabaptist, Evangelical, or Evangelical Anabaptist." *Brethren Life & Thought* 61 (Summer 2016) 36–48.
———. "The Ecclesiology of Gottfried Arnold." *Brethren Life & Thought* 28 (1983) 91–100.
———. *"A Gleam of Shining Hope": The Story of Theological Education and Christian Witness at Ashland Theological Seminary (1906–2006) and Ashland College/ University (1878–2006)*. Ashland, OH: Ashland Theological Seminary, 2007.

---. "The Life and Thought of Gottfried Arnold." *Brethren Life & Thought* 26 (1981) 135–51.
---, ed. *The Lord's Supper: Believers Church Perspectives*. Scottdale, PA: Herald, 1997.
---. "Nineteenth Century Background." Studies in Liberalism and Fundamentalism. Class lecture notes, Ashland Theological Seminary, Ashland, OH.
---. "Prelude to the Controversy: Liberal Trends." Course lecture: Church History 6637: Christianity in America. Ashland Theological Seminary, Ashland, Ohio, n.d.
Sutton, Matthew Avery. *American Apocalypse: A History of Modern Evangelicalism*. Cambridge, MA: Harvard University Press, 2014.
Turretin, Frances. *Institutes of Elenctic Theology*. 3 vols. Translated by George Musgrave Giger. Edited by James T. Dennison Jr. Phillipsburg, NJ: P&R, 1997.
Van Bragt, Thieleman J. *Martyrs Mirror: The Story of Seventeen Centuries of Christian Martyrdom from the Time of Christ to A.D. 1660*. Translated by Joseph F. Sohm. Scottdale, PA: Herald, 1938.
Vanhoozer, Kevin J. *The Drama of Doctrine: A Canonical-linguistic Approach to Christian Theology*. Louisville: Westminster, 2005.
Ward, W. R. *Early Evangelicalism: A Global Intellectual History, 1670–1789*. Cambridge: Cambridge University Press, 2006.
Warfield, Benjamin B. *Inspiration and Authority of the Bible*. Philadelphia: P&R, 1948.
Weaver-Zercher, David, ed. *Minding the Church: Scholarship in the Anabaptist Tradition*. Scottdale, PA: Herald, 2002.
Wells, David. "The Debate over the Atonement in 19th-Century America Part 2 (of 4 Parts): The Shaping of the 19th-Century Debate over the Atonement." *Bibliotheca Sacra* 144 (July–September 1987) 243–53.
---. "The Debate over the Atonement in 19th-Century America Part 3 (of 4 Parts): The Collision of Views on the Atonement." *Bibliotheca Sacra* 144 (December 1987) 363–76.
Wenger, J. C., ed. *The Complete Writings of Menno Simons*. Translated by Leonard Verduin. Scottdale, PA: Herald, 1956.
Wicksteed, Philip H. "Abraham Kuenen." *Jewish Quarterly Review* 4 (July 1892) 571–605.
Willoughby, William G. *Counting the Cost: The Life of Alexander Mack*. Elgin, IL: Brethren, 1979.
Witter, C. Orville. "The Message of Science in the Twentieth Century." *Brethren Evangelist* 23 (January 3, 1901) 8.
Worthen, Molly. *The Apostles of Reason: The Crisis of Authority in American Evangelicalism*. New York: Oxford University Press, 2016.
---. "The Reformer." *Christianity Today* 54 (2010) 18–25.
Wright, Christopher J. H. *Cultivating the Fruit: Growing in Christlikeness*. Downers Grove: InterVarsity, 2017. Kindle.
Žižek, Slavoj. *The Sublime Object of Ideology* . Essential Žižek. 2nd ed. New York: Verso, 2009.

www.ingramcontent.com/pod-product-compliance
Lightning Source LLC
Chambersburg PA
CBHW060602230426
43670CB00011B/1928